SOUL-U-LAR EVOLUTION

A Mormon Woman's
Transcendent Journey to Love

Angel Lyn, MSW, Soul Mentor

Joan of Arc Publishing

Soul-U-lar Evolution
A Mormon Woman's Transcendent Journey to Love
Copyright © 2023 by Angel Lyn

Cover design and page layout by Elizabeth Gunter from Creative Well Design. The illustration features the Soul-U-lar Evolution logo, depicting the harmonious balance of nature across space and time—sun and water, earth and sky, wind and fire. It embodies the force of creation, in constant motion, ever-evolving, and symbolizing our transcendent journey towards love.

All rights reserved. No part of this publication may be reproduced, stored in a retrieval system, or transmitted in any form or by any means, electronic, mechanical, photocopying, recording, or otherwise, without written permission of the publisher or author, except for the use of brief quotations in a book review.

Although the author and publisher have made every effort to ensure that the information in this book was correct at press time, the author and publisher do not assume and hereby disclaim any liability to any party for any loss, damage, or disruption caused by errors or omissions, whether such errors or omissions result from negligence, accident, or any other cause.

Adherence to all applicable laws and regulations, including international, federal, state and local governing professional licensing, business practices, advertising, and all other aspects of doing business in the US, Canada, or any other jurisdiction is the sole responsibility of the reader and consumer.

Neither the author nor the publisher assumes any responsibility or liability whatsoever on behalf of the consumer or reader of this material. Any perceived slight of any individual or organization is purely unintentional.

The resources in this book are provided for informational purposes only and should not be used to replace the specialized training and professional judgment of a health care or mental health care professional.

Neither the author nor the publisher can be held responsible for the use of the information provided within this book. Please always consult a trained professional before making any decision regarding treatment of yourself or others.

To request permissions, contact the publisher at publish@joapublishing.com or the author at soul.u.lar.evolution@gmail.com

Paperback ISBN: 978-1-961098-16-9
eBook ISBN: 978-1-961098-17-6

Printed in the USA.
Joan of Arc Publishing
Meridian, ID 83646
www.joapublishing.com

GRATITUDES

To my friends and family, including my clients, whom I consider to be far more than the word denotes. They are my tribe, my people, my greatest teachers, and my soul family. Thank you all, for allowing me to be in your lives and for everything we have experienced together.

To my mentors, therapists, guides, and coaches: Shelby Smith and Kami Mitchell (The Unicorns), Richie and Natalie Norton, Diana Dokos, Christopher Stubbs and Megan Darger, Brent Wade, and Pam and Neil Fisher. I have had conversations with each of you that were pivotal, creating major bifurcations in my path. Every one of you is an angel in my life!

To some of my favorite authors—Brene Brown, Wayne Dyer, Louise Hay, Wendi Jensen, Marianne Williamson, Michael Singer, Byron Katie, Debbie Ford, Deepak Chopra, Paul Ferrini, Neal Donald Walsh, Gay and Katie Hendricks, M. Catherine Thomas, Stephen R. Covey, and Viktor Frankl. Thank you for writing about concepts that enabled me to move past what I thought I knew and begin to comprehend ideas beyond what I ever thought possible.

To the team:

Beta readers: my friends, Daria Peterson, Rachel Skousen, Julie Chew, and Ravyn Wright.

Editors: Jamie Borup and Rachel Skousen of Style Guides Editing, thank you for your patience and remarkable skills.

Graphic Designer: El Gunter

Publisher and Coach: Keira Brinton of Joan of Arc Publishing

To my parents, Paul and Dana Mathews. Thank you for believing in me, supporting me, and encouraging me every day of my life! You two are my heroes! I love you! And to my siblings, Lisa (who moved to heaven), Michelle, Marcia, Adam, and Aaron—thank you for a lifetime of loyalty and kindness.

To my Wasband (a.k.a. former husband). A sincere thank you. There are no accidents. I believe we came into this life with a promise to each other to help one another experience the things we did. I have no regrets. You were my mirror and catalyst.

To my boys: Sikeli, Aisea, Maika, Josaia, and Malakai. Thank you for raising me into a parent. Thank you for your love, loyalty, and forgiveness. I am incredibly honored to be your mom. I love you!

To King Eric, the love of my life. God delivered you into my life with the most amazing timing! Thank you for facilitating so much of my healing in mind, body, heart, and soul. Thank you for buoying me up throughout this entire book writing process. You have believed in me, held me, and championed me every single day, even the days I wanted to quit writing and bury this material. I never dreamed love, friendship, and companionship could look and feel like this! I love you! And thank you for bringing me three incredible bonus daughters: Alyssa, Adrianna, and Aubree.

To my readers: Thank you for picking up this book and stepping into my mind and heart. May you find something here that uplifts you.

To God/Spirit/Creator/Truth/Love: I have got to hand it to you, you are really good with plot twists! And I love the humor with which you speak to me and the fact that you don't seem to care what name I use to address you, you always answer. Thank you for answering all my questions—this mortal thing has been a most exceptional experience so far!

"Any human statement or belief might lack a portion of truth, as it has been filtered through that mortal's understanding, life experience, and limited vocabulary. Truth in its purest form comes directly through the pure sensation and intelligence of the mind, heart, body, and soul. It appears in the space of silence and stillness, full of love and peace. In the absence of words and their connotations, it remains pure and powerful."

— Angel Lyn

TABLE OF CONTENTS

AUTHOR'S NOTE	XI
PREFACE	XIII
INTRODUCTION	XVII
TERMS	XXIII
SOURCES	XXVII

SECTION I: MEMOIR

1	Confusion: Darkness and Light	1
2	Awareness: Error and Truth	23
3	Sources: Fear and Love	45
4	Aliveness: Sadness and Joy	63
5	Transcendence: Chaos and Peace	83
6	Being: Captivity and Freedom	113

FREEDOM POETRY	**149**
REFLECTIONS FROM "THE UNICORNS"	**152**

SECTION II: PRINCIPLES OF SOUL-U-LAR EVOLUTION

	INTRODUCTION	169
7	Discerning: Darkness and Light	173
8	Separating: Error From Truth	191
9	Perceiving: Fear and Love	203
10	Experiencing: Sadness and Joy	223
11	Observing: Chaos and Peace	241
12	Playing: Captivity and Freedom	257

EPILOGUE	**277**
FOR FURTHER READING	**281**

AUTHOR'S NOTE

WHAT IS SOUL-U-LAR EVOLUTION?

In 2017, I read *The Godseed*, by M. Catherine Thomas. Page after page, I found myself feverishly writing dates, noting my own past experiences that paralleled and illustrated the stages of spiritual development outlined in the book. I felt as if I were putting pieces together, connecting the corresponding dots of my own spiritual journey as quickly as they appeared in her text.

As I observed and noted the rapid unraveling of everything I thought I knew, and the subsequent unfolding of discovery after discovery, I asked, "What is happening to me?"

That is when the words showed up as an inspired thought, spelled out for me this way: *"It is soul-u-lar evolution—the spiritual evolution of the soul."* I wrote those words in the front of that book, and the thought that came next was, *"You'll write a book about it one day."* Years later, here it is!

PREFACE

When I was born, my mother looked at me and said, "You precious little Angel!" And that's how my name was chosen. You may think Angel would be a fun name, but it came with an inherent invitation for others to comment, "Angel, you are such an angel." Or, "Are you *really* an angel?"

To be honest, my name did not always align with my thoughts and behaviors. I was a clever and witty child, sarcastic and often fearless with my tongue. At times, I was devious and manipulative. My dad often said that I loved to "stir up trouble." And I did. I found it entertaining to get a rise out of people. I remember, as early as elementary school, feeling powerful when I was able to make a grown adult, a teacher, lose their composure in front of the classroom as a result of something I said or did.

I am a middle child—the fourth of six—and often bullied my two younger brothers. My older sisters called me "The Destroying Angel," due to my compulsion to break others' belongings when I felt angry. My nickname from my fifth-grade classmates was "Lucy," which sounded cute until I found out it was short for "Lucifer" . . . the opposite of an angel! In my early teens, one cousin called me "Fred" because, as he told his parents, "I just can't bring myself to call her 'Angel.'"

I certainly did not always feel like an angel, and having the name only enhanced my sense of guilt. I lived many years in anger, defensiveness, sarcasm, and fear, and did not understand why I felt a lot of what I felt. It has been a decades-long journey to find my true self, the Angel inside of me, and set her free. What helped me the most in this process of liberation was first recognizing who and what I *was not*!

The deconstruction of my *ego identity* (the who and what I thought I was, and then realized I was not) began in 2016, when I was thirty-eight years old. Through miracle after miracle, I discovered I was not just living a lie but living many lies. The lies came from what I was telling myself I had to do and be. I had become a product of my environment. I was living a life programmed and conditioned by external voices of authority that had systematically separated me from my authentic, spiritual self.

I have been commissioned by God to write and share my experiences. I am here to assist in the unraveling and separation of the wheat and the tares of life: the *wheat,* meaning truth and unconditional love; the *tares,* meaning the fear-based "philosophies of man," including the misinterpretation of truth by mortals.

My words are not intended to condemn or criticize any individual or group that I identify as contributing to my external programming and conditioning. I see others' innocence and I comprehend their intentions. I have come to believe it is each individual's opportunity to examine what they have been taught, no matter how authoritative the source, by taking every idea and concept *inward and upward* to inquire of the Divine and know for themselves.

This story is about my awakening to truth and how I came into *right relationship* with myself and my Creator. My objective in sharing my story is to inspire anyone wrestling with confusion or seeking to find and become their true and authentic self. I have written this book to share the methods of inquiry I have learned and invite you to experiment with this process alongside me.

I'm convinced that you were Divinely designed in perfection and that you being *you* is exactly what the world needs right now. You have nothing to prove and you don't need to earn your worth and value. It is inherent and infinite. The fact that you exist is evidence that you are worthy to exist. It is that simple! So rise and shine, baby! It is time to love yourself, all parts of you, one hundred percent. May you find and fall in love with the real you!

And P.S. Mom, thanks for believing in me, and thank you for naming me Angel.

INTRODUCTION

My Story

There it is again, I think. Peace. Like a soft blanket draped over my heart, a warm light filling my lungs. I notice a simple sense of joy in just being. I pause my morning walk to breathe in the peace and joy and savor it. It seems hard to believe that these feelings were not often a part of my life in years past—they were blatantly absent, in fact, despite all I was doing "right" to try to find my way to them, create them, earn them, or achieve them. I used to feel I was forever working towards peace and joy; I was chasing them, yet never quite able to catch up to them. Now they are a familiar and frequent part of my life.

Peace is the undercurrent of my days now. It is a state of being I intentionally and frequently access. That space is the *eye of the storm,* always present amid the chaos of life. This peace is a substance as real and delicious to my mind, heart, body, and soul as chocolate coconut milk is to my tastebuds—it has yet to grow old! I relish these moments when my awareness rests on the peace that is present within me and I didn't even have to work for it—it's simply there! I pause and notice the difference in the way I experience life now, because just a few years ago, my life was anything but peaceful.

In those days, I wore my stress around like a lead jacket. The jacket represented everything I was committed to: it was my purpose, my drive, my reason for being, my identity. Those weighted commitments included the expectations of society, family, church, community, and myself; it was the shoulds, beliefs, and values of all of the above. I was focused on being a stellar and spiritual human being. My goals were structured around doing life "right"—doing everything "right"—and being the best I could possibly be, in every role. It seemed noble. It seemed righteous.

I mentally put that lead jacket on every day. It kept me focused, dedicated, and driven—bulletproof. For years I was completely unaware of the mental and emotional weight it brought. I was unaware of the pervasive and destructive implications of the stress that came from relying on my own accomplishments for a sense of worthiness. Indeed, that was the cultural norm. I fit right in with many women around me—all of us constantly carrying the weight of striving for perfection to protect us from our fear of not being enough. I was consciously aware of frequent sensations of overwhelm and fatigue, and I thought they were just a normal part of life as a mom.

Between my quest for perfection, the physical, mental, and emotional toll of birthing five sons in eight years and educating the children at home, and the stressful, unhealthy patterns in my marriage, I hit a breaking point. Though I thought I was doing everything right, I felt like I was drowning—suffocating under feelings of unhappiness in my marriage, confusion from not knowing what else I could do to "fix" it, frustration and resentment, and fears of failure. In 2016, this season of burnout reached a climax when I received news that shattered my world completely and triggered an existential crisis.

That is when everything fell apart . . . and simultaneously came together.

INTRODUCTION

About the Book

SOUL-U-LAR EVOLUTION: A Mormon Woman's Transcendent Journey to Love is the retelling of my spiritually-guided journey—the awakening that exposed the disconnect between my body, mind, heart, and spirit. Through the crisis of 2016, I was led to a series of spiritual encounters in which the root causes of my emotional roadblocks and dissatisfaction with life were revealed to me. In a word, that root cause was self-betrayal.

I learned it was not my *circumstances* that caused me stress, unhappiness, confusion, frustration and resentment. Instead, it was the judgmental and fearful *thoughts* I had about my circumstances that caused me to feel stressed. These thoughts stemmed from many unconscious, fear-based beliefs absorbed from my surroundings, including societal beliefs, family and community ideals, and common practices and beliefs of the culture of the religion I belonged to, The Church of Jesus Christ of Latter-Day Saints—often recognized as "Mormons." (Also referred to as "LDS," for "Latter-Day Saints").

I discovered I had abandoned my true, spiritual self and operated primarily in my religious ego identity, trying to prove and earn my worth and value. This period of awareness led me through a process of *re-membering* my soul—systematically reassembling all of the fragmented *members* of my being: body, mind, heart, and spirit. I began learning more about my original Divine design. It was then that I learned how to start listening to God's direct impressions as they came to me, over and above what any human wanted me to believe.

Over the span of a few short years, I gained an ability to recognize and observe my ego, learned truth from my body, discovered my emotions are my friends and the alarm clocks of my awareness, and became familiar with my Higher Self (a.k.a. soul). This rapid growth has encompassed and shifted my entire world. I call it, simply, *Soul-u-lar Evolution*.

Part one of this work is a memoir. Part two seeks to clarify the principles illuminated by the Divine through my personal experiences. The latter part of the book is laid out for the reader as a self-help section. You may choose to read this book from front to back, or you may opt to read one chapter of the memoir, then the corresponding chapter in the self-help section—whatever feels best to you.

After each principle, I have included experiments you can use to try on these concepts for yourself. There is no right or wrong, good or bad way to apply these experiments. You cannot fail. Anything you choose will provide you an experience. That experience can be informative. I hope you enjoy getting acquainted with your miraculous internal compass — mind, body, heart and spirit—through the experiments offered here as well as others you might be guided to.

Disclaimer

As I have conversed with the Spirit, I have felt the desire to write down what I'm learning. I was surprised to find that the truth doesn't come in the form of words. I translate the truth into words for my own mortal comprehension, creating analogies and metaphors to help me explain the downloads I have received. I have been shown that if any human says anything, including myself, it must be acknowledged that there is inherently a potential margin of error. Any human statement or belief may lack a portion of truth, as it has been filtered through that mortal's understanding, life experience, and limited vocabulary. Truth in its purest form comes directly through the pure sensation and intelligence of the mind, heart, body, and soul. It appears in the space of silence and stillness, full of love and peace. In the absence of words and their connotations, it remains pure and powerful.

The purpose of this book is not to declare that I know or have the truth for anyone else, but rather, to share my personal experiences and

INTRODUCTION

encourage readers to practice receiving truth directly from the Divine in its pure and powerful form.

Thank you for receiving this book. May it serve your greatest good in this moment.

Love,
Angel Lyn

TERMS

In this work, you will encounter terms that may be new to you, or that are defined non-traditionally in this context. This is because I sometimes make up words or alter their meanings to communicate concepts. Here are a few key terms and their definitions:

Drama Triangle: A term introduced by psychologist Stephen Karpman in 1968. It refers to a pattern in relationships in which individuals cast themselves in three primary mental/emotional roles: hero/rescuer, villain/persecutor, and victim. "Heroes" believe they gain worth from helping others. They tend to disempower others by "saving" them. "Victims" believe they are helpless and incapable, and that others must do things for them. "Villains" tend to be aggressive, judgmental, and spiteful. They blame and criticize others without seeking to offer solutions. These are all ego-based roles, and most humans play into these roles from time to time.

It's important to note the healthier counterparts to these roles, found in the Empowerment Triangle: coach, creator, and challenger. "Coaches" support, encourage, and empower others. "Creators" know that they are the captains of their own ship. When challenging situations arise, they accept and respond, rather than resist and react. "Challengers" seek to learn from setbacks and mistakes and identify lessons to apply going forward.

Ego identity/Natural Man: I do not use the word "ego," in connotation and reference to its origin from Freudian analytical psychology.

Instead, I apply the term from the perspectives found in writings of consciousness and spirituality. I also use the words "Ego" and "Ego identity" synonymously with the LDS religious term "Natural Man."

"Natural Man" is a reference from The Book of Mormon. Mosiah 3:19 reads, "For the natural man is an enemy to God, and has been from the fall of Adam, and will be, forever and ever, unless he yields to the enticings of the Holy Spirit and putteth off the natural man and becometh a saint through the atonement of Christ the Lord, and becometh as a child, submissive, meek, humble, patient, full of love, willing to submit to all things which the Lord seeth fit to inflict upon him, even as a child doth submit to his father."

The connotation of "ego identity" in this work refers to the persona an individual develops over time. It is the conceptual image of oneself, based on how she/he thinks they measure up to the expectations, judgments, and standards of others. This "ego" is a deceptively convincing yet tainted perception of oneself, and is the result of the conditioning and programming of external authorities, including social norms and one's own fear-based interpretations (a.k.a. limiting core beliefs) of every life experience.

Enlightened Ego: I use this term to refer to the common human temptation to see oneself as more spiritually advanced or enlightened than others. It is a belief that one's education or experience sets him or her apart from others. While these knowledge-seeking individuals desire to be "conscious" in all they do, and are acutely aware of many of their external behaviors, they still often deny and project their own shame and fear onto others.

God, Source, Creator, The Divine, Spirit, and the Spirit of Truth: These are terms I intentionally use interchangeably to refer to a power greater than myself that answers my questions and guides and directs my life. I use these words as synonyms to refer to the same entity.

Jealous Judgment: Harboring a hidden sense of jealousy for another person or persons, but being unable to recognize or accept jealousy as a trait within yourself. In a deflective response, you seek justifications for your judgments in order to defend your own values, opinions, and choices in relation to the person being judged. This is one manifestation of projection.

Mis-giving: Saying "yes" when you truthfully want to say "no." Doing things because you are capable of doing them and think you "should," not because you want to. Doing things for others from a place of fear, guilt, shame, shoulds, or judgment.

Priesthood: Referring to a male ecclesiastical leader, and/or specifically, to the power and authority ordained men are bestowed by Church leadership.

Projection: Attributing a condition, trait, behavior, attitude, or habit to another person while ignoring, denying, or being innocently oblivious to the presence of that same trait within yourself.

Radical Accountability: The ability to lovingly embrace any situation, concept, personality trait, or emotion that surfaces through self-awareness. In these moments, opting in with a choice to expand in love through humility, rather than restrict through fear in humiliation.

Self-Betrayal: Engaging in behaviors and practices that don't align with your true desires and identity. Resentment is a sign of self-betrayal.

Shadow: The behaviors, propensities, and characteristics in yourself that you have deemed to be unacceptable and have repressed. These lost parts cry out to be recognized, acknowledged, and healthfully integrated into the conscious self.

Spirit/Soul: The ageless, fearless, egoless version of yourself. A conduit of truth and an agent who will not lie and can communicate directly with God, the Source of Truth.

Story

The set of assumptions, perceptions, and judgmental conclusions a person has compiled for their interpretation of any situation.

Trigger

An experience, thought, circumstance, and/or person that brings about thoughts and emotions that remove you from your natural state of peace and love. Noticing that you are no longer inhabiting a loving energy—a.k.a. that you are in a state of judgment—provides an opportunity to uncover the programming (beliefs and attendant thoughts) that created your emotional distress.

Transmutation

This word can simply refer to changing one thing to an entirely different thing; I often use it to signal healing that occurs because the energy of unconditional love has changed the very nature of something.

Truth

Any message from a Divine (non-mortal) source, such as thoughts and impressions that create resonance and alignment of my mind, body, heart, and spirit with feelings of light, love, joy, peace, and freedom.

SOURCES

Many authors and mentors have guided and inspired me throughout the course of this journey. Direct quotations and references to specific works will be cited whenever applicable. A large majority of my learning came through personal communication with my body, mind, heart, and spirit. I periodically felt comforting and assuring impressions from unseen presences and recognized them as individuals from the scriptures I grew up studying, including the Bible and the Book of Mormon. Another significant portion of my growth resulted directly from dialogues between myself and a Higher Power, a Being of Love and Wisdom. In my most comfortable words, I will refer to this power as my "Creator," "God," "Source," "the Divine," or "Spirit."

PART ONE
MY STORY

CONFUSION: DARKNESS AND LIGHT

"Light is the symbol of truth."
- James Russell Lowell

What would you do if you learned, with no prior evidence or suspicion, that there was a warrant out for your spouse's arrest?

This scenario came into my life in May of 2016, and it was the beginning of a great spiritual awakening. These challenging circumstances brought me the gift of an ever-increasing exposure to light, which began to illuminate pockets of my life formerly blanketed by darkness, deception, and disconnect—not my husband's, but my own.

To help you understand how it all came about, let's back up a little more than a decade to 2005, just prior to the birth of my second son.

My husband was informed that he would be let go from his job, his first out of graduate school, in three months' time. I do not know that I ever understood the full reasoning for his termination, but the timing was scary. Gratefully, his company extended his termination date out of consideration of the fact that I was pregnant and they were providing our health insurance coverage.

In light of his impending unemployment, my husband decided that we would return to Oahu, Hawaii, where we had met as undergraduate students, so he could go back to school for a second master's degree. I questioned his logic, noting that we were living financially month-to-month, had no savings, and didn't have a place to live in Hawaii. I sought to understand his vision of how this second graduate degree would benefit our family. He dismissed my concerns; he had made up his mind.

From that point on, I kept my fears on this matter quiet because I believed it was my role to submit to his priesthood leadership in our family, to trust and support him, and to follow him wherever his education or career would lead us. This perspective on the wife's role within marriage was based on my understanding of our religion's teachings. In church, we were taught the role of the husband/father is to be the provider and leader of the family, and the role of the wife/mother is to be the bearer of children and the primary nurturer in the home. My husband and I agreed upon these roles. My husband did not want me to work outside of the home and, while we had small children, neither did I. I felt I was fulfilling my role in the "right way," and I trusted, hoped, and prayed that he would pull through and fulfill his commitment and duty as the provider as well. I wanted to be a good wife and believe in my husband's abilities.

The lease for our Salt Lake City apartment was up a month before my husband's employment ended, and coincided with the approaching due date of our second baby. Relatives kindly agreed to allow us to live in their basement apartment for the final month of my husband's employment. As we were loading our moving trailer, I went into labor. I left one apartment, gave birth in the hospital, and two days later, entered into a new and temporary place with a newborn baby and our seventeen-month-old son.

That month in the basement was difficult. I was determined to breastfeed my second child exclusively. When my first son was born, I was in the final semester of graduate school in a clinical social work program. I felt exhausted and forgetful, and my baby was losing weight, so his doctor advised me to give him formula. No one told me (or perhaps it didn't sink in) that sometimes breastfeeding is hard; I'd assumed it would be intuitive. When it didn't work out the way I'd planned, I felt broken. When my second child was born just seventeen months later, I wanted to do it right. It was a struggle. He cried a lot, so I chose to supplement with formula to keep him satisfied. I felt like I had failed again. I was isolated in a basement apartment, overweight, tired, and afraid for the future. I stayed in the basement for most of that month, fighting against feelings of depression and suppressing my anger and resentment toward my husband.

My husband completed his final month of work and left for Hawaii to look for a job and housing before beginning the graduate program. With my two boys, I moved again, this time into my parents' home, to wait until my husband found a job and a place for us to live. I called daily to ask about his progress. Often when I called, he was visiting friends or reading a book in a hammock. He told me he had not been able to find a job and did not think he could be a full-time student and work too. I felt disbelief at what I was hearing, and I was furious! I felt that working to provide financially was not optional for a husband and father of two children; a second master's degree did not seem like a necessity, nor even a priority, over providing for the basic needs of our family.

As the weeks rolled on, his answers did not change, and we ran out of money. I felt I needed to reunite with my husband to "help" motivate him to take care of the essentials, so I applied for my first credit card and purchased plane tickets to take me and my babies to Hawaii.

From this point onward in our relationship, I pushed and pulled my husband towards what I thought were our shared goals. My husband and I often talked about each area of responsibility in our lives, such as finances, parenting, household duties, strengthening our marriage, etc. We set joint goals based on corresponding doctrines from our church. In theory, I felt we were on the same page in our marriage; in application, however, I felt he did not follow through with his responsibilities, so I had to jump in and pick up the slack. I didn't know it at the time, but I was contributing to a dysfunctional relationship structure often referred to as the *drama triangle*. Moving through various roles, I'd repeatedly rescue him (hero), expect him to change and feel let down when he didn't (victim), judge, resent, and shame him (villain), then rescue him again (hero). It wasn't until much later that I recognized how my behaviors in this cycle reinforced his limiting beliefs, shame, insecurities, and fears of failure.

I did not know what else to do to strengthen our family other than "try harder" to do better at my wifely and motherly duties. I had never before been presented with the simple awareness and ability to distinguish and operate from a place of love instead of fear. I only knew what I had been taught and seen modeled about duty, obligation, expectations, shoulds, right and wrong, good and bad, and true and false. I did not know anything about listening to my body, processing my emotions, or honoring myself. I felt helpless and trapped.

I confused my emotions, especially nervousness and stress, with the physical sensation of hunger, and used food to avoid, escape, numb, and distract myself in order to cope with my life. Due to my commitment to my church's health code, consumption of alcohol or drugs was not an option as a form of escape; instead, I justified eating whatever I craved, indulging in a more socially acceptable addiction.

I used my fear as a source of toxic motivation, staying busy to cover up my emotions and take my mind off the unhappiness of my marriage. I lived by a never-ending task list. I knew how to take initiative, get things done, and make things happen. I was driven and ambitious. (In retrospect, I made up my own word to describe myself: amBITCHous!) I was a woman seeking to do the "right" thing. I wanted to BE good and DO good and succeed at life. I wanted to achieve, accomplish, "win the race," and be worthy of God's love and Kingdom.

During this time, as our family continued to grow, my anchor was my church. Being a member of the Church of Jesus Christ of Latter-day Saints was not simply an affiliation, it was a way of life. It was the center of my life. My membership in this church was at the core of my identity. It gave me a sense of security and meaning. I attended three hours of church every Sunday and consistently donated ten percent of our income to the Church. I wore the recommended modest clothing, including special undergarments. I read my scriptures frequently and spent time performing rituals in our temples. I had not engaged in any sexual relations prior to my marriage. I served in volunteer positions within my congregation from age twelve on. At the age of twenty-one, before I married, I served an eighteen-month proselytizing mission in southern Spain. I centered my whole life around "keeping the commandments."

I operated like a pressure cooker: the steam of frustration, anger, and fatigue would build up inside of me, and then periodically, and without warning, release itself as impatience, blame, and rage onto my family. I did not know then that frustration and anger were masks for the fears in my unconscious mind. I believed my husband and sons were the reasons life was hard and I was stressed, tired, and unhappy.

I thought I could control my family's happiness, success, and righteousness by "teaching" (forcing) them to do the right things all the time. I thought that if they did things the "right" way, I would be happy and not so tired. I was seeking to prove my worth and value by producing a family well-grounded on the pathway to "perfection."

Unconsciously, I believed that my family's accomplishments (or lack thereof) reflected back on me. If one of my children did not "measure up," it meant that *I* did not measure up. I believed that if the boys were falling short, or if my husband was not progressing in his work and life, it was because I had not done enough, and was failing at parenting and partnering. And if I was failing in these most important mortal roles of wife and mother, then it meant that I was failing God, too! *I should be more. I should be better. I should be able to do more.* I carried this unconscious stress, guilt, and shame for years without reprieve. These fears presented in my conscious mind and body as frustration, resentment, hostility, impatience, judgment, and shame. Looking back, I can see I was angry and condescending a lot of the time. Yet I was not aware. I didn't even notice the pressure! It was just normal.

A desire to perform, achieve, and excel felt normal to me. I was a self-starter from a very young age, influenced heavily by the concept of Positive Mental Attitude[1], which my father studied and believed in. Outgoing, competitive, and academically inclined, I motivated myself to excel in various areas of my life by setting goals and applying positive self-talk. When I was born, my family, and other families in the neighborhood, hadn't had a baby in five years, so I got a lot of attention, and I thrived on it. I performed early on and experienced the thrill of applause. As a three-year-old, I sang a solo at a community talent show; at five, I auditioned for a drill team that normally only accepted seven-year-olds and made the team.

---

[1] PMA was a popular concept in the 80's, taught by Napoleon Hill and W. Clement Stone, among others.

CONFUSION: DARKNESS AND LIGHT

Looking back on my school years, I think I was always covertly competing: going for the top grades, the most friends/followers at recess, the winning team, trying to be the most funny person in class. Attention and achievement brought praise, recognition, privilege, and a sense of power—I caught on to that in grade school. In first grade, I was chosen for an advanced reading program; in third grade, I was chosen to be a peer tutor to children with special needs; in fifth grade, I actively competed for the highest test scores in my class. Even at recess, I played with the goal of winning in every activity and sport.

As a teen, I created a spreadsheet that hung on the back of my bedroom door. It had six categories listed across the top of the chart: physical, mental, emotional, social, spiritual, and financial. Down the left-hand column I had listed daily tasks to complete for each category, such as: run thirty minutes, read a self-help book for thirty minutes, practice the piano (music was an outlet for my emotions), visit a friend, read my scriptures, and allot ten percent of my income to tithing and fifty percent to savings. I prided myself on checking those boxes daily.

I took this mindset into my adult and family life. I believed that achievement equaled progress, which brought happiness. The larger my family grew, and the more experiences we were involved in, the more expectations I put on myself (and my spouse and children) to achieve and progress. I would get the kids involved in things like community classes, Boy Scouts, and sports, and my drive to excel at everything dictated that I also be as involved with these organizations as possible: fundraising, recruitment, teaching, coaching, planning, etc. Whatever I was capable of, I offered. I also pressed my husband to seek to improve in his career, in parenting, in our relationship, in his financial dealings, and in his physical health.

After my first two sons were born seventeen months apart, my weight was the highest it had ever been and I did not like my body.

I also experienced periodic waves of depression. I was determined, however, that if I did the "right things," I could fix these issues. I was aware that my personal health had to be a priority in order for me to "keep up," so I continually sought to increase my health and wellness by setting personal goals in the six categories I had learned to focus on in my youth.

Frustrated about my health after my second baby, I was inspired by a friend who had four children and ran marathons. I asked her how she did it. She described her early morning training schedule, discipline with food and hydration, and experiences running races across the country. That day, I left her house determined I would run a marathon, and I registered for one in my hometown that was five months away. When I shared my goal, friends expressed their doubts about the time constraint, telling me maybe I should start with a half marathon. I didn't know that was a thing; when I heard this, I decided half marathons must be for the weak—those who would settle for less. That wasn't me, I told myself. Five months later, I ran my first full marathon, proving those doubters wrong. I lost the baby weight and my mood changed substantially for the better. Nine months later, I had baby number three. This time, I knew how to lose the weight—train for another marathon!

For about five years, between 2008–2012, my ambitious lifestyle had me on top of the world. I fed my mental health with mentors. I was attracted to motivational speakers and life coaches, both online and in person. I read their books—and any books they recommended. I completed five marathons between having babies. I became passionately involved in a multilevel nutrition company. With colleagues from this company, I created an online wellness game that served over 2,000 participants, and blogged daily for this group. I discovered Crossfit and was instantly hooked; I fit my workouts in by attending the six a.m. classes before my children woke up. On the way to the gym one morning, I happened upon K-LOVE Christian radio station and felt my soul come alive! I would start these early mornings by jamming to dance tunes about Jesus, complete an intense workout, fuel my body with high-density nutrition, and then celebrate by saying out loud, "I feel like a million bucks!"

In August of 2012, I gave birth to my fifth son. I was aching to get back to Crossfit—so I went to class just a week after he was born! I felt very proud of myself and sure I could "feel like a million bucks" again. I was ready to pick up all my tools and get right back on the wagon of wellness with daily exercise, good nutrition, uplifting music and books, and scripture study! However, two months later, I felt worse than ever: tired, depressed, alone, and scared. This was not what I expected! I tried harder and harder, but I felt more and more fatigued and more depressed. I remember feeling like a hamster on a wheel—running faster and faster and going nowhere. Never getting a rest. Never feeling finished, accomplished, or successful for long. There was always more to do!

My husband and I became very distant. I asked him to join me for couple's scripture study, hoping we might cultivate a connection. He responded with, "I think we can just study them separately." I noticed that when he came home from work, I felt nervous. The moment he walked into the apartment, I felt stress and worry. The house was messy, the kids were fighting, the baby was crying, dinner wasn't ready, and I was tired. I felt ashamed for how things were spiraling, and for some reason, I felt repelled by his presence. I kept trying to get on top of my wellness routine, but I was not getting the same results.

In March 2013, I was thirty-five years old, my baby was seven months old, and I still did not feel like I had recovered from pregnancy and childbirth. I felt like I was slowly dying physically—my body growing weaker and weaker; I was simultaneously dying emotionally—subtly losing the will to live. I was not suicidal, but I did not enjoy being alive. The fire in my soul was going out. My personality was stale. I was not funny anymore. I did not feel like dancing. The emotion of joy was a distant memory. I often felt upset and frustrated with my children and spouse, and then guilty and ashamed for feeling that way because it was not Christlike. I felt overwhelmed and stressed every day about my to-do list that never got completed. I was in survival mode, just barely functioning in the tasks my life's roles required.

I sought help at a women's regenerative health clinic, and after lab results came in, I was told, "You have stage two adrenal fatigue and the beginning stages of Hashimotos. You're prediabetic and you have chronically elevated cortisol levels." A treatment regimen was prescribed. I left that appointment feeling somewhat relieved at having received concrete evidence for what I was experiencing. The lab results served as validation that I wasn't just "crazy and lazy."

And yet, I also had a feeling these diagnoses were only a part of the whole picture. I had an inner prompting to *look beyond*. It told me, "There is more to understand." I prayed and asked God what was at the root of my physical health challenges and what to do with the doctor's recommendations.

An inner voice responded concisely, in the form of a thought: *"This is a spiritual problem at its root."*

That was all I received at that moment. Although I comprehended the words, the overall message felt vague. I lingered in that space of ambiguity for months, then years, as I repeatedly returned to ponder that insight, seeking to gain clarity on what my spiritual problem was.

In the fall of 2014, I felt impressed to return to my hometown so that my children could have a closer relationship with their grandparents. Within a year of my return, all of my siblings moved back as well, bringing three uncles, four aunts, and ten cousins for my children to enjoy. My husband, who by then had a job in Aspen, Colorado, stayed and worked in Colorado for nine more months, but in the summer of 2015, he left his job and joined me in Utah. He began mentioning enthusiastically that he had an interest in starting an airport shuttle business. Around this same time, my sister and her husband gifted us a twelve-passenger van they no longer needed. My husband saw that van as the perfect shuttle vehicle, and he launched a business transporting passengers the two hours between our town and the nearest international airport.

Shortly after the shuttle business opened, I could see that there were far too many details for one person to handle successfully. I feared if my husband didn't have help he would fail, and I fiercely wanted him to succeed. At this time, I did not know that I was playing the role of rescuer in my relationship with my husband. I did not understand that by constantly stepping in to "help" him, I was inadvertently communicating my belief in his inadequacies and ultimately perpetuating his role as a victim in our relationship. I thought I was being helpful and supportive. I ended up taking on the business branding, marketing campaign, online reservations process, and public relations. It was all new to me; it was challenging, yet very invigorating. Once business picked up, I even got my taxi license and drove the shuttle once, and sometimes twice, a day.

Adding these business responsibilities to my daily routine was wild. As is common in our culture, I was solely managing the household cleaning, meals, and routines. I was also homeschooling our five sons, ranging from three to eleven years old. The round-trip shuttle route was five hours. I would leave at 4:00 in the morning and return home at 9:00 a.m. My husband would then take the next shuttle run while I took care of kids, meals, and the home, and then I would hit the road again at 4:00 p.m. and return home around 9 p.m. There were several occasions when I went thirty-six hours without sleep because the shuttle business was especially busy.

Despite the intensity of my daily schedule, I experienced tremendous joy in interacting with our customers. I loved meeting new people every day, finding thoughtful ways to make their travels convenient, and seeing the familiar faces of repeat customers. I relished engaging in conversation with passengers, and would intentionally instigate dialogue, which often led to connections among the travelers, who would delight in discovering genealogical ties and mutual interests. At the end of these rides, it was not uncommon for passengers to hug each other (and me) good-bye!

With my background in social work, I have a passion for human behavior and relationships. My conversations during these rides were never centered around small talk—I had real curiosities. I inquired about people's lives and feelings, and I was continually amazed at the willingness of my passengers to be vulnerable. I heard about college and career plans, recent deaths of loved ones, divorces in process, fears of flying, parenting issues, past abuse and trauma, and so much more. My academic and career passions would often come up in conversations. When people found out I had a master's degree in clinical social work, they would ask me, "Why are you driving a shuttle?" (They didn't realize I was also co-owner of the business.) I enjoyed responding, "I get the best of both worlds! I get to host group therapy right here in the shuttle, but I don't have to write case notes, and I don't have to follow up with your psychiatrists!" The passengers would laugh, but it was true! I felt energized by the presence of others and their openness. Their life stories left imprints on my mind and in my heart.

I remember one ride I was taking at 3:30 in the morning, having felt so tired prior to picking up the passengers, but as I talked with them I noticed how energetic, awake, alive, and excited I felt. This brought a light of awareness about my personality: I could have any job and be truly happy and fulfilled, as long as I could engage in free-flowing conversation with people regularly. I felt energized by connection with others, and it mattered more to me *that* I connected with people than *how* I came into contact with them. I was grateful for the sense of fulfillment I got from these interactions and from the experience of building a business with my husband.

Months went by, however, and we were barely breaking even. We relied on government assistance to feed our family and sought financial assistance from our church to cover rent on our five-bedroom home. This was the first actual house we had lived in during our marriage, and I desperately wanted to stay in it. Although asking for help was humbling (and triggered a sense of shame in me), I wholeheartedly believed that we were gaining traction for a profitable business that would help us eventually enjoy the freedoms of entrepreneurship. Business appeared promising: our reputation was growing quickly, with over 100 five-star reviews online, and we were becoming a viable competitor to the two large corporate shuttle companies in our area. We believed that if we could cross the profit threshold, we could afford to outsource several duties and eventually have a very successful business.

During an interview with the two of us, our bishop told my husband, "The Church is not in the business of floating people while they work on start-up companies. You may need to get a job to be able to cover your rent." It was not the first time he'd said this. Although the counsel made sense logically, it felt like we were being guided back into the rat race we had been working so hard to escape. It also felt impossible to find time for employment outside of running the shuttle business. We had dismissed the counsel previously, and when it surfaced again, I felt deeply ashamed. I felt as though we were being seen as taking advantage of the system and operating a business that was destined to fail.

Approximately nine months after launching the shuttle business, in May of 2016, we had exhausted all of our financial resources and were still not profiting enough to pay the rent on our home. We knew we needed to move. My kind sister and her husband graciously stepped in once again. They purchased a modular home for us to rent from them at a minimal rate, mobilizing a crew of friends and family to repair and clean it so we could move in.

Despite my deep and sincere gratitude for the assistance, moving into a trailer home felt very shameful to me. I had been raised hearing the phrase "poor white trailer trash" used to refer to people who lived in trailer homes, and there I was: thirty-nine years old, a mother of five with a graduate degree, a God-fearing, faithful, and active Mormon woman, and I felt like "poor white trailer trash." *How did I get here?* I wondered.

While church members, relatives, and friends did the work to make the trailer livable, my husband and I were hardly present; we were constantly operating the shuttle business and taking care of our kids. During this time when so many people were helping us by working on our home, as well as helping me pack and clean the rental home we were moving out of, I often felt heavy guilt and shame about my life being in such a mess and seeing myself as a "service project."

I would pull up to the new trailer house between shuttle trips and see volunteers busy at work fixing and painting the house I was going to move into. At these times, I noticed that I would not look the volunteers in the eyes. I wanted to sneak away, unseen. I saw this as a red flag that shame was present. The emotion of shame came with a physical sense of restriction in my body, a tightening and heaviness, particularly in my chest area.

Even as life grew heavier and more difficult to manage, I continued to seek mentors and strive for personal growth. Shortly after moving back to my hometown, I reconnected with a friend I'd grown up with, and she and her business partner became powerful mentors in my life. Their very presence was so magically impactful, I began to call them "The Unicorns."

One of the first things they taught me was to challenge my thinking, and through this process I began to recognize that hardly anything I told myself was actually true; rather, it was a fictional story my ego identity had created from a place of fear.

In the face of heavy emotions, I learned to pose the question in my mind, "What am I telling myself right now?"

Applied to the situation with our modular home, I noticed my thoughts included, *I should be here working on this,* and, *These people are working so hard. I don't deserve this much help.*

I inquired of my spirit further, "What does this say about me—that others are working so hard on my behalf and I am not helping?"

I uncovered a deep-seated belief that I had to earn the right to be worthy of love and service. I believed if I was the recipient of service and charity from others, it was because I was needy, not doing enough for myself or others, and that I was failing.

"Who or what taught me to think this way?" I asked myself.

I thought back to many experiences serving in leadership positions in the women's organization of the Mormon church. Service projects were often organized by leadership councils. These projects often seemed created for people who could not help themselves. If someone needed help, it felt to me like they were not living one of the core principles of the gospel of Jesus Christ: self-reliance. I judged the people we served, and now that I was a recipient of service, I was judging myself.

I had shame around our financial situation and I felt helpless to do any more than I was currently doing. It was embarrassing to be in such a needy position. Despite the kindness of these volunteers, my thoughts were negative and fearful, souring my ability to receive the love and generosity of those serving our family.

In the middle of May, the trailer remodeling was complete and we moved in. I remember crying that first night because the shame from the thought of being "poor white trailer trash" plagued me. I felt like a failure. *I am almost forty years old and I live in the ghetto of my hometown! After all I have worked toward my entire adult life, here I am, with nothing to show for it!*

My bike was stolen from our driveway the first week we lived there, and there were cops on the street almost daily, which was not something I had ever experienced before. This provided evidence for the idea that I lived in "the ghetto." I also discovered that some of my most treasured belongings had been mistakenly hauled off to the thrift store by the volunteers helping us move, including two trash bags full of my favorite clothes and a box of my best kitchen appliances.

Each experience felt like compounding evidence pointing to a pathetic life—I had sunk to the bottom of the socio-economic barrel and I felt as though I had nothing, which meant I was nothing—nothing but a failure! The shame felt suffocating.

One evening, within the first week of living in this hell hole, I was alone in my bedroom and I allowed the rage inside to have full expression. I had been learning more about emotions and especially about the nuances of shame from the works of author/researcher Brené Brown. I was learning to allow myself to feel my emotions.

CONFUSION: DARKNESS AND LIGHT

For quite some time I cried as I looked at my surroundings, mentally screaming my judgments of my husband. I felt like I was living in a cardboard box, and I blamed my husband for our circumstances. I ranted to myself, *He is so bad with money! He doesn't provide for us! He doesn't know what he's doing in business! If I had gone to work after receiving my graduate degree, I am CERTAIN I would be financially successful by now and be providing for this family! I would own a home like the rest of my friends—something he has yet to be able to provide for us!*

Self-righteous indignation continued to spew forth from my mind. I was very aware that I was raging, and though I had learned that rage is an expression of shame, I was unable to clearly see the shame story I was telling myself. Instead, I continued to elevate myself with piousness: *But I didn't choose a career path! Instead, I rightly sacrificed professional opportunities to take on the stay-at-home mother role. Because, heaven knows, "No success can compensate for failure in the home."*[2] I believed I had done the *right* thing, according to my religious teachings about the roles of mothers and fathers, and he had done the *wrong* things and had *failed* us.

After I had exhausted my anger, I paused and took a deep breath. "What now, God?" I asked. "What can I do to change things? What wisdom can You offer me?"

The answer came quickly and clearly. *"You co-created this experience with your husband."*

I was astonished, and then a little bit ticked off. "I have done everything I possibly can to help my husband succeed, to raise our family, and to obtain our shared goals. How is this situation *my*

---

2   This is a popular quote often recited in church lessons on motherhood and parenting. It is often attributed to Mormon prophet David O. McKay. I have only recently discovered that this quote was actually written by J.E. McCulloch in his 1924 book *Home: the Savior of Civilization*.

17

creation?!" With these questions, I noticed a feeling of resistance in my body—a slight restriction of the cells in my chest area.

I breathed again. The Unicorns had taught me that the depth to which I breathe is the depth to which I can receive. I had inspiration coming to mind in that moment, and I wanted to intentionally and mindfully receive it.

After that breath, I asked a follow-up question: "What was my part in co-creating this life in the ghetto?"

A series of moments from my past came to mind like scenes of a movie, strung together by themes of self-deception, self-betrayal, and projection. I saw how I chose to "submit" to my husband as the leader of our family while inadvertently enabling, rescuing, and resenting him. I saw myself motivated by the approval and acceptance of my religious ideology—I was acting the part of the "good" wife and mom, the "righteous" one, but in reality, I was co-creating drama in my marriage by drafting a martyr-victim identity for myself, penning him as the villain.

I had ignored and relinquished my aptitudes and income-earning abilities, forsaking them in the name of the "righteous choice" to be the stay-at-home mom, and placing the burden of providing for the family on my husband. It was his responsibility, I believed, to make my dream of owning a home come true—something that would surely make me feel happy and secure. And when he did not live up to those expectations, I resented him deeply, and my words and actions often reflected that pain.

As I reflected on all this, I was shown through my spiritual eyes, in full detail, my accountability for the circumstances I was currently in. I was shown how these beliefs and values provided me with strict expectations that offered me a pious platform from which to judge my husband. My part in this co-creation was that I *shoulded* on him a lot—in the same ways I *shouldded* on myself. *You should do this! You shouldn't do that! You should be this! You shouldn't be that!*

"Well, holy shit," I thought. And then I laughed. *Perhaps this is a "HOLY SHIFT"!*

It felt like heavy curtains covering a large window were pulled back and a bright light cascaded into the room of my mind. The light of awareness came with such peace and love that I was not tempted to attach to shame. In place of judging myself, I could see how I had simply and innocently responded in the only ways I knew. Following the examples I'd seen around me, I'd inadvertently helped to bring poverty and a scarcity mindset into the life we'd created.

I marveled at the awareness washing over me. It felt liberating, and my chest relaxed and expanded. It felt true, and this truth dissipated the anger and rage I had been feeling in response to the lies I was telling myself. I lay in my bed and breathed deeply, reveling in the peace, awareness, truth, and love present in my room.

I turned my attention back to the process of inquiry: "If I co-created this, then what does that say about me?"

The answer was empowering: *"Look no further; you are already a creator!"*

I realized that, for the past decade, I had been reading books, going to personal development seminars, and seeking to learn how to become a creator, how to live in abundance and have the life that I wanted. I had studied these concepts and felt very capable of employing them, but I had abandoned my personal drives and ambitions, instead passive-aggressively trying to "teach" or "inspire" my husband to apply the concepts I was studying.[3] I had been chasing this desire to become a great creator without knowing that I had been a creator all along!

---

3   This is a classic relationship blunder: believing if HE did xyz, then I would be happy!

Again, I laughed out loud, then said, "All this time, I have had the traits of a creator within me, and I have been using them—just unintentionally?!" I could see in my mind a downward spiral of energy, a force I was contributing to by adding my own fears, guilt, shame, judgment, resentment, hostility, blame, and ignorance. "Well, that definitely seems like a recipe for disaster!" I acknowledged." If it is true that I co-created this situation, unintentionally, what might happen if I begin to create with intention?" I wondered.

No more books, no more workshops, no more longing to be something that I thought I wasn't. I chose to acknowledge what I already was: "I am a creator." I acknowledged my Divine design. I immediately focused my energy on being very intentional with my choice of words and how I treated my husband. I began to look for the blessings of my situation. I chose to believe that I could contribute different "ingredients" to this relationship recipe to shift that downward spiral into an upward spiral with expansive creation energy.

Two weeks later, I had a phone conversation that would put my creator-self to the test.

It was a typical business day and my husband had not returned from his shuttle run on time. It was closing in on the time for the next trip's departure, and I wondered if I needed to get someone to watch the kids so that I could take a second van and make the shuttle run, since he was delayed. I called my husband and asked where he was.

"I'm at the library," he told me.

That was odd. "What are you doing there?"

My husband told me his former employer in Colorado had contacted him about some accounting issues and missing funds from a prior year. This didn't feel suspicious to me since he had been the company's accountant; I assumed somebody was auditing records and they naturally turned to him for the information they were seeking.

I asked him if he was going to be ready to drive the next shuttle as scheduled.

"No," he said, "I am meeting with a lawyer."

A lightning bolt of awareness struck my body. "Did you take money from your former employer?"

A pause.

"Yes," he said quietly. "There's a warrant out for my arrest."

Right then, I had an experience in a quantum realm; in a nanosecond, I perceived his whole soul and the last few years of our lives together. My husband had been the leader of our religious congregation while working for this company and embezzling their money. He had been preaching the doctrines of Christ and enforcing religious practices in our home while living in direct opposition to those teachings. There had been many odd occasions when I'd questioned him about our finances and his behaviors, but his evasive responses left me confused, questioning my own sanity.[4] These moments suddenly made sense.

In that same instant, I was gifted the ability to temporarily feel his pain and see him clearly. I felt the weight of his guilt and shame pressing on my chest and observed the mental justifications, the self-deception, that allowed the embezzlement to occur. I comprehended his upbringing in an island nation that operates on subsistence living, and how the money philosophies of the western world were entirely foreign to his relationship with money. I saw the cultural shame-driven emphasis on a reputation of respectability and responsibility. Being male and the oldest in his family came with specific responsibilities, including the expectation that he financially support members of his family and clan living in Fiji.

"I am so sorry," I told him, "I feel nothing but compassion for you."

---

4   I later learned the term *gaslighting* from my therapist, which explained these moments further.

"I did not expect you to say that!" he replied.

Me neither!!! I thought incredulously.

Those were not the words of the wife I had been even just weeks prior! Those were not judgmental words. Those were not persecuting words. Those were not shaming-him-to-hell words. I surprised myself! As I spoke those words, I felt a Power greater than I had ever known—much greater than myself—speaking through me. I felt that I was operating merely as a conduit of that Power, which was the essence of light, truth, and love.

That moment initiated a new aspect of my spiritual awakening—the ability to *behold* another. That lightning bolt of awareness was a spiritual light that allowed me to see my husband in his totality and in truth, without judgment, and it felt peaceful, expansive, and freeing. In this spiritual spotlight, I also discovered things within me that I could no longer unsee. Awareness does not allow us to go back without suffering, so I chose to go forward intentionally, to live in a state of *Soul-u-lar Evolution*—the discovery of my true Being through an intentional process of deliberate attention and presence.

AWARENESS: ERROR AND TRUTH

"He who knows nothing is closer to the truth than he whose mind is filled with falsehoods and errors."
-Thomas Jefferson

After that phone call with my husband, I walked into my bedroom and glanced at my bookshelf. It was filled with the books I had been taught to use as spiritual references for my life. Most of the books on the shelves were written by leaders of my church. There were also sets of scriptures, including copies of the Bible and Book of Mormon in both Spanish and English. There were magazines published by the Church, and doctrine-filled lesson manuals from the classes I attended regularly on Sundays. Scanning the shelf, I thought, *I'm pretty familiar with all of that material, and I can't think of one chapter, not one verse, where it says what to do when there is a warrant out for your husband's arrest.*

I took a deep breath—and then I did something spontaneous and new. Rather than reach outside myself for external sources to lead me to God, I turned *inward and upward.* Instead of folding my arms, bowing my head, or kneeling on the floor, in what I had been taught was the "proper" way to pray, I simply began a conversation with

God from my raw and honest heart. It was unlike any prayer I had ever offered.

"Dear God, if you exist—and I'm not totally sure that you do at this moment, since my marriage feels like a myth, and it wouldn't surprise me to discover that you are a myth too—without any expectation, I am just going to take this opportunity to let go of everything I have ever believed in or wanted to believe in and surrender it all. Here you go!" I mentally dumped all the things I "knew" from my brain, laying all my beliefs out on an imaginary table.

"Apparently, I have been wrong about many things that I believed. I believed in my husband. I believed we were partners. I believed in his priesthood and leadership in our family and at church. I believed we were working together toward common goals. I have been mistaken. And if I have been mistaken and deceived in this most intimate relationship, I can only imagine how many other relationships I have wrongly trusted in as well. I am here to acknowledge that I have been wrong about my husband and my marriage and possibly wrong about everything in my life. I now admit that I know nothing—NOTHING AT ALL!

"If I know nothing, then I cannot expect any other mortal to know anything, either. Right now, I cannot think of a single person whom I can trust to guide me from a place of truth and love, rather than fear and judgment. Normally, I would turn to my parents at a time like this, but I believe if I tell them what my husband has done, my rancher father—the epitome of honesty, integrity, and hard work—might want to shoot my husband, and that would not be good for anyone. My friends will want to villainize him for his wrongdoings and seek to feed my ego and self-deception. So it looks like it is just You and me. God, if you exist—a Being of greater wisdom than myself, whatever that may be—tell me, what shall I do next?"

AWARENESS: ERROR AND TRUTH

Immediately the answer came as a clear thought: "*Put chicken in the crockpot.*"

That was unexpected. *Did I really just have that thought?* I remember chuckling a bit as I repeated the words out loud: "Put chicken in the crockpot?!?"

Yet there was a recognition present. I realized that these words came to mind immediately following my question offered up to God. How could it *not* be an answer? My ego-mind wanted to discount the ridiculous, seemingly irrelevant, immediate answer, and ask again. Yet, as I considered that choice, I noticed an impression that said it would be arrogant and egotistical to do so.

"*Did you not just ask a question?*" the thought said.

My quickness to dismiss the thought felt very familiar. *How many times have I turned to God with a question, rejected the immediate answer—as I am tempted to do now—and then asked the question again?*

Evidence of my past rejection of personal revelation flooded my mind. I was astonished at my own past ignorance. The pattern of error became clear: when spiritual impressions came in as new thoughts, my ego often contradicted and dismissed those thought-impressions because they did not make sense to my logical, mortal mind. The messages often felt unfamiliar, uncomfortable, or inconvenient. I would then ask the questions again and feel stifled when there was no recognizable answer. I noticed during this reflection that each time I believed I was not getting an answer to my prayers, I did one of two things commonly practiced in my religious culture:

1. I assumed that I needed to be more spiritually worthy to receive an answer from God, so I would do more of the things I had been taught equal worthiness: pray more, fast for

twenty-four hours, read my scriptures, and/or attend the temple to participate in religious rituals, then pray and ask again; or
2. I would pacify myself by repeating a phrase I heard often from others at church: "Prayers are answered in God's timing."

Both assumptions were erroneous explanations for what I did not know I did not know: answers and inspiration were available to me *all the time*—and I was innocently ignoring and rejecting them! I truly did not know how to recognize truth in the form of personal revelation. I had been conditioned to restrict my definition of *truth* to the thoughts, principles, doctrines, and teachings sanctioned by my church—those published by the church, preached from a pulpit, and commonly accepted in church culture. When I prayed, if thoughts came to my mind that did not fit within the familiar practices and boundaries accepted as doctrine by my religion, I dismissed them and clung to prescribed teachings. I was shown multiple accounts from my past where I had dismissed revelation for these reasons. It was disturbing.

As I followed the unusual prompting to put chicken in the crockpot, I looked over at the table and saw my boys busily engaged in their drawing and playing with Legos. I humbly remembered I had little people to feed that day—real life was still continuing around me! The world had not stopped, despite the disruption that had just occurred inside of me. In a few hours, my boys would be hungry for dinner, and I would now have something ready for them to eat. I took this miracle in with a deep breath and expressed gratitude for the wisdom that had been provided to me. I realized I could trust myself to trust God.

When I turned to God for guidance and visualized myself dumping all I knew onto an imaginary table, like an altar, I dumped with it my own common sense—something I had prided myself on (one of the ego's favorite phrases) since childhood. I surrendered all former logic and reason. My mind was left blank, curious, and unattached, like a fresh canvas, a wide open space. My certainty had vanished, and along with it, my fear of being wrong. Releasing my fear of being wrong was one of the most fundamental shifts I needed to make in learning to source and receive truth.

After this experience, I could no longer freely say that I "knew" anything anymore without experiencing a physical reaction: my body would cringe and constrict whenever I was tempted to claim any former thought, belief, or idea as right or absolutely true. It was as if those cringing sensations were my body actually speaking to me, saying, "Check in. Is it true?" The acute awareness of these physiological changes led me to ask the Spirit what was happening, and I was told that nothing had changed other than my awareness of my body. The more effort I made to observe and challenge my thoughts, the more aware and connected I became to my body's signals and reactions.

Practicing this *check in*, as I call it, led me to discover how easy it is to develop an *enlightened ego*. Having been conditioned to value believing I know things and I am right about things, even as I had new and powerful spiritual experiences, I noticed that the same old paradigm would try to return and tell me that I now knew how to be "spiritual"—sneaky ego. By *checking in* with my body and soul continuously, I am reminded by that cringing feeling and the whispers of my soul that I don't actually need to know anything—which is the perfect invitation to keep turning to God for everything! And, when I do, there is always an answer to the question, "What is true in this moment?" Moment by moment, situation by situation, the spiritual direction I receive changes. What I personally think is true is consistently different, when I pause and *check in*, than what God thinks is true.

My former attachments to my identity, security, and meaning were obliterated by this process. Up to this point, my identity had been anchored to my membership in the Church and my marriage to a priesthood leader in that church. My life's purpose was in living all the Church's teachings and raising my sons to follow in our footsteps. This was the core of who I believed I was. This religious identity guided every decision in my life and gave shape to the direction of every day. When I abruptly discovered that my husband of fourteen years was not really who I thought he was, I found myself questioning the truth of everything tied to him. *If our relationship is based on fallacies, what else is not real and true?* I wondered.

I felt alone and isolated, but I did not know where I could go for effective support. I did not feel ready to talk to others, as my perspective was frequently impacted by my fluctuating emotions. Without a spouse to talk to, and believing that friends or family could not help, there were times when I wrestled alone with a flood of emotions stemming from my disillusionment and the disruption of my identity.

It was interesting navigating outward "normalcy" while inwardly experiencing something so new and unusual. Having been trained as a clinical therapist, my mind periodically referenced symptoms of psychosis and other potential mental disorders; I asked myself if my process of asking questions inwardly and receiving answers from an unseen source meant that I had schizophrenia. I wondered if the periods of intense bliss and love followed at times by physical exhaustion and a lack of motivation meant that I had bipolar disorder. Trust me, these were legitimate questions, and I took the time to evaluate myself and to confer with professionals to ensure that I wasn't developing a serious mental health condition. I wasn't.

As I contemplated my options, I felt guided away from pursuing typical forms of advice, counseling, or support. I felt compelled, rather, to continue to seek the truth: the truth about my husband, the truth about myself, and the truth about our future. It felt imperative that I turn directly to the Source of Truth. As I continued to converse with the Divine in lieu of speaking to mortals, the Spirit comforted me and continued to provide insight regarding my husband's choices. Despite my growing understanding and compassion, my life going forward felt unclear and foreign. The straightforward path to eternal happiness and salvation that I thought I was on had disappeared.

I recognized, in psychological terms, that I was experiencing an existential crisis: a severe disruption of my identity, security, and meaning. *I do not know who I really am. I do not know where I fit or with whom I belong. I do not know what my purpose in life is. I do not know where to go or what to do next.* I felt like I had been stripped down and was wandering in a desert wilderness inside myself, lost, alone, and disoriented—yet I wasn't afraid. Instead, I was curious.

I felt tempted by my mortal programming to attach to fear, but instead, I chose to allow myself to just be in it. I was learning that I could ask questions and receive answers from God, and I chose to trust that. *So, I am naked and alone in a wilderness. I'm not the first. The scriptures are full of accounts of children of God who wandered in the wilderness. I guess it's my turn. This is new. I wonder what will show up next?*

I began to intentionally seek to align my mind, body, heart, and soul with truth. If you had run into me in the grocery store at this time and greeted me with, "Hi Angel! How are you?" I would have honestly responded, "I'm having an existential crisis. How are you?" or, "I'm wandering in the wilderness. What's new with you?" I was choosing to be truthful, even in my words. No shame. No judgment. While I searched for truth inwardly, I wanted to reflect it on the outside, too.

I cannot adequately explain this phase of my experience without expanding on the preparatory mentoring that had taken place earlier. Beginning in 2015, nearly a year before my existential crisis, I had been seeing a therapist for my depression and learning from "The Unicorns," whom I mentioned earlier.

My therapist helped me see the degree to which I lived in self-betrayal. He pointed out that I was loyal and obedient to all of my external voices of authority, but that I ignored my intuition and had no voice in my marriage. To be clear, I was not afraid to speak up, speak my mind, and speak what I thought was true—sometimes I would yell these things at my husband and kids—but what I was yelling about were the things I had been programmed to call true. I tried to command others to be obedient to church teachings and what I felt was common sense. And I was ignored. My husband dismissed most of the ideas or concerns I brought to him regarding our relationship. (I have since realized that ignoring a hostile, angry, resentful wife is a pretty common response from a husband who feels like he's not good enough.) Despite feeling repeatedly ignored in my attempts to address issues within our marriage, I pressed on. I continued to labor, *enduring to the end*, as I was taught to do at church. I believed that if I kept doing the right things, one day everything would click: I would feel in love with him, we would be friends, and I would be happy.

Seeking to understand self-betrayal revealed to me that I habitually forsook my inner knowing, my own "truths," in exchange for obedience to what I was taught to do: *choose the right* was a motto I heard often in church from childhood, and *the right* it refers to is the specific steps outlined by the church for all areas of one's life. I was obedient to the laws of the gospel as taught at church and in the scriptures, and to my husband's counsel (although I secretly did not see him as the "leader" of our family. While he wore the suit and tie and carried the title of "priesthood leader," my perspective was that I was guiding the spiritual direction of our home and leading *him* along). In this headspace, I was deceived. I was disconnected from my own epicenter, my soul.

Wanting to heal from self-deception and self-betrayal, I went in search of ways to reconnect to my true self. That is when I found The Unicorns. These two boisterous women held retreats and invited me to participate. They made it possible for me to attend, even when my finances didn't allow for me to pay in full. At these retreats, I learned to recognize my own emotions and to allow myself to feel them without judgment. I learned how to give myself permission to feel and to be a witness of myself and my experiences.

I had suppressed so many emotions and red flags in my marital relationship that resentment, anger, and hostility brewed within me. There I was, trying to *choose the right* every day, and concurrently experiencing anger and bitterness, primarily towards my husband. These mentors taught me to connect to my inner child, to play again, to find joy in life, to love myself, and to believe I was not failing at life—I was enough, I was lovable, and I was worthy. Somehow, these keys to happiness had been lost in my pursuit of righteousness.

I also came across the book *Loving What Is*, by Byron Katie. Although it took me three times reading through it, across a couple of years, I finally quit arguing with the author and began to approach life through her prescribed lens, which is to question your thoughts with, "Is it true?" Byron Katie taught me there is a vast difference between what I was thinking (telling myself), and what reality was portraying. She helped me learn how to be curious about life and ask questions. I was able to utilize this approach and take my sincere questions, my longing for truth, to God.

I feel it was a miracle that these resources were placed in my life at this time. They laid a foundation for me to operate from a paradigm of love instead of fear. The Unicorns taught me to challenge fear and shame with the mantra, "I love me, and I'm learning." That attitude guided my journey, opening my heart and giving me the ability to accept and embrace the challenging truths life was delivering to me, rather than being fearful and resistant. I had been practicing these concepts and developing the skills that helped to anchor me to peace, even amidst the chaos of my circumstances.

Thus prepared, I felt an overwhelming sense of fascination with the experience of being stripped of everything I once thought I knew and understood about life, while wandering in a wilderness mentally, emotionally, and spiritually. I intentionally focused on the present moment. I could clearly see that worrying about the future consequences or fallout from this situation would only lead to panic, anger, and rage. It didn't make sense to create drama for myself. When I allowed myself to *just be* in the wilderness, to wander and explore, to feel all my feelings, it felt safe, peaceful, and oddly familiar.

It seemed like I had a best friend inside that kept assuring me, *"You're okay. The truth is, you're naked and alone in the wilderness. And the truth about that is, you are totally okay being naked and alone in the wilderness."* I decided to trust this "friend" inside of me as I continued to seek truth. I decided—tentatively, because I felt I did not actually know anything—to call this friend my *soul*.

I no longer felt that I needed to know anything. Even in my not-knowing, I still existed; I was still there, waking up every day, so why did I need to know anything? This was a tremendous relief. If I did not have to *know* everything, nor anything, then I did not have to *do* everything, nor anything! Instead, I could simply consult my soul daily, "What are we doing today?"

I would close my eyes and picture my soul—the ageless, fearless, egoless version of myself. I saw my soul as a conduit of truth and an agent who would not lie to me and could communicate directly with God, the Source of Truth. And day after day, my soul guided me consistently with directions that felt true. These directions, which came as ideas or thoughts, produced feelings of love, joy, peace, and freedom. My heart space seemed to expand daily into realms it had never known. The burden of years of depression and fatigue began to fade. And what I was labeling as *truth* felt pure, like love and light.

I wondered if this process of looking inward was simultaneously taking me upward, into a communicative exchange with a Higher Power. My best guess, my assumption, was that the source of the answers was God, the Creator. I chose (and continue) to use those words because they were the best words I could find when sharing my experiences with other people. However, in my private spaces, I admitted and accepted that I did not know who or what exactly I was communicating with.

Daily, I took every definitive thought through this process. I directed those questions to my soul and, simultaneously, to God. I said, "Here's what I am telling myself . . . " I felt that my soul was in constant contact with, and would deliver answers from, what felt like God. I was amazed and delighted to find that not only could I receive answers immediately, I could trust those answers! Nothing I have ever heard or read has impacted my awareness of my worth as much as following these simple steps:

1. Ask a question
2. Receive the answer
3. Trust myself and the Divine
4. Act with courage & commitment

A.R.T.A.—Ask, Receive, Trust, Act—became my mantra. I listened with my whole being. I trusted. It was a playful experiment with explicit reliance on the Divine. My core desires for my life came into focus: to seek truth; to open my mind, body, and heart to receive it; to trust it; and then to act on it with courage and commitment.

This questioning process carried a different energy than my lifelong, religiously influenced practice of praying in a rote manner.[5] I was examining an alternative for communicating with God. Rather than praying by kneeling on the floor, folding my arms, and bowing my head to send a message outside of myself to a God in an unseen space, I was taking my words, my thoughts, and my feelings inward to my own soul and being escorted right into the presence of God. Up to this point in my life, I was used to deferring to voices of authority to guide me to truth. Now, rather than going *outward and upward* to God, I was going *inward and upward*.

It was particularly interesting to notice how necessary it was for me to detach from the need to know in order to receive the truth, because it was so contrary to how I was raised. I had been taught that having a testimony of God was something I demonstrated by the ability to stand in front of my congregation and say things like, "I *know* this church is true. I *know* we have a true prophet on earth today. I *know* the Book of Mormon is true." *Knowing* doctrine, *knowing* right from wrong, *knowing* good from bad was paramount, it seemed.

God gave me a new perspective: in every area of my life where I was telling myself that I knew something, I was actually in my ego, attached to receiving mortal approval. My focus on "knowing" had capped my growth: I was not probing those spaces or seeking an increase in understanding because I thought I already knew. Throughout my teens and into adulthood, I kept thinking and speaking the same

---

[5] People are great at asking God questions, but can lack the skill of receiving and trusting themselves to be worthy of communicating with God. I work with people who have been religious for decades, doing ALL THE THINGS "right," but they often don't know how to receive answers and don't trust themselves as conduits of God's love and word.

concepts that I had learned at church as a child—with almost zero expansion. That was why everything seemed so monotonous in my church experience. I saw how I had been on a merry-go-round of thought—not learning, not growing, not expanding, not experiencing life. Instead I repeated the words of others, calling them "right," "true," "knowledge," and "testimony." In this environment, I wasn't progressing.

This discovery was such a relief. It explained why I could go to church, week after week, for a lifetime, and feel so emotionally stuck. I practiced consistent religious study, yet I was still carrying the psychological fallacies that created my emotional roadblocks: *I'm not good enough, I'm not lovable, I'm not worthy.* I couldn't seem to move past the anger, shame, resentment, and self-doubt created from these beliefs. Despite all the sermons and scripture discussions, I did not leave church on Sundays feeling like "a new creation in Christ."[6] Instead, I left thinking I knew the gospel extremely well. The repetition in basic church teachings taught me there is only one right way to view and interpret scripture, doctrine, and Church policy. Therefore, I was either doing it all the right way, or, I was doing it wrong. This all-or-nothing, right-and-wrong, good-and-bad way of thinking perpetuated my psychological, emotional, and spiritual stagnation.

I experimented with taking ideas to God and asking, "What more is there?" as a way to stay humble and teachable, like a child. I started actively visualizing taking every concept, idea, belief, or thought into my hands, approaching it like a toddler picking up an object for the first time. I would consciously suspend my mortal judgment—anything and everything I thought I knew—and I would present the concept to God with openness, asking, "What is this?"

One day while visiting family at my mom's house, I was observing conversations and family dynamics when I realized I perceived

---

6 The Holy Bible, KJV, 2 Corinthians 5:17

everything differently than I had in the past. I asked God, "What is going on with me? What is this process that is changing me so much?"

The Spirit replied, *"You are separating the wheat from the tares."*

In church, I had heard lessons about "separating the wheat from the tares" in the last days prior to the Second Coming of Jesus Christ, and I had understood it to mean that the righteous people would be spared and the wicked people would be destroyed by floods and fires and other calamities.

"More, please?" I asked, seeking clarification.

"The separation of the wheat and the tares is happening within you; you are seeing and separating the fear-based philosophies of mankind from the truth. You are distinguishing your ego's voice from your soul's voice. The 'wheat' refers to the truth; the 'tares' are the fallacies."

I felt so much joy! These experiments with thought separation were enlivening! My former understanding of the wheat and tares phrase came with a little paranoia. While I had always assumed that, since I was doing everything right, I would be among the righteous followers who would not get swept from the earth, I did—hello, cute little ego!—feel sad for the sinners who were going to burn. Now this phrase, when given a personal application, switched my focus away from judging others toward my own quest for distinguishing truth from error.

Letting go of former, mortally-programmed beliefs allowed me to reconsider everything about my life from a fresh, uncluttered, and emotionally neutral space—without fear, judgment, guilt, and shame. I considered myself engaged in a personal research experiment to explore, discover, understand, and describe the mechanics of truth. I gave myself permission to ask and ponder everything about life anew, especially the topics I was taught in absolutes as a child. I wondered:

- Does God—a Creator of my being—exist?
- Can I communicate directly, and at all times, with this Creator?

- Is the Creator a source of absolute truth?
- Is it truly possible to verify everything I learn through this source?
- What other inaccuracies and misunderstandings exist in the concepts I have learned and believed?
- What truths might exist in ideas I have previously discarded as false or wrong?
- What else is possible if I really can connect with a Higher Power and source of truth and wisdom whenever I choose?!

In order to fully align with truth, I had to give myself permission to admit that every concept I was taking inward and upward was being contradicted or augmented by God. It seemed like I had misconstrued nearly everything I had drawn from church teachings. My church indoctrination had presented gospel principles like an open bag of Twizzlers licorice on a family road trip. They began as delicious truths, then got contaminated by a wet mist of mortal fear, rolled on the dirty floor of guilt, shame, and judgment, and finally handed to me with the expectation that I would ingest them as enthusiastically as I would have when the bag had first been opened. Unraveling these concepts often felt sticky.

It's pretty humbling when God shows you that something that you have believed and built your life around is, quite frankly, not true. Allowing God to teach me made me laugh at how egotistical I had been. My whole life, I had listened to other people teach me the "doctrines" of God, and I had obediently taught those same ideas and interpretations to others. I had unknowingly perpetuated the passing on of "philosophies of man mingled with scripture!"

I love this scripture: "Yea, I know that I am nothing; as to my strength I am weak; therefore I will not boast of myself, but I will boast of my God, for in his strength I can do all things."[7]

There are many principles, values, and ideas from my church involvement, family, and past experiences that continue to resonate as truth. These elements remain within me, and I love and cherish them. I am grateful for all of these experiences; each of them have helped lead me to further light and truth. However, I am no longer attached to the residue of principles, practices, or programs I perceive to be wrapped in fear, guilt, shame, or judgment. I am no longer afraid to challenge my beliefs.

I can only laugh now at how sure I have been and how much I thought I knew, only to discover that what I believed were Absolute Truths From God were actually mortal ideas and human philosophies. *"Angel, if a human taught you to believe or think anything, even if they said it was from Me, there is a potential margin of error."* I have come to understand that when you recognize that the source of a belief you espouse is human—even if that human says, "God said . . ."—there is an opportunity to reconsider it.

Applications of this concept show up daily. Sometimes I am shown my own erroneous thinking by Spirit; other times, I am the observer of this behavior in others. Once I was at a stop sign, preparing to turn right. I was looking to my left awaiting a break in traffic. The next car approaching on the left had its right blinker turned on. Knowing their turn at the intersection would give me the room I needed, I pulled out. Suddenly, a horn honked aggressively behind me. Glancing in my rearview mirror, I saw that the car had not made the expected turn and was close behind me, blinker still on. I quickly moved into the left lane and the honking car pulled up in the lane beside me.

---

7   The Book of Mormon, Alma 26:12

I checked in with Spirit quickly and asked to understand what was true. I was given the understanding that the driver, unaware her blinker was on, thought I had recklessly pulled out in front of her. What seemed true to her justified her emotional reaction. I could perceive her innocence—she did not know what she did not know. I was filled with compassion for her. With a smile of understanding, I rolled down my window and told the woman, "Your blinker is on." She looked down at her dashboard, and her look of anger quickly transformed to confusion, then shock, as she shut off her blinker and sheepishly apologized for blaming me for the situation.

The Spirit used this experience to teach me the truth about my own perceptions. I have often felt and behaved like this woman: blind to my own problematic behaviors while criticizing someone else for theirs. In practicing going inward and upward to the Source of Truth, seeking to identify my errors, I have been shocked repeatedly by my own ignorance and then filled with grace and compassion for myself and others.

What made this process especially fun was that all the corrections I received from God were gentle and loving. It became very clear that God saw me as innocent. As shocking as the truth of my ignorance could be, there was no room for shame, guilt, or regret regarding my ignorance and misunderstanding. There is no place for any of that in the presence of God. It is just a joyful space in which to play, explore, and expand.

Now that I have lived these concepts for several years, I have become unable to think or speak an untrue word or sentence without feeling physical restriction, a resistance in my body. It is an immediate alert that happens like an alarm system.

The first time I noticed this, I was giving a presentation and began to stumble, stutter, and struggle to speak, mid-sentence. Rather than panic or feel ashamed, I stopped and noticed. "What is this?" I asked.

"What you are saying is not true."

I breathed deeply to center myself and accept the message without attaching to fear and shame, then asked, "What is true?"

A slight correction to one or two words in my sentence altered the meaning from error to truth. Then I was able to speak it without hesitation. To onlookers, this looked like a brief pause, slight correction of my previous statement, and return to seamless speech; but for me it was the beginning of an astonishing awareness. It seemed as though my body began to declare, "You're lying," whenever I spoke a fear-based, and therefore untrue, statement.

Practicing this on myself and learning to catch and release my judgmental words in order to anchor to truth has resulted in a surprising ability: I am *really* aware when someone else is not telling the truth! My body feels it. Sometimes I can even perceive others' thoughts and feelings before they speak them, and understand the lies they are telling themselves.

I thought this was my little secret until I was on a walk one evening with my youngest son, and he said, "You know Mom, you have something like Spidey-sense."

"I do?" I asked, very intrigued.

"Yes, but it's . . . *Spirit*-sense. You just know when people are lying!"

I laughed so hard! My secret was out! This darling little guy had somehow picked up on the truth that no one can get away with lying in my presence, and he saw it as my superpower!

As it had become so easy to discern lies versus truth, I wondered how I had lived oblivious to the lies and deceit of my spouse for fourteen years. I took that question inward and upward, and was gifted this little prize in humility: *"You could not recognize the lies of your partner because you lied to yourself all the time."*

"Well, dang!" Once again, I had to choose to breathe deeply and receive this moment of truth. Truth is no respecter of persons; truth exposes everything and everyone. I employed a question the Unicorns had taught me: "Can I love myself through this?"

This question calls for a pause and a return to truth. It is posed to my own soul and therefore overrides the potential for self-betrayal through an attachment to judgment and shame. My soul always answers this question with, "Yes, you can love yourself through this." That answer restores my whole being with peace. Truth and love are then able to continue to flow to me.

Having settled back into a space of love, I inquired further, "Am I willing to see and accept that maybe I am a liar, just like the person I am annoyed with?"—and again found that I could.

Once my heart was open and ready, I asked, "What more is there? Where was I lying to myself?" Several examples were brought to mind. The ones that stung most were, *"You told yourself that if you did everything right, one day you would be happy and in love with him,"* and, *"You lied in telling yourself you were married; you co-existed, you were never one."*

It became easy to see how subtle lies start. They start as thoughts, particularly "shoulds," and become more and more entrenched. I sat in vision with the former versions of myself, seeing that younger me on my wedding day, back in 2002, when I told my friend, "Keep driving," as we pulled up to the place for the marriage ceremony. My stomach was tight; I assumed it was just nerves. As she drove around the neighborhood a few times, I summoned the courage to *do the right thing*. I was getting married in the temple. I *should* be happy. This was what I was *supposed* to want: a forever family.

That young lady did not know what being in love was; she had never felt it. She had never experienced passion and did not believe in romance. It felt like a silly concept depicted in cheesy movies. Truth was, she did not feel beautiful or desirable or good enough to have her pick of men, so the first man to show interest in her won the prize.

I gave that younger, innocent version of myself so much love and compassion as I saw her on her wedding day. She did not know she was lying to herself. She was just trying to do the right thing. "It's okay," I whispered, with tears flowing. "You are perfect." I held her in my vision and let go of judgment around whether she made the wrong choice, the right choice, a good choice, or a bad choice. The truth was, she made a choice.

Cleansed by this vision, my thoughts were directed to my husband. "Maybe it is possible he did not realize he was lying. Maybe he is as mortal as I am." The compassion I had tapped into for that younger version of myself extended beyond me and flowed in his direction.

During this transition in my way of being and relating to life, I felt tucked away in a cocoon. Life was happening around me, but I was all wrapped up in my soul and God; it felt cozy, warm, and comfortable there. I felt supported, like a newborn babe in one of those tightly wrapped hospital blankets. I had lived with illness, stress, and fatigue for many years, and suddenly felt healthy, relaxed, and energetic. It was like a mental vacation from life, and God and I were hanging out at the beach every day! I asked all kinds of questions and received the most thought-provoking, paradigm-shattering, illuminating responses; I would ponder them for hours and days at a time. I felt like I was attending "God University." What some might refer to as a "faith crisis" felt like a "great awakening" to me.

I experimented with using various names to reference the Source offering me guidance and was surprised and pleased to find that, regardless of the name I used, It did not seem to get offended—at least

AWARENESS: ERROR AND TRUTH

not offended enough to stop answering me. This came as a delightful surprise! This was just one more area where I realized *I can't get it wrong*. One of the doctrines I was taught through church was that there was a proper way to refer to God when speaking about "Him" and when speaking to "Him" in prayer. These "proper" terms were used by everyone around me growing up. They were stated as absolutes and taken very seriously. I was taught the use of any other terms was considered blasphemy. Until this time, I had no idea that I was afraid of getting it wrong, of talking to God in the wrong way, and that this unseen fear actually impeded the quality, sincerity, and vulnerability with which I addressed my Creator.

Once, in a conversation with a couple of people of my faith, I casually remarked, "I sometimes wonder if God is a woman. If so, so many things about life would make sense!" The following day, I received a text from a woman who had heard about the conversation secondhand, saying she was disturbed by my comment. She told me that what I had said about God being a woman was blasphemous, and that if I wanted to gain any insight into the nature of God, she would be happy to educate me.

When going inward and upward, I continually received answers that reframed my previous beliefs. The act of challenging these beliefs felt like the greatest risk I had ever taken. Trusting myself and the Voice of Truth took more courage than anything I had ever done.

I checked in with myself often. "Do I love God enough to believe the answers I'm receiving, or do I love my ego and my reputation more?"

In order to truly love God, I would need to trust in the answers I was receiving while giving zero credence to any contradictory thought, belief, teaching, or practice that stemmed from a mortal origin—regardless of that source's authority. As I explored the possible implications of this particular step, I had a gentle thought enter my mind: *"This is what faith is."* These words resonated deeply in my body. My reaction? "Oh shit! We're talking *total faith,* one hundred percent faith in God! Holding nothing back! Oh boy!"

Oddly, everything I had thought was an "act of faith" previously was actually me following the religious crowd, fitting in, conforming, and believing others in order to receive validation and approval. The concept of faith began to look like asking God questions about everything, and staying totally open to any possibilities, rather than seeking to reaffirm answers, beliefs, and ideas I had been taught were "right" and acceptable. This faith feels like an act of love; it is loving myself enough to trust in my ability to communicate with the Divine. Faith really does cast out fear, as it suggests in the Bible.

These moments seem simple as I write them, but as I was going through it, I tell you, they felt as scary as facing my own death! Everything my entire life had been founded on was being peeled back and stripped away, one layer at a time. I had to make a choice regarding how to be with this deconstruction. I could: 1) love myself and be humble and teachable, or 2) fear what I stood to lose, judge myself, and reject these opportunities. "Bring it," I kept saying to the Divine. "Even if, in a few years, I discover I was wrong about all my new perceptions, I am willing to love myself through that, so I have nothing to lose—other than my attachments to my ego!"

SOURCES: FEAR AND LOVE

"Light is to darkness what love is to fear; in the presence of one the other disappears."
-Marianne Williamson

As I began to discover how often I rejected personal revelation in favor of what I thought I knew, my religious ego identity began to crumble. I had thought of myself as a "faithful member of the Church." I'd prided myself in this, actually, although I would never have admitted it—after all, I had been taught that "pride cometh before the fall." In reality, I was following what others had told me to do, afraid of being "wrong" or "doing it wrong." Whenever I felt an impression that didn't "follow the program," or what I expected in my own proud certainty, I rejected it.

My current hypothesis is that *all* beliefs, thoughts, feelings, and actions come from one of two sources: fear or love. There are many scriptures that instruct us to cast off fear, and they demonstrate that fear does not exist in the same space as love and truth. I began asking myself, "Are my thoughts, feelings, and behaviors (or those of others around me), coming from a place of love or fear right now?" Fear was present more than I could believe. It felt so strange to acknowledge because I had considered myself a "faithful" person. *"How can I be fearful and faithful?"* I wondered. The truth was, *I couldn't!* The deconstruction of my pharisaical identity was now well underway!

I have heard it said that you cannot change what you are not aware of. That was certainly true for me with fear. I did not think of myself as a nervous, anxious, or worried person, so I could not see that fear was driving me, but for thirty-eight years it propelled my every action. I feared the range of consequences, including disappointing my parents; not being accepted among the other members of my church congregation; not being deemed worthy to enter our temples, go on a mission, or attend a church university; and ultimately, not being worthy to live in the presence of God. I had no idea I was fueling up and operating on the energy of fear as often as I was putting unleaded gasoline into my vehicle. It was a wild discovery!

All this time, I believed I was a spiritual person. I did not realize there could be a difference between *spiritual* and *religious*. But now I stood, face to face with the truth: I was actually a fearful and doubtful member of the Church who frequently rejected the answers to my prayers! The beliefs I was challenging were the cornerstones of my ego identity. Everything I had done, every goal I had set, had been founded on these beliefs and values; and, one by one, they were confounded by emerging truths. I felt like I was shedding layers of old skin. Sometimes, when really deep-seated beliefs or values were confronted and no longer held true, I experienced grief and loss, like losing a loved one. I cried, I moaned, I curled up in the fetal position and mourned the "death" of parts of myself.

Who am I? I wondered. *How did this happen? Who is this person I have become?*

It was a moment that held the potential for shame. I felt naked as I was stripped of my ego identity. Thankfully, I had been prepared for this moment. "Can I love myself—rather than judge, guilt, and shame myself—through this?"

A miracle occurred as I was able to first notice the temptation to feel shame, then pause and foresee the result awaiting me if I chose to attach to it: a downward spiral of compounding darkness resulting from fear, guilt, and negative self-judgment. By asking the question, "Can I love myself through this?" I received an answer from within. *"Yes. You can love yourself through this. Keep seeking."*

It was necessary, in order to stay open and learning from the Divine Source of Love—imperative to the continuation of the process of receiving Truth—that I choose not to judge or condemn myself each time responses to my questions arrived and contradicted my previous beliefs. I recognized that I could choose to meet each new insight with love, rather than fear—I could feel *humble*, rather than *humiliated*. Both options were always present when awareness showed up.

One of my Unicorn mentors, Shelby Smith, pointed out to me, "Our choices are either *expansive* or *expensive*." Choosing to love myself and be humble throughout the process of gaining awareness allowed me to be meek and teachable, growing and expanding in my awareness and actions. Humiliation tempted me to feel stupid, blind, betrayed, and full of rage towards myself, others, and institutions. All of these responses cultivated and perpetuated fear-based beliefs and actions—they cost me learning, peace, and freedom.

There is a famous quote often attributed to Viktor Frankl, a psychologist and Holocaust survivor: "Between stimulus and response there is a space. In that space is our power to choose our response. In our response lies our growth and freedom."

There is profound guidance in this statement. Before my awakening, my emotional reactions between stimulus and response went from zero to sixty in one-point-two seconds. As a child, my go-to emotion was anger. I got intensely angry and reacted quickly. I broke stuff, I threw things, I yelled at people. As an adult, my default setting drove me from stimulus to stress, overwhelm, and anger just as fast.

When I discovered breathwork—the simple act of intentional breathing—I found that I had the power to push the "pause button" on life and extend the space between stimulus and response. The power to choose is our greatest gift; this freedom can never be taken from us, but many of us throw this gift away by reacting in the moment, rather than choosing our response. As I used the breath to broaden the gap between stimulus and response, I learned to give myself more time to consciously and intentionally enact my agency. By utilizing my breath to pause, I can look at my options and choose the source of my response.

In my commitment to stay humble and open, I asked seeking questions, such as, "What would you have me do next?" In one of those moments, my soul's voice told me, *"Now is the time to see your doctor and get an antidepressant."* The directive seemed even more bizarre and unexpected than *"Put chicken in the crockpot."*

Two years after I was married, I completed a masters degree in clinical social work. After confronting a series of ethical dilemmas in the workplace, including the role the pharmaceutical industry plays in affecting legislation for the diagnosis and treatment of individuals, and the standard operating procedures of insurance companies, I left the profession and immersed myself in research and science from the fields of nutrition and fitness. Discovering the extensive mind- and mood-enhancing power of vitamins, minerals, and physical activity, I had grown skeptical and critical of psychotropic medications. They seemed to me to be a crutch and a pathway to dependency rather than a solution to an underlying problem. Now I was asking for guidance and my soul was telling me to request a prescription for antidepressants.

I acknowledged my resistance when it surfaced, and I chose to suspend judgment and offer myself grace. *What if the perceptions and judgments I have held in the past are simply not true? What if, at this moment, this is what I need? Can I love myself through this?* I trusted my soul and God, so I did not hesitate to act. I simply said, "You got it, boss!" I followed through with scheduling an appointment with my doctor, who prescribed me an antidepressant.

These small and simple shifts continued to significantly alter my life course. As I continued to separate the wheat (truth) from the tares (error) and replace fear with love, I felt like I was undergoing a personality transplant. It was becoming easier to actually *be* like Christ—to feel the compassion, lack of judgment, and the unconditional love of Christ for others.

One day, mid-June, just three weeks after that critical phone call with my husband, I was hanging up laundry in my bedroom closet and contemplating the events unraveling in my life. Now and then, judgmental thoughts would pop into my mind, such as, *I would never steal. I have never stolen anything. How could he be so stupid?* In my closet on this particular day, those stories returned. I paused to notice them, acting as an observer of my thinking. "I am in judgment." I said to myself. "I wonder what is going on in my unconscious mind."

I decided to investigate my thinking, setting my ego's voice and judgments aside, and inquired of God to find out what was true. I was telling myself I had never stolen money from my employer, and therefore had no ability to access understanding or compassion for my husband regarding his stealing.

"I'm telling myself I have not stolen. Is it true, or is it my story?"

A thought appeared, *"It is your story."*

Then I asked, "Show me what I have stolen."

Memories rolled to the forefront of my mind. They were memories from moments as a parent, as a wife, and as a high school student.

The message came, *"You have stolen the hearts of your children when you have yelled at them."* I saw their scared faces in past moments when I was in my anger. I recalled their innocent eyes and the force it took for me to ignore those eyes and allow my fear and pride to justify my yelling. I sat with this awareness, receiving the truth while suspending the temptation to attach to the guilt and shame that wanted to swallow me up. I acknowledged that I had stolen their hearts at times. I felt sadness.

"Can I love myself through this?" I asked. I felt the answer, *"Yes, you can."* I breathed several deep breaths until it felt like the heavy sadness in my chest lightened.

"What more is there?" I asked my soul.

"You have stolen the spotlight." My mind went to my teen years and moments from school and social settings where my sarcasm took center stage. I was often so afraid of being teased or bullied that I harassed others in an effort to deflect negative attention away from myself. I was quick-witted and loud, and I could steal the spotlight at any moment. I saw the faces of my peers and my close friends in the moments when I was more concerned with my own reputation than with their feelings. I had stolen the safety of others in those moments. I had stolen the love from those spaces.

In this awareness, my guts wrenched. Agony. I wanted to crawl into a hole. But instead, I breathed. "Can I love myself through this?" I asked. Again, the answer was, *"Yes, you can."* Every intentional breath I took was a conscious effort to remember, *I love me, and I'm learning.*

I had been practicing this mantra often to stay open and receptive to truth, instead of retracting in shame.

When my stomach muscles began to relax, I asked, "What more is there?"

The answer was, *"Every time you take something that isn't yours to take, it is stealing."* Like frames in a movie, I saw moments of myself taking someone's space or their time to speak, crushing their ideas with my opinions, talking over people, making decisions for others... so many examples of my stealing surfaced.

My ego returned and shouted, "But these examples are not *nearly* as bad as stealing money from one's employer! That is ILLEGAL!" This thought was my ego's last-ditch effort to preserve itself. It was pure deception and deflection. I laughed out loud, noticing what I was doing: I wanted to moralize my stealing as being *better* than his stealing?!

"Aren't you so cute!" I said to my ego.

Then I acknowledged the truth. "I am a thief."

I breathed deeply and sat with the sadness that accompanied the awareness of my actions. God had delivered the answer I was seeking; the evidence came to light through my soul, and there was no denying it. Breathing helped me to assimilate the awareness and decrease the physical sensations of contraction throughout my body. Fear, guilt, shame, and judgment seemed to seize upon me like a cramp in my guts, around my heart, in my chest, and sometimes in my throat. As I took deep breaths, I sent love to those places in my body and noticed they were able to relax.

Although this had not been conscious knowledge beforehand, my identity as a thief lived inside of me, in my *shadow*. I refer to my shadow as the "junk closet" of my mind. It is the place where I stuff anything that does not fit the way I want to see myself. I had hidden my forms of stealing from my own view because there was unconscious shame around it. Shame loves to avoid being noticed, and it often deflects attention by blaming someone else. My initial judgments about my husband's stealing money from his employer were direct projections of my unconscious shame around my own moments of stealing. This light of awareness annihilated my self-deception. It led me to the truth about myself.

This moment called for repentance. I sincerely desired a change of heart and wished to never repeat these egotistical behaviors again. I turned to a Hawaiian spiritual practice I had learned called the "Ho'oponopono Prayer." It is a simple, yet complete transitioning process, guiding one from awareness to forgiveness to acceptance to gratitude and love. The prayer includes these four simple steps:

1. I'm sorry
2. Please forgive me
3. Thank you
4. I love you

I spoke these words, adapting and directing them toward the past versions of myself who had stolen the hearts of my children, the attention in the classroom, the emotionally safe space from my peers.

"Angel, I am sorry that you felt less than others and afraid in all of these memories. I'm sorry you felt you had to control these situations by demeaning others to maintain your sense of safety.

"Angel, I forgive you! You were doing the very best you knew how to do, with what you had, in each of these moments. I see you as purely ignorant and completely innocent.

"Angel, Thank you for being willing to see yourself and acknowledge these things.

"Angel, I love you!"

Upon completing these words, I felt a sensation in my body I would describe as an excretion.

I inquired of the Source of Truth, "What is this?" and the answer was, *"This is shame, guilt, and judgment leaving the body."*

I was fascinated. It felt as if those emotions were substances being extracted from within me by an overbearing force, followed immediately by the rushing sensation of a substance entering me, filling the spaces in my body that had been occupied by those heavy emotions.

"What is this?" I asked, referring to the sensation of a new substance entering my body.

"Compassion," was the response.

The substance of compassion permeated my being. I mean to say that an energy I recognized as compassion passed through my cells, and I could feel it in my body. I followed the direction of its flow, charting a course through my body, and recognized with a chuckle, "Wow, even my bowels are filled with compassion!" a phrase I had heard used in scripture, yet never before experienced. I settled into it. Compassion felt so yummy to my entire being! It resonated with my soul, just like the harmonious resonance of a musical chord, with the words, *"This is Christ. Christ is compassion."* It was so clear and easy to identify. The "knowing" who Christ was, from all I had learned about Him growing up, was a disconnected, intellectual understanding, residing only in my mind; but now, it had transformed into a true knowing—in my whole being.

Then I returned my awareness to the thoughts that had begun this whole process. I had been wanting to understand how my husband could steal. As soon as I returned my thinking to that question, a flood of understanding and compassion surrounded him in my mind. *HOLY SHIFT!* I thought! *From judgment to compassion—just like that?!*

From criticism to kindness? That was the simplest act of forgiveness of another person I have ever experienced!

The quote, "You cannot give what you don't have" came to mind. *"But now,"* I was told, *"you have compassion, so you can give it!"*

Prior to doing my own shadow work, I did not have the awareness around the subject of stealing that would enable me to give him total compassion. I thought I had some compassion initially, but it was kindness that lacked true understanding. I was able to be kind to him, but I still told myself I could not understand why he would do what he did; therefore, judgment remained. Without the awareness of my own stealing, I could not have compassion for myself nor forgive another person for the same thing. It was a mind-blowing epiphany!

Well, huh! Would you look at that? I thought. In releasing fear, I was able to receive the love God was offering me in an attitude of curiosity and wonder, rather than resisting it from a framework of shame. I chose compassion for myself as I learned, and this expanded my ability to love others unconditionally.

I sat with this experience, reflecting on the ease, grace, and flow of it all, and the following ideas percolated in my mind: Having been raised a Christian, the topic of forgiveness was a frequent theme of lessons and Sunday sermons. Despite this, I had often heard others say, "It is so hard to forgive," and, "I'm praying to be able to forgive someone, but I am not there yet," or, "I am really trying to forgive." Forgiveness was often portrayed as an arduous task. I often heard people talk about their struggle to become a person who could forgive someone else.

The lessons given at church on forgiveness always pointed to the example of Christ, encouraging us to forgive and love as He did. But I noticed a contradiction in the culture, underscored by common statements such as, "No one but Christ is perfect." This "escape clause" justified our inability to forgive and love others, because we all believed we were not as great as He.

Now I had just done it; I had truly experienced a "mighty change of heart."[8] It came about first by cleansing my own inner vessel, and then simply aligning with truth. There was no room for judgment once I purged myself of erroneous beliefs. I had found, for myself, the missing steps in how to complete the process of forgiving others through shadow work and self-forgiveness.

I was astonished and in awe! *God, you are brilliant!* I thought. *This whole embezzlement thing is so beautifully designed!* Had my husband's issue been with pornography addiction, an affair, or a substance abuse problem, I felt I would have more easily understood those temptations. As a social worker, I had a background in addressing those subjects, and could have supported my husband in finding professional treatment and the tools to overcome any of them. However, having been raised with the examples of my honest and hard-working parents, it felt impossible for me to comprehend why or how anyone would steal money from their employer. It was the thing I was most judgmental about—it seemed like the most unnecessary and idiotic choice ever!

With a sense of awe, I saw how the very challenge my husband had with lying and stealing was the one thing that cut straight to my core. I noted how perfectly orchestrated this experience was for the refinement of both of us. Because my husband embezzled money, I was led to examine and acknowledge my sources of judgment, shame, and projection, while my husband got to face his own demons. As my mind expanded deeper into reflective understanding, I felt joyful and grateful for everything we as a couple were experiencing.

---

8   The Book of Mormon, Mosiah 5:2

Noticing the gratitude I was feeling, I thought to pause and specifically articulate my thanks to God, out loud. Standing there in my closet, a hanger in hand, I paused and said, "God, thank you for entrusting me with this experience and my role in all of this." These were the exact words I spoke. As I said the words "my role," I perceived that I had been assigned a pivotal role in this well-orchestrated experience.

Powerfully and unmistakably, a response came into my mind. *"Angel, I DO trust you."*

BAM! An explosion hit my being, sending shockwaves throughout my body. I felt like I had been electrocuted in a way—what I experienced in that moment is beyond words.

My next thought was a question. *Did God—the Source of all creation—just tell me that It trusts me?! Little, mortal, insignificant me?*

Tentatively cradling the supposition that this message may be true unsealed a portal of possibility and potential for me. A hopeful if-then thought emerged: *If God, the Source of all creation, trusts me, then wouldn't this mean I can trust myself too?*

An affirming response to my query came through: *"YES! You can absolutely trust yourself!"*

I reflected on the dynamic pattern shift that had occurred in the way I was processing my thoughts, feelings, and actions in recent weeks. *I see it now! This is exactly how I have been living lately: trusting myself to communicate with God and trusting the answers I have received every time I ask a question!* I saw the consistency in the simple equation:

Faith = Ask + Receive + Trust + Act

This formula is absolutely devoid of fear. Energies of faith and fear cannot coexist in the same space within me at the same time. I have found that I can only hold to one and reject the other; I fuel one while ignoring the other. I remembered the Bible verse, "You cannot serve God and Mammon."[9] I got it.

I said, "I DO trust me. And, God, I trust you, too!" I meant this with every part of me. I did not need anything or anyone else, ever, to connect me to God. I had come to an awareness of what was really true: it's just me and God, at all times, and in all things, and in all places; there is one source of truth, and it is available for me to access directly.

A new and radical sensation then struck me: I closed my eyes and noticed a feeling of warm water cascading over, around, and through my entire being. It felt so real I opened my eyes to see if water was leaking from the ceiling. There was no waterline break above me. I closed my eyes again and explored the sensation. This waterfall was cleansing my mind, body, heart, and soul, and I could feel the palpable material of fear leaving my body through my toes—the sensation felt like they were bleeding. I was simply aware—it was a *knowing*—that fear was draining out of me. The sensation revealed that fear could not remain inside of me with the substance that was entering.

"What is this washing over me?" I asked.

"*Love*," was the immediate reply.

I felt as if I could track and calculate the shifting quantities of love and fear, like tangible, measurable elixirs in my body: one increased in volume as it poured in through the top of my head, and the other decreased as it drained out through my toes. I also felt surprised by the thorough saturation of the substance of love moving through every area of my body. I paused and expressed, "Wow! You even love my fat cells?!" I experienced the waterfall drenching my fat cells, permeating and penetrating them at the same uninhibited rate as it passed through all of my organs and bones.

---

9   The Holy Bible, KJV, Matthew 6:24

As the energy of love continued to push the fear out of my body, curiosity emerged. *How is it possible that I have been so filled with fear?* I wondered. *If I have been operating out of fear for the majority of my life, and if fear and love cannot coexist in the same space, have I been devoid of love all this time?*

In church settings, I had been taught that "no unclean thing can enter the presence of God." I had assumed that meant anyone who had "sinned" or who had not "done enough" could not enter the presence of God. *But what if* fear *is the "unclean thing"? What if it's* fear *that cannot enter the presence of God?* I reflected on my experience. I felt I had entered the presence of God many times in recent weeks, and I realized that each of these connections began with a choice to surrender my fear in order to trust the answer that came.

God's love for me was imprinted permanently on my heart that day. The truth about the worth of my soul rose to the surface: it was not linked to my *doing*, it was innate in my *being*. My relationship with God was sealed. My love and trust in myself was branded on my heart, too.

Life presented many opportunities to confirm my commitment to this newfound love and trust. On a rare, unscheduled morning in early July 2016, I lingered in my bed enjoying a conversation with my sons, who were piled all around me. In this moment of being mentally, physically, and emotionally present, I felt a surge of love, connection, and gratitude for my boys. I verbally expressed my feelings to each of them. I remember seeking to savor the moment, deeply appreciating the unique absence of feelings of stress, pressure, and overwhelm from an endless to-do list.

As I continued to go about my day, I began to experience a severe tightening in my chest. It quickly escalated to difficulty breathing. I was confused by what was happening, and afraid because I was the only adult in the house. I was gasping for air and began to emit sounds of sobbing with each exhale. When I felt a bizarre sensation as if my soul was separating from my body, I fearfully wondered, *Am I dying?*

I called to my oldest son, telling him, "Call Grandma!" He called and handed me the phone. Between gasps, I described what I was experiencing.

"Hold on!" my mom responded, "We are on our way!"

I hung up the phone, gasping between sobs, and worried about what my kids were thinking. It had to look terrifying to them as I held my chest and struggled to breathe. I felt like I was suffocating. Only when I heard the sirens of an ambulance halting abruptly outside my house was my attention diverted from my painful fight for oxygen and fear for what my sons were going through.

One of my sons opened the door and let paramedics in. Almost simultaneously, my parents entered the home and began calmly ushering my kids to their car. I wondered if they had run every stoplight to arrive at my home so quickly.

As a paramedic began asking me questions, I closed my eyes and sank into a deep sense of relief. I felt as though I could relinquish the care of my body. Now, I could just let go. The paramedic's assurance that I was going to be okay triggered a simple explanation. *Oh no, not that.*

I inquired, "Am I having a panic attack?"

"Yes. It appears so." He said. "But we are going to take you to the hospital and have you checked out."

The next thing I remember is sitting in the hospital room, feeling deeply embarrassed for causing such a commotion. I noticed my embarrassment and I repeated in my mind, several times, *I love me.*

The words brought me back home to truth: I am lovable—even when I think I'm dying and it is actually a panic attack. Intentionally claiming love for myself with these words cast out the fear that caused the embarrassment. I had feared that I was a burden, feared that I had inconvenienced others, feared I had traumatized my children. All these fears subsided when I commanded my mind, body, heart, and soul to return to love, with the simple words, "I love me."

My mom and sister sat with me in the hospital room, offering support and compassion. My mom knew I was always busy. She had seen my pattern of operating as a highly stressed mother and business co-owner, but she did not know about the added measure of the pending arrest warrant.

A doctor came in and cleared me to go home. He handed me a prescription for an anti-anxiety medication. *What does this say about me?* I asked myself. *Am I weak? Am I broken?* I felt sorrow and shame swell within me once again, riding on the waves of old stories I had believed about needing medication to manage one's emotions. Those beliefs engendered more feelings of shame and created tension in my body—my stomach region physically tightened. I intentionally responded with the words, "I love me. It's going to be okay."

I filled that prescription and kept it in my purse, to take if I ever experienced the onset of another panic attack. I was two months into taking an antidepressant daily, and now I had added this anti-anxiety medication.

I chose to let go of my judgments around medication and replace them with gratitude. In the year that followed, there were just two occasions when I felt those heart-attack-like symptoms swelling within me and utilized the medication. I was delighted at the instantaneous neutralizing effect it had, and I felt grateful to have access to medication when I needed it. I admitted to myself that I did not fully understand how everything in my life was impacting my mind, body, heart, and soul, but I did not need to know all of that in order to simply be grateful for everything happening exactly as it was.

The more spiritual experiments I conducted, the more dramatically my ways of thinking, feeling, and behaving shifted. The basic truths in the scriptures became tangible for me. I found so much truth in the scriptures regarding fear and love.

I experienced the literal truth of the verse, "There is no fear in love; but perfect love casteth out fear: because fear hath torment. He that feareth is not made perfect in love."[10]

The shift from fear to love is a major example of the "small and simple things" described in the Book of Mormon: "...by small and simple things are great things brought to pass; and small means in many instances doth confound the wise."[11] I started to use these powerful principles every chance I got to find truth and direction in my life, forgive myself for misconceptions and past mistakes, and gain true compassion for others. As I stepped out of the energy of fear and called in the energy of love, I began to develop (or rather, recognize) my spiritual gifts. Life felt like a celebration. Surprises just kept showing up! It was like God was throwing me a surprise birthday party every day—perhaps more accurately, it was a *Rebirthday party!*

---

10   The Holy Bible, KJV 1 John 4:18

11   The Book of Mormon, Alma 37:6

ALIVENESS: SADNESS AND JOY

> *"When you do things from your soul,*
> *you feel a river moving in you, a joy."*
> -Rumi

While my husband was contending with his legal situation and court dates, we continued to operate a barely-breaking-even shuttle business and raise our kids. I found direction and peace by going inward to ask my soul questions throughout each day, especially, "What would you have me do next?" Every time I asked, I received an immediate answer, and I acted without hesitation. I continued to follow the mantra, *A.R.T.A. Ask - Receive - Trust - Act.*

Sometimes the answers eclipsed my wheelhouse, and I did not know exactly how to carry out what I was directed to do, so I would ask for assistance. *"What* do I need to do next to accomplish this? *Where* do I go to find the knowledge, mentors, skills, or resources necessary to accomplish this?"

The ability to receive and recognize spiritual thought-impressions came with a sense of ease and a growing frequency. Day after day, my soul guided me consistently with directions that felt pure, like love, light, and truth. My heart space seemed to expand daily into realms it had never known.

Answers came for every aspect of my life: physical, mental, emotional, social, and spiritual. I received a range of impressions. *"Start the laundry." "Release your ego and humble yourself." "This particular son needs you right now, go hug him." "Look into your eyes in a mirror and connect with your soul." "Forgive this person and forgive yourself."*

After four months of asking daily for direction, an answer that had come twice in recent months showed up a third time. I asked, "What do I do next?" and the answer was, *"Fire your husband from the business, tell him to move out, and tell him you are filing for divorce."* I had resisted this mandate because my programmed mind blocked it with thoughts like, *We were married for time and all eternity. You don't just get a divorce, you work through things. We made covenants to support and love each other.*

I did not come from divorced parents. None of my close friends had divorced parents. Divorce felt taboo in my culture, like failure, like a sin. My feelings toward my husband during this time were genuinely neutral. I was not angry at him and did not carry a grudge. My conversations with God had illuminated my husband's motivations for what he had done. They were culturally influenced in part, and they were also a product of his personal fears, pressures, and insecurities. Divorce was not my goal; I did not think I needed to divorce him.

When this directive came again, I knew it was the third time, and rather than reject it instantly, I began to negotiate with the Spirit. I remember saying out loud, "Is there no other way?"

When those words left my lips, a presence appeared next to me. It was invisible, yet palpable. My mind was drawn to Mother Eve, and her moment in the Garden of Eden as she was presented with a choice that seemed to oppose everything she had been taught.[12] The presence standing next to me offered compassion, "*I get it.*" She communicated with me instantly without words, like a direct conveyance of intelligence. I cannot find the words to describe all that was explained to me by this unseen being, but it was clear I was not alone, and that was comforting.

There was a distinct absence of fear in that moment; there was no space for fear because love and truth filled the room. It became clear to me that what was taking place in my life was part of a much grander design. It was not just about me making choices in regards to my physical world. It was not about me choosing to stay married or choosing to get divorced. This moment was about me choosing my own ego as my idol of worship or choosing to surrender that part of me and give everything I had to God, in total trust.

I followed that prompting, and my husband did leave our home, quite reluctantly. My next question for God was, "What now?" I was directed to leave St. George for a time to be in nature and get centered. "Where do I go?" I asked. The "where" showed up two days later when a long-time friend invited me to visit her at her new home in Maui. I jumped online to look up the cost of a round-trip flight: $590.

I immediately reverted to my fearful, programmed mindset. I thought, *HOW can I afford $590 dollars? I have no savings, I am literally bankrupt!* As I believed these thoughts, additional fearful assumptions appeared and my fictional story anchored deeper.

Even if I sell my plasma to earn the money, what will my bishop say

---

12   In LDS Doctrine, the Fall of Adam and Eve is taught as being a necessary part of the human experience. It is taught that Eve needed to choose to taste the forbidden fruit in order to be able to perceive that all things have an opposite: light and dark, good and evil, pleasure and pain. This gave her, and all mankind, the power to make conscious choices that would provide opportunities for learning and growth.

when he hears I went to Hawaii? I can just imagine him asking, "HOW can you afford that after asking your church congregation for help with food for your family?" How will my mom react? She'd say, "WHY would you leave your kids at a time like this and go on a vacation?!"

My mind flooded with words of imagined judgment from others.

I felt swallowed up and suffocated by fear. Immediately, I felt like a large steel door had shut above my head and I was in a very cold room; it was reminiscent of being in an underground cellar.

While I had been living and breathing every day in total trust in my communication with God, asking, receiving, and acting with courage, a sensation of warmth and love had surrounded me. This new sensation provided a shocking contrast. When I noticed that this feeling came in response to my thoughts, I asked for an increase in understanding. "What more is there?"

The Spirit taught me that the feeling of a steel door shutting above my head was the sensation of disconnect: I had unplugged from communication with God.

The pattern I had been following became clear: *How* and *why* questions carry an energy of doubt, an element of fear. They are looking for proof that the answer is right, certain, and safe. When I ask these types of questions, I turn away from faith toward fear; I disregard the answers God sends me, to the point that I don't even recognize them.

When I ask *what* and *where* questions, I am in an attitude of faith, trust, and love. The answers show up; I receive them and act with courage and commitment, demonstrating my love for God. God delivers the *how,* and explains the *why* afterwards.

I call this *The What-and-Where Pattern for Co-Creating Miracles with God.* Following this, I have lived nothing but miracle after miracle. I used to believe that God was not giving me answers to prayers much of the time, either because I was unworthy or because

He had His own reasons for withholding them and I just needed to be patient. I learned that changing my questions prepared me to receive the answers God was *always* eager to give.

I had asked *what* I needed to do next, and was given a directive to go away into nature. I asked *where* I needed to go, and I was invited to Maui. Then I shifted away from love and trust, and approached my Creator with a limiting, fearful question: "*How* am I going to afford this?" My story spiraled into fear from there.

Words from the Bible came to mind: "Oh ye of little faith!"[13] After all the miracles, the comfort, the love, and the guidance I had been receiving from God for months, did I have any room for concern, or any legitimate reason to doubt that the Creator of all things had this figured out? As I reflected on this, it just felt natural to apologize.

I humbly approached the Source of all Truth and Love and said, "I just realized what happened: I attached to fear. I am SO SORRY! Please forgive me! I promise I'll focus on *what* and *where*, and trust You, because I KNOW in whom I have trusted, and there's NO REASON for me to doubt, fear, or need to know the *how*!"

A flood of warmth returned again, as if that steel door slid open. It felt like light entered the top of my head and flowed throughout my entire body, restoring my feelings of peace and connection to the Divine.

That's when I realized, *I just repented of fear!*

That was a first for me. I had always repented of "sins," but this truth came as an instant knowing: if I continually repent of fear—recognizing and apologizing when the energy of fear is present and I am believing it—I may NEVER need to repent of anything else! This really nips things in the bud: I can escort fear out of my mind, body, heart, and spirit by turning to love and trust before my fearful thoughts

---

13   The Holy Bible, KJV, Matthew 16:8

and feelings evolve into fearful actions—a.k.a. "sins"!

The very next day, my son handed me a stack of mail. I shuffled through it and came to a letter from a commercial car insurance company. Expecting a bill, I opened it.

And there in my hands was a letter and a check:

"You overpaid your commercial vehicle insurance for the last quarter. Here is a reimbursement check in the amount of $590."

It was the *exact amount* of a round-trip flight to Maui! I almost said, "I don't believe it!" But I caught myself. Instead I said, "I DO believe it. And God, I RECEIVE IT! THANK YOU!" Within minutes, that check was deposited and I was booking my flight to Maui.

Sometimes impressions that came would guide me, not to change my behavior, but to examine my motivations. This new way of operating was definitely a major mental shift. Prior to this time in my life, I had believed that I *was* my thoughts, and that my thoughts were accurate, true, and right; I simply trusted them. Now, every time I encountered a conviction, such as *I should make breakfast for my kids right now,* I would catch it, notice it, and challenge it: "Is this true, or is this my story?" I would receive a response to my question, telling me that it was my story. Then I would ask, "What is true?"

The truth that came about making breakfast for my kids was, *"You can choose to make breakfast."* Over and over again, I was reminded that I am free to choose.

When I asked the additional question, "What more is there?" I was given insights into parts of myself that were wrapped in fear, judgments, and the worries I harbored in my unconscious mind.

In this instance, the Spirit asked, *"How would you feel about yourself if you didn't make breakfast for your kids?"*

"I would feel like a bad mom."

ALIVENESS: SADNESS AND JOY

"Then your motivation for making breakfast is to prove something . . . You are trying to prove and earn your worth and value by doing something you think will make you a 'good mom.' At this moment, you are doing it because of the shame that would surface if you didn't do it—not because you love your kids."

This insight resonated through my body, clear as a bell; I knew it was true. I was shown that the motivations behind my choices could easily vary from moment to moment and day by day. One day I might wake up and be motivated by love to make breakfast for my children, while another day guilt and shame would be driving me.

But it doesn't really matter, as long as breakfast gets made, right?

That is not what I was shown. I was taught that it absolutely matters! The energy in which I do the things I do has an effect on me, on the people around me, and on the very things I am doing with that energy. I began to notice that when I did things motivated by fear, I held degrees of resentment about doing them. I then carried that energy and projected it onto others.

I behaved with covert hostility and an increase in sarcasm when operating from the energy of fear; I would suddenly snap at someone in overt rage when the energy built up. All of that garbage was eliminated by learning to choose love over fear as my source of motivation for doing (or not doing) anything!

The mysteries surrounding my health issues came to light as I began to pay attention to the energy in which I did things. I learned that my physical health conditions were all symptoms of my beliefs. I was guided to find writings on the physical impact of beliefs, thoughts, and feelings. I was led to inspired works of women healers that opened my eyes to a whole new spiritual realm.[14]

At first I met these resources with disbelief: *Oh, this stuff can't be*

---

14   See "Further Reading" section at the end of this book.

true. This was my ego-mind talking. My ego loves to reject anything different or uncommon; it likes to stay safe and cling to its pre-existing beliefs. But my soul drew me in to read these women's words and converse with the Divine about them. As I experimented with what I learned, incredible physical healing occurred, and I made mental connections as well.

I realized that if we are beings that have a soul, a mind, a heart, and a body, then of course all these parts of ourselves are connected to each other and to their Creator! It is only our modern, western belief system that has fragmented and isolated these aspects of us. I learned about cultures across the globe and throughout history that viewed health holistically and spiritually. I had been raised in ignorance, in a system driven by money and power that had divided and compartmentalized the body, mind, heart, and soul, falsely conditioning me to dismiss these concepts as "woo-woo."

God showed me that my body is a vessel of truth—it cannot lie. I can lie to my body with false beliefs, but my body is a billboard of truth. It will manifest my beliefs in physical form to help me see. In our medically-focused society, we are conditioned to constantly address the *symptoms* of poor physical health, rather than finding and treating the root causes. Many of us go from doctor to doctor, trying one prescription and treatment after another, never finding anything that works. Few people understand this truth—that the body's symptoms are a result of our beliefs; we must go deeper. As you resolve the lies you are telling yourself and remove the fear you operate from, you can come into truth and love, step out of chaos into peace, and witness your own healing.

In these divinely inspired books, I found powerful truths that unlocked my medical mysteries. For example, Louise Hay says, "Resentment affects all organs in the body." Because it was true, that one sentence had a greater healing effect on my physical, mental, emotional, and spiritual healing than the combination of hours, days, weeks, months, years—and lots of dollars—I had spent on doctor visits and lab work.

I carried unresolved resentment towards my husband through most of my marriage. Resentment drove me to try to fix things—to fix him. I thought if he worked harder, if he read self-help books and parenting books, if he worked on progressing and changing himself the way I did, even just a little, our marriage could be better. He did not want to. My resentment grew over time, and I made myself ill with it.

My therapist told me resentment is a red flag for self-betrayal. My ego was certain this was not me. The word *betrayal* sounded like deception, like someone who is a liar. That did not fit my view of myself. "I value living in integrity." I told him. "I have had the definition of 'integrity' memorized since I was a young woman: *Integrity is having the moral courage to make my actions consistent with my knowledge of right and wrong.*"

He looked at me. "Who or what are you in integrity with?"

I stared. The truth of my delusion came like a slap in the face.

In an instant, I surveyed my entire life. I saw that I had been living in integrity to all of the rules, the shoulds, the expectations of the people around me. "Be obedient"—this was the way I had been taught to do life. I obeyed others while betraying my inner self because I never paused and asked what my inner self actually wanted. That wasn't even a consideration! I was too busy fulfilling external demands, striving to become all the "right things" and really believing at the time that I wanted to be those things!

I realized I had no idea who Angel really was. If I wasn't trying to live someone else's template, script, or program, who would I be?

What would I want? Where would I go? What would I do? It felt scary to learn that I had no answers to these questions. I had never looked inward before! I also felt very curious, wanting to find answers. I wondered what might be there if I was willing to look. But how? I began seeking to know how to connect with myself.

During this season, I was reminded to "be still, and know that I am God."[15] I did not know how to give myself permission to just BE! Whenever I stopped *doing*, even for a moment, I would fall asleep. Then I would feel guilty for taking a nap because there was so much I "needed" to do. Stillness was foreign to me. I had to explore the meaning of *being* instead of *doing*. As I searched for guidance on learning to be still, I read about "woo-woo, hippy-dippy, baloney" practices like meditation, yoga, and mindfulness. *This is some weird shit,* I thought. *Who has time to just sit around?*

After resisting and complaining, I turned to God and asked for help. "I'm telling myself I can't sit still and don't have time for that. What is true?"

"Angel, you do not have to prove or earn your worth and value. Just be. Breathe. Relax. Play. Rejuvenate."

I did not know how. I had forgotten how to do all of those things.

For years, the primary way I betrayed myself was by trying to prove my worth through "doing." As I woke each morning, my mind immediately went to my *to-do-list*: all those things I believed I needed to get done that day.

Ironically, some of the heaviest items on my to-do-list were my "spiritual to-dos." We had been taught at church to "search the scriptures, ponder, and pray" every single day, and I had interpreted those activities as tasks on my checklist. They were work items, steps to climb on my stairway to heaven. When I missed these steps, I felt

---

15   The Holy Bible, KJV, Psalm 46:10

guilt and shame, believing I was not "keeping the commandments." Practices that could have brought me peace were accompanied instead by my own mental pressure—*I have to do these things daily to be righteous and worthy.* I tried so hard to do all these things and to tell myself that there was joy in completing these tasks (because I was taught that there *should* be joy in doing these things), but I was *not* feeling the joy from this list. In fact, before my existential crisis led me to conversing with God, it had been years since I had felt lasting joy! Instead, I often felt its opposites. I felt numb. I felt dead inside. I felt like I had lost my personality.

Years earlier, a therapist had asked me to make a list of ten activities that lit me up. He called it a "Passions List." I remember staring at that blank paper and then glancing up the clock and then back down on my paper, totally frozen; I could not think of one thing! I left the therapist's office that day wondering what had happened to me and where I had gone—when had Angel died and a "momster" appeared in her place?

I never rested because my job of being a perfect wife and mother and Latter-Day Saint was never done. I did not play—there was always work to do, and I thought play was frivolous. I did not do things for me or spend money on myself—that was selfish. I only did the things for me I thought I *should;* therefore, I lived in denial. I did not do the things my heart and soul wanted to do, like dance and sing, or play my guitar. I did not go cliff diving or swing on rope swings. I did not write about my ideas. I was busy doing the *right things.* I was caught in the trap of a doing-addiction and thought the way to feel better was to do more, do it right, do it perfectly. I thought *doing* would earn me blessings of health and happiness; in reality, it brought me resentment and health issues!

One day, the Spirit asked me to look at my list. "Here it is." I said. "My to-do list." The Voice responded, *"Looks more like a 'do-do list,' to me."*

I laughed out loud. "You are right—it's my shit list!" (I have called it that ever since!)

"Does that list make you happy?" asked the Spirit.

"No. It makes me tired and ornery and bossy. There is so much to do, I feel like there's never any time for anything else. I never get to the bottom of my list, and items that don't get done just get carried into the next day and added to. I am so busy *doing* all the time! Every once in a while, I experience burnout, and then I hang out there until guilt and shame motivate me to repent of my slothfulness, pick up my list, and start chipping away at it again."

"What are you trying to prove?" Spirit asked me.

I had to stop and think about it. "That I am faithful. That I have a testimony. That I am righteous and worthy. That I love God." These were all the programmed answers, the reasons I thought I should do these things.

Then came the wrecking ball. The Spirit said, *"This is your modern-day Tower of Babel."*

Mic drop, Jesus.

It was so interesting to think back on the many times I had heard a lesson at church about the Tower of Babel. The account depicts people who were building a tall tower, believing its height could get them closer to heaven. Anytime I heard this scriptural account, I wondered, *What was wrong with people from ancient times? Were they less intelligent than humans today? How could anyone think that you could actually build a tower to get closer to heaven and God?*

When the Spirit revealed that I had been building my very own Tower of Babel, using my to-do list as a structure to get me closer

ALIVENESS: SADNESS AND JOY

to heaven, I found myself standing in a puddle of my own humility. *That's cute,* I thought, rolling my eyes at my religious ego once again. My next thought was, *Time for demolition!*

One of the major pieces of my list was "keeping the commandments"—not just the Top Ten that came through Moses, but every commandment ever given to a prophet throughout the history of the world, including all the modern-day ones. These weren't just a part of meaningless *doing,* were they? I went inward and upward, asking God how I could learn to keep *all* the commandments. I was aware that, although I kept some, there were always others I was inevitably breaking.

God taught me, *"Angel, what have been called 'commandments' are examples; they are patterns. They are records of what I told other individuals to do in their present moments of seeking direction from me. You are not expected to carry out every commandment I have given to every mortal throughout all time. What I speak to you in this moment is your commandment. That is the one thing for you to keep right now. Can you do one thing?"*

"Yes!" I answered with a feeling of tremendous relief.

"That is keeping the commandments."

Stress and overwhelm—the pervasive emotions I lived in for years—vanished instantly.

To break my addiction to doing and stop living in self-betrayal, I began to ask myself often, "Why am I doing this?" I took that question into every moment and situation. It was an enlightening experience to see that my entire life was being dictated by *shoulds.*

While pondering the process of shifting from *doing* to *being,* I remembered the Bible story about Mary and Martha. The more I reflected on the story, the more annoyed I got. In the story, two sisters, Mary and Martha, are preparing their home for a visit from

Jesus. When Christ appears at the door, Mary sits down and begins talking with him and listening to him. Martha, however, stays busy. Apparently, there are things left undone and she is the only one left attending to them.

Martha's resentment builds until she finally approaches Jesus and starts to vent. "Aren't you going to say anything to my sister? She is just sitting here while I do all the work! Tell her to get up and help me!" (That is what I got out of it, anyway.)

Jesus responds with love and compassion. "Martha, Martha, thou art careful and troubled about many things: But one thing is needful: and Mary hath chosen that good part, which shall not be taken away from her."[16]

This is where I needed some expanded understanding. I turned inward and upward and said, "God, this story really annoys me. Of course I want to be like Mary and spend my days close to Christ, studying the scriptures and pondering spiritual things, but who would take care of my to-do list? Who would do the laundry? Who would make food for my kids? Who would clean up the dinner? Who would take my kids to the park? It just does not seem feasible. Tell me, what is the meaning of this story?"

The response came with love. *"My dear one, Mary and Martha were both preparing for the Savior's visit. They made food together and straightened the house. Both were helping. When the Savior arrived, Mary knew when to quit."*

Practicing meditation helped me develop mindfulness—the ability to observe rather than engage—and begin to challenge my thoughts instead of attaching to them. I discovered *to meditate* meant *to be present*, having mind, body, heart, and spirit all attuned to what is happening *right now*. Developing a practice of arriving in this state

---

16   The Holy Bible, KJV, Luke 10:41-42

illuminated for me how often I did not live there. My mind seemed to vacillate between ruminating on the past and obsessing about the future, taking me out of the only moment in which I can take action—the present.

A simple way I realized I can bring myself into the present is through awareness of what I am experiencing in my body. One day while developing my meditation practice, I made the connection with a popular trauma treatment approach in clinical therapy called EMDR—eye movement desensitization and reprocessing. I remembered learning about it in graduate school fourteen years earlier. My professor had told us, "We don't know *why* it works, we just have evidence that it *does* work."

In EMDR, a therapy client will share details and emotions of a past trauma while using their eyes to follow the therapist's fingers as they move them back and forth. Afterwards, the client is asked to notice and share how they felt during the process. Clients report being able to talk about the past trauma with a decreased sense of emotional intensity. The process, therefore, reprograms the client's experience with memory recall, and can halt the recurrence of a debilitating emotional trauma response when memories are triggered.

As I was meditating and curiously contemplating the tenets of EMDR, the Spirit explained to me why this process works, and how it is connected to meditation. The Spirit asked me, "*Can you see yesterday?*"

"No."

"*Can you hear tomorrow?*"

"No."

"*Can you touch yesterday?*"

"No."

"*Can you taste tomorrow?*"

"No."

"*Can you smell yesterday?*"

"Well . . . sometimes." I jokingly said. But of course the answer was "no."

"*You cannot experience the five hard senses in the past or the future; they are experienced in the present. Most people mentally live in the past or the future. Traumatic memories are from the past. Anxious thoughts are about the future. When a person is truly operating in the present, there is no sensation of trauma because the trauma is not happening right now. There is no fear in the present. Stimulating any one or more of the five hard senses is the quickest way to bring a person mentally, physically, and emotionally into the present moment and elude emotional reactions from past or future thinking. That is why EMDR is effective.*"

I sat reflecting on these thoughts, fact-checking them against my experience. It resonated as truth—the Spirit had a great point.

The Spirit then added, "*Can you hear the voice of God yesterday or tomorrow?*"

"No. I can only hear the voice of God now."

"*That's right, in the present. When you arrive in the present moment, you bring yourself into alignment with the frequency of truth.*

"*Like listening to a radio station: when you can hear a song you love, but find it's slightly blocked by static, you can adjust the dials and arrive on point with the exact station broadcasting the song. The static is then removed and the song comes through loud and clear.*

"*So it is with your thoughts. When you are thinking about the past or the future, there is static disrupting the signal from God. For clarity, you must come into the present moment and tune in to God's radio frequency.*"

ALIVENESS: SADNESS AND JOY

This awareness sent shockwaves through me as I considered its implications. In all the years I spent performing my religious rituals in an effort to get closer to God, 99.9% of the time I was thinking about the past or the future—I was not even tuned to the same frequency that could access the voice of God!

Learning to be present has made it feel like I have a 24/7 live stream broadcast available directly from God. It is an easy choice to plug in or unplug from that broadcast.

When I am plugged in, or *in tune*, God answers my questions about what to do in the moment. Because I can go directly to the Source any time, it has become unnecessary to rely on a long *shit-list* of items to determine what I "should" do. It is such a shift in faith!

Another important part of my journey to joy was learning how to experience my emotions. I had to be *taught* to give myself permission to feel! Before this, I had just done what others around me did: avoid, escape, numb, and distract myself from feeling. I didn't think I had time to feel; I had shit to do! Sleep and food were my drugs of choice.

My mentors The Unicorns worked with me over time, giving me the space and the encouragement I needed to fully feel my feelings. They coached me through movement and emotional expression activities that normalized and helped me understand my emotions. In the beginning, it was extremely awkward to move my body or dance to different intensities of music and allow myself to feel whatever emotions naturally surfaced. Once I chose to love myself through the experience, rather than attach to embarrassment or insecurities, I began to be able to fully experience and honor my emotions as messengers.

After I'd been practicing emotional expression for a little while, I attended a yoga class, and while holding the final pose on my mat I began to cry. I witnessed it and let it flow, rather than attempting to hold it back. The crying swelled into sobbing. I did not know what it was about, or why it was happening. I did not have any research at the time to explain the connection between movement and emotions, but I did not need it. I am my own research. It happened. It was a release. It felt healing.

The physical release of tension through this kind of expression is notable, but emotional expression does more than simply "let off steam." Giving emotions a sound expression has helped me self-validate by being a witness of myself: I see me, I hear me. This allows me to effectively fill my own need for emotional support. While consciously expressing emotion, I have made sounds (like groans of agony) that surprised me. They sounded like nothing I had ever heard before—especially not coming from me! As I am able to hear and physically feel the depth and intensity of the emotions I carry, I become more aware of the way my beliefs and thoughts have impacted me, and I feel more compassion for myself.

I also learned that expressing and witnessing my emotions in private prepared me to honor my emotions anywhere I chose. Once I was in a clinical staff meeting, where I worked as a Life Coach, surrounded by my colleagues (all therapists). Something that was said struck me and I noticed that emotion was coming up in me; tears were moving to the surface. My first egoic, fearful thought was, *You can't cry at work.* I challenged it: *Unless I can!*

I was instantly reminded by my soul that I did not need anyone else's approval, acceptance, love, or belonging—I just needed my own.

A few of my colleagues made eye contact with me, and I said out loud, "I'm going to cry now." I then talked, sharing my thoughts while allowing myself to cry. Everyone else listened silently. I realized not one person felt the need to interrupt or console me after I gave myself verbal permission to cry!

I have continued to operate this way since that time. I choose to not shame myself over my feelings. I have discovered that feelings connect us to each other in the deepest ways. They also lead me into examining my stories. When I stuff my emotions, I disconnect from myself and everyone around me, and I perpetuate the cultural emotional constipation. Learning to love and honor my emotions has brought joy into my heart and helped to cultivate deep and richly connected relationships.

It took me three years of consistent focus to fully unravel my programmed addiction to doing. I learned to make fun and play a part of my life again. When I released my ego's need to do it all "right" in order to be worthy of God's love, I allowed myself the pleasure of doing things for the sheer joy of doing them. I learned the importance of doing nothing, through meditation and stillness, and found I was much more available to hear the messages of my body, heart, and soul. I felt like I was coming alive again!

TRANSCENDENCE: CHAOS AND PEACE

*"Peace is not the absence of chaos or conflict,
but rather finding yourself in the midst of that
chaos and remaining calm in your heart."*
-John Mroz

During the eighteen months I was separated from my husband, I was closing up our business and working out the details of filing for bankruptcy. Throughout this process, I discovered more hidden financial transactions, and even some large debts incurred under my name without my knowledge or consent. When I tried to address these findings with my husband, I was met with denial and deflection. I was accused of inappropriately "bringing up the past" and "not forgiving him." These conversations went in circles and often ended with an accusation that I was "destroying our family." I felt enveloped in a cloud of confusion every time I approached him. Attempts to converse never brought clarity—rather, they brought more confusion, doubt (in myself and in him), and disbelief around the entire situation.

While the circumstances of my life were unraveling and sending shrapnel in every direction, I found it was getting easier and easier to anchor to peace by turning inward and upward in all things. One day my mom said, "I don't know how you do it. How do you keep going when your life is in such chaos?"

Her comment made me stop and reflect. I realized what my reality must look like to anyone on the outside: a total tornado, chaotic and destructive. I could see the evidence and understood her perspective, and yet, I knew: *I am at peace. I have more stillness than ever before.* I had found a safe place in the eye of that tornado, a calm refuge within the chaos.

My old ways of thinking would persistently try to intrude on this sacred space. Many of these thoughts began with, "What if..." They were worries about a possible problem in the future. As soon as a thought like this appeared, I would feel constriction in my body and a wave of emotion. Such questions carried a lot of baggage with them. Stress, fear, and anxiety came rushing right in, like some sort of package deal: buy one thought, get a cluster of emotions too!

It did not make sense to disrupt my newfound peace, especially when the fearful thoughts were only my imagination trying to predict the future. *How ridiculous of me to try to stress about something that does not exist,* I would remind myself. *If that does happen, I'll do what I have been doing every day: I will pause and say, "Soul and God, here's what's up. What do You think I should do at this moment?" Based on my track record since I began this practice, I can trust that I will receive a response.* This made sense to me, and it brought me peace. I was learning to live in *being* versus *doing*.

As I practiced noticing my position within my own storm, I was taught that the ability to navigate from the windswept chaos of the storm to peace within the eye requires the recognition and removal of judgment. Judgment contributes to chaos, drama, and contention, tossing up the debris of false stories in our minds and blinding us to the truth.

The awareness and suspension of judgment is an integral part of communicating with the Divine, yet it first has to be truly understood in order to be consciously removed. I find that many people, like I was, are in denial of their own judgments. Before I went through these experiences, if anyone had asked me if I was a judgmental person, I would have told them, "No, I am not judgmental! I am very open-minded! I'm a Christian, a social worker, I have a gay friend, and I watch Oprah!"

However, around 2015, I came across a book called *Loving What Is: Four Questions That Can Change Your Life*, by Byron Katie. It took about three years and three times through her book to digest and apply her message, but her work exposed me to myself and changed my perspective. I was judgmental—not just a little, but full-on, hard-core, pharisaical judgmental.

Byron Katie asserts that every single thought we have is a *perception*, unique to us, and that perception *cannot* be the same as truth. Every thought has been skewed, altered, filtered, impacted, and contaminated by our limited mortal experiences and biases. As such, it is a judgment.

And yet, we almost always believe our thoughts are true! We confuse our thoughts with truth and reality when they are often worlds apart. As I listened to this audiobook over and over again, I frequently paused it and argued with the author. Ultimately, though, my ego would always end up tapping out. Truth won every time!

These judgmental thoughts can be sneaky, but it's easy to recognize when I'm in judgment because of the red flags that show up in warning. Mental pressure—we often call it stress—is one red flag. Tension or tightness in my body is a second red flag. Any emotion other than peace is an obvious third red flag. The fourth and final red flag comes when I check in with my soul and God to receive the truth—which is always in opposition to the judgments that are causing me distress.

Mind, body, heart, and spirit are the elements of my internal compass; I check in with each and utilize them to help me navigate my course from chaos to peace.

I had been married to my husband for fourteen years when we separated; we had created five children together. We had made plans and goals together. We had committed our lives to each other. Now talking to him felt like talking to a total stranger. *Who are you?* I would sometimes wonder while we conversed. I often thought of the phrase "sleeping with the enemy," and shuddered as I reflected on our past together. My plans to build a "forever family" had shattered; I could almost see the pieces of my family vision scattered on the floor like broken glass.

I periodically felt waves of rage emerge in which I wanted to punch or break something; this was my shame seeking an expression. It came from my thinking, *How could I have been so stupid, so blind, so ignorant, to be married to this lying man?* Sadness washed over me from a sense of defeat, grief, and loss. *All this effort and intention in creating our family . . . I have given everything that I have, to the point of my own exhaustion, and for what?!*

"All suffering comes from our thinking," Katie says. I argued with that concept my first two times through her book. I believed that suffering was the result of being acted upon, of conditions or circumstances outside of my control. But I could not ignore her message. As I examined my thinking, I gained an acute awareness of certain words that can contaminate an entire thought, shifting it from truth to error. As I seek to think and speak truth, I have extracted words like "good," "bad," "right," and "wrong" from my vocabulary. Initially, this felt delusional and I feared I was becoming amoral; those words were central in the vernacular used in my religious upbringing. However, the practice has proven powerful and led me to more peace.

I intentionally toggled back and forth in my mind, exploring the two perspectives: that my life was chaos, and that I was peaceful. I noticed feeling that I had to choose one right answer, a perspective that put me into a state of cognitive dissonance. When I thought, "My life is chaotic, *and* I am at peace," I felt resonance, complete alignment. Both were true! I learned that judgment locks me into either/or thinking. It is definitive and absolute, consistently limited, narrow, and lacking a fullness of truth. Allowing for contrasting realities allowed me to suspend judgment in each moment.

Gratitude flowed into my life when I embraced the paradox of chaos and peace, removing judgment from each experience. I felt as grateful for the chaos as I did for the peace; it was one whole, perfect experience! The chaos in my life had spawned my search for peace.

If I had never learned what my husband was secretly doing in his financial life, my life would have continued in a state of homeostasis; I would have remained unaware of my own self-deception. I would not have started asking God questions in the manner that I was now employing. I would not have known I was in chaos. Without an awareness of the chaos, I would not have begun to cultivate peace. I would not have uncovered the pattern that light led to truth, and then to love, and then to joy, and then to peace.

This shift in thought sent rippling effects through my perspectives about myself and my husband. He was not "bad" and I was not "crazy." We both simply . . . were. He was doing life the way he did life, and I was doing life the way I did life. Together, we created a state of confusion in our conversations because we both brought self-deception, self-betrayal, and projection into our interactions. We were not aligned with truth!

I laughed as I realized this—truth makes my stories seem so hilarious! *I can't believe what I was thinking and felt so sure was true;*

that the confusion was from him; that the dishonesty was in him. That the only one hiding anything was him! I hid things from myself. I lied to myself. I couldn't help but be deceptive to him too!

Meanwhile, almost daily, the atmosphere inside my home was as turbulent and chaotic as a tornado. My five sons, ages six to fourteen at this point, frequently brought all of their emotions—including anger, grief, fear, and rage—to the table. I just wanted peace. I wanted peace in my mind, in my body, and in my home. There was so much violence, yelling, and arguments over seemingly insignificant issues, I felt more like a referee than a mom.

During one instance, before I "blew the whistle" and intervened, I decided to pause and go inward and upward for advice on my next move. I expressed my exasperation to God and asked for insight. "God, what can I do to stop all this fighting?"

This time, the answer came in a visual metaphor: I saw myself holding a large mixing bowl with a whisk in my hand. I was stirring some type of batter in a clockwise direction. I mixed the batter into a smooth and creamy consistency and I whisked it until all of the substance was swirling in the same direction. Suddenly, I switched directions with my whisk and began to stir the batter counterclockwise. I noticed something: not all the batter shifted direction at once. I had to consistently maintain the momentum of my stirring and stir into all the parts of the bowl, until, over time, all the contents shifted direction and moved together.

For years I had been a contributing factor to the chaos in our home. My stress, overwhelm, depression, resentment, and anger combined with their father's unhealthy behaviors to create the momentum in which the boys had learned to flow. As parents, we were like the whisk; the children were the batter. Just because I had begun to operate in a different direction did not mean that the entire system could turn on

TRANSCENDENCE: CHAOS AND PEACE

a dime. It had taken time to create a flow of contention and volatility, and it would take time and consistency to redirect that momentum.

This understanding replaced my frustration with deeper trust for the journey I was on. I had a new sense of compassion for my children, and a deeper commitment to keep bringing myself back to the eye of the storm.

My experiences have shown me that whenever I commit to a new degree of integrity toward any principle, life will provide the opportunity to be challenged on that principle. It is as if the universe is saying, "Are you really committed?"

I was now seeking to apply all that I was gaining from my spiritual experiments to my parenting techniques—there was a lot that needed to change! I wanted to parent from love instead of fear. I wanted to operate from truth instead of error. And I was provided with many opportunities to test my commitments to those principles.

One day, my thirteen-year-old and nine-year-old were in a fight. I chose to remain calm, simply observe them, and stay out of it. I was focused on breathing and switching my internal state of being from fear to love. Seeking to stay calm while the boys shouted at each other, right up in my face, was challenging. I finally said, "Go outside. Take this chaos outside." I ushered them out the door and into the driveway.

Within a short time, I glanced out the window and saw the younger one running down the driveway and up the sidewalk. Not too far behind him, the older son was walking at an aggressive and determined pace as he raised a machete high above his head. This particular son had struggled with rage from the time he was two years old. I felt that if I ignored this moment, there would be a serious physical injury.

I darted to the nearest door, flung it open, and ran out into the driveway just as he was beginning to swing the machete down over the top of his brother's head. I hollered, "STOOOOOP!" And he stopped.

I walked toward the boys and gestured to the younger one to get into the house. I reached out and took the machete by the handle. My son resisted releasing it. I told him, "Give it to me." The fury in his eyes was evident.

I took a couple of deep breaths and went inward and upward, "What do I do for him?" I asked.

I was given an understanding that, at thirteen years old, this boy, moving into manhood, was carrying and dealing with a great deal of pressure. And that this was not the time to have yet *another* talk about contention in the home. This was a time to make a serious move. The Spirit told me, *"Call the police for backup and report the attempted assault."*

In a split second, all of my egoic beliefs rushed in: *I never thought we would be one of those families with so much violence in the home that it wasn't safe to live there. I feel so embarrassed and ashamed to be calling the police on my own child! What does that say about me? I'm such a failure as a mom. Is our life in such disarray it has come to this?*

These thoughts were full of darkness, error, and fear. I allowed them to flush right through me as I pulled my thoughts consciously back to the directive the Spirit had given me—I took action and called the police. I ended up following the procedures that allowed the police to take my son to juvenile detention for the day. As the cop car drove away with my son in the back seat, peace entered our home. Okay, maybe the other boys were shocked into silence, but, either way—it was quiet, no one was headed to the ER with a fractured skull, and I could finish making dinner.

I got a call later in the evening and was told that the detention center was ready to release my son and I could pick him up. I was able to have a conversation with him before we left the detention center, and he told me it had been a positive experience for him. He had been able to talk with a counselor, they gave him some food, and he had free time with no brothers there to trigger him. He was calm and collected. I expressed love to him. I did not lecture him. I simply took him home. From that day forward, he has taken accountability for his emotions and actions; he has demonstrated emotional intelligence far beyond his years. My soul had led me to a solution I never would have found when living in my ego.

As I have learned more about peace-driven parenting, there are two questions I ask over and over again as I interact with my children:

1. God, what is true in this moment about my relationship with this child?
2. If I were to operate from love right now, what would I think, feel, and do next?

The answers that come are consistently the *exact opposite* of how I parented in the past, and they are liberating! As I have chosen to parent from love over fear, my five sons and our relationships have healed immensely. They trust me, respect me, appreciate me, and turn to me for advice and support—and I do them, as well.

My former self believed, *I am the mom. I want to be a* good *mom. A good mom does this, this, and this. A good mom should do this and shouldn't do that.* I rescued and felt like a martyr, misgave and felt like a victim, self-betrayed and became an angry villain—playing all three roles in the drama triangle over and over again. I lived in fear, fought them for control, acted out of anger, and "relied on the arm of the flesh"—all the societal and cultural norms around "good parenting." All the while, I felt like I was failing as a mom and I would never be enough!

Throughout my journey, I noticed a powerful force in the tornado, a torrent of fear that could easily tear me from the peace I found in its center: it came from my worries about the thoughts and opinions of others—particularly as they related to me. Many experiences were lined up to help me learn how to detach from these concerns.

The first came when I chose to follow God's directive to end my marriage. I approached my husband and told him flat-out that he was fired from his business, I wanted him to move out that day, and that I was filing for divorce.

"Why are you doing this?" he asked, "Why won't you forgive me?"

I wanted to help him understand. "It is not about forgiveness, I have already forgiven you."

"Then why would you talk about divorce?"

I hesitated, wishing I could mentally export to him all that I had experienced in the spiritual realm over the past few months. I felt a deep yearning to explain, to help him see and validate my perspective.

"It is not because I hate you," I offered. "It's because this is what God has told me to do."

"God would never tell you to do such a thing!" he shouted.

I stopped attempting to explain myself.

This was the first of many vulnerable conversations I would have with him, and with other people—friends, family, church leaders, and even acquaintances—in which I would be told that God would never tell me to do the things I said God was telling me to do.

One day the phone rang, and when I answered it, I was surprised to hear the recognizable voice of one of my best friends from high school! It had been years since I had seen or heard from her. I was so excited to hear that familiar voice and that fantastic laugh of hers on the other end of the phone.

She jumped right into the purpose of her phone call, "Angel, I heard that you are getting divorced."

It felt like my head spun around in a 360 degree circle. "Where . . . ? What . . . ? How . . . ?" I had not told anybody that I was separated and moving toward divorce. I felt totally ill-prepared to have this conversation.

"Where did you hear that?" I asked.

"Well, my mom sat by your mom at a funeral, and . . ."

The gossip circle had begun. Word was out.

What do I say? I wondered. I felt comforted by the familiar voice on the phone. It was nice to have a friend reach out. I decided to tell her my story.

I explained some of the basic details and the true reason divorce was on the table: I felt led by God in that direction. She was very nice to me; I did not feel judged, I felt heard. The phone call ended, and I was grateful we had reconnected. I thought it would be nice to have an old friend by my side as I moved through the stages of divorce. But the days, weeks, months, and years passed, and, though my phone number stayed the same, I never heard from her again.

When I told myself the story that the phone call was more about gathering information and details to spread the gossip, rather than real friendship, I felt terribly sad and lonely. I felt a lot of anger every time I thought about that call. *She had a lot of nerve to just pop into my life to grab the juicy details and then disappear—offering zero support during the toughest period of my life!*

Not long after, another old friend called me and said she wanted me to come over to her house. She too had heard that I was going through a divorce. I sat on her couch and shared the circumstances that had lead me to the decision. She was only the second person outside of my family I had discussed these details with. It felt nice to be looking into her sweet face, to feel listened to, and to feel like she cared.

But as soon as my story was over, she said, "I do not share your perspective."

She began to tell me about her relationship with her husband: how they had experienced some struggles the previous summer and had turned to their scriptures and to God. With faith, she told me, they had gotten through it.

It felt like a punch to the gut. I was so embarrassed; I felt so much shame and so much judgment. It felt like she was trying to proselytize, like she thought she could save my marriage if I would just listen to her and do as she did. I wanted to stand up and bolt from the house. I have no idea where the conversation went from there because I shut down and shut off. As soon as I could, I left her home and cried all the way back to my house.

"Is this what it's gonna be like? Am I gonna have to relive these embarrassing and empty scenarios with every friend that finds out I'm getting a divorce? Am I going to be the topic of all the gossip? Am I going to be the lucky recipient of everyone's unsolicited advice?" I cried out loud in the car. I screamed and raged, and I judged and I blamed my friend as well.

After releasing that tidal wave of emotion, I was able to get still. "Can I love myself through this?"

The affirmative answer from my soul was followed by a reminder, *"It's your choice."*

I asked God to help me see what had truly transpired in these conversations with my friends.

"You were in your ego."

Me? *I* was in *my* ego? I had to breathe a few times to release my indignation and humble myself to prepare to receive more. Then I asked, "What more is there?"

"Both times, when you were explaining your situation to your friends, you were in the energy of trying to prove something to them. You shared certain details of your marriage and divorce because you wanted their

acceptance, approval, and love. You were sharing with the hope and intention that they would offer you sympathy and a confirmation that you still belong. When you tried to explain your decision to your husband, you were trying to prove to him that your decision was good and right; that was your ego wanting to be heard and affirmed. You were seeking the validation of mortals, and you don't need it."

When the Spirit speaks, there is no confusion. It was so very clear to me. In those moments, my idols of worship were friendship and reputation. I was trying to manipulate and control how I was seen by others, I had placed my reputation as a god above God. This clarity removed the stories and judgments I had made regarding these friends, and the pain that accompanied them disappeared as well. The fears I'd had became irrelevant. They were products of my own self-deception.

I felt grateful for those experiences. They had triggered portals to incredible growth. My love for myself and my friends increased—they had played vital roles in my awakening. I was astonished at how quickly a feeling of complete peace replaced the anger and resentment I had felt.

I was intrigued, so I asked the Spirit for more.

I was told that I was going to face many more experiences like this in the future. *"Everyone is going to have their own interpretation of your experience. They will assume, they will judge, and some will even persecute you."*

That pronouncement felt tight in my body as I resisted it. I began to imagine various people I knew and the interactions we might have. As I thought through these exchanges, fear, guilt, shame, and judgment came into my mind, heart, and body.

"God, what can I do to withstand these experiences and not crumble under the weight of the shame of it all?"

In answer, God gave me a vision. I was standing on the sidelines of the streets of Jerusalem in a large crowd. I had a pair of pom-poms in my hands. Jesus entered the street with an entourage. There were all kinds of shouts going up towards him. I lifted my pom-poms in the air and I was cheering, "Go Jesus! Go Jesus!"

As the procession reached me, Jesus stopped and looked at me. He said, "Drop the poms-poms. Come, follow me." I did as I was told, and I stepped out into the street, walking several feet behind Jesus.

Then I noticed not everyone was cheering in favor of Jesus. A rock hit Him and then it ricocheted and hit me. People were spitting on Him, and sometimes they missed and it landed on me. I heard crude and vulgar terms shouted out at Him, and my head dropped; I looked down at the ground in shame. So many voices; so many different opinions, both of praise and of condemnation.

The longer I walked in His steps, the more I understood: neither approval nor disapproval had any effect on His worth. The opinions of men were not a reflection of Him in any way. They were a reflection of *them*. He attached to nothing because He knew exactly who He was and what guided Him.

Following Jesus in this vision allowed me to notice the disparity between His consistent emanation of love and my reactions to all the cruel, unkind, and hurtful words and gestures being thrown His way and mine. I felt sadness, but my awareness would bounce back and forth between my sadness and His joy.

I telepathically handed Jesus all my worst fears concerning my potential persecution while getting divorced. These included being a poor, single mom and looked down upon by society; no longer being accepted in the Polynesian culture; and having religious friends think I had "been led astray" or "lost my testimony."

Christ responded, "Angel, if you are judged and persecuted for following God, you are in good company. Sadness is the result of your story; let it go. Anchor to truth."

I took a deep breath and kept walking. As the stones and spit and shameful names continued to fly, I turned inward, "Can I love myself through this?"

"Yes," my soul responded, *"Loving yourself in all moments, and especially through the moments of the darkest persecution, is where joy, peace, and freedom emerge. Persecution is your opportunity to expand! There is no need to fear it; it's a beautiful gift, a catalyst for your harnessing of unconditional love. Be excited about it!"*

That was an unexpected twist. *Be excited about persecution!? Okay!* I developed a new motto: "I WILL DANCE IN YOUR PERSECUTION!"

I came back to the present. The whole thing had happened in a moment. I thought about those pom-poms I'd set down; I was done being just a cheerleader for Christ. I learned more about myself and what it means to be a disciple of Jesus Christ in that one vision than I had learned in thirty-eight years of attending church, my four years of seminary classes, my mission, and a lifetime of reading and teaching from the scriptures combined.

"Drop the pom-poms," is one of my favorite lessons! I discovered in that vision that the love of Jesus Christ transmutes all energy—He is able to alchemize anything projected towards Him—and I was beginning to learn to apply that process. I had feared judgment, shame, and persecution; I had wanted to run and hide from it because I attached my worth and value to it. I bought into the idea that judgments and persecution were a reflection of me—of areas where I was not good enough, not lovable, or not worthy. I believed they could cause me sadness and harm, and therefore I gave them the power to

do so. I learned that the only way judgment and persecution can hurt us if I believe they are accurate reflections of my worth and value.

The lesson pointed to this: believing in the ideas of man and placing them above what God thinks of me is idol worship. That was not what I sought. My soul was aching to be free of my stories and fears, free to love and serve God, and free to dance while doing so! As promised, I got a lot more opportunities to practice.

I held a teaching position at church in the women's organization known as the Relief Society. God was guiding me daily to find inspiration from people around the world and throughout history who spoke spiritual truths. Many of their words penetrated my heart and often significantly expanded my understanding of gospel teachings. *Oh wow!* I'd think, *That's what it means to "love thy neighbor as thyself!" I must first love myself!* I delighted in looking at things differently and gaining new perspectives.

One Sunday, I shared quite a few of the ideas and experiences that had recently brought me a sense of greater depth and love for the gospel. Many of the women in the room were wiping tears from their eyes, and when the hour ended, there was a line of women from the front of the room to the exit door waiting to talk to me about what they had felt during that lesson. I will never forget the woman in her eighties who stood in line and pulled her oxygen tank along so she could tell me, "In all my years attending church, I have never had a lesson that changed me like that one. Thank you."

I felt so much joy seeing these diligent women—from eighteen to eighty-plus years old—moved to tears of joy. It removed the masks they wore and broke open the flood gates to emotions they had buried and carried so deeply within. It brought their limiting, fear-based core beliefs to the surface and eradicated them with the light of truth and love! Many were liberated from years, and even decades, of hidden fear and sorrow. The love in the room was palpable.

Later, my bishop asked to see me in his office. I sat down in a chair across from his large, wooden desk. He informed me that I had been reported for teaching and sharing information that was not from church-published sources. I was chastised and reminded of the policy for the lesson material. I was told that I was supposed to stick to the assigned article, written by a "General Authority," a leader in the hierarchy of our church.

The article was a speech that had been televised worldwide in our semi-annual General Conference, then published a month later in our church magazine. I was assigned to teach it, apparently verbatim, in the women's class. I wondered, *If the women have watched this talk and had access to read it as often as they desire, what purpose am I serving by once again repeating this man's words? Indoctrination? Making sure they know what they are supposed to think on this topic?!*

The contradictions in our church's teachings would not leave me, either. "Bishop, are we not trained as teachers in this church to 'seek inspiration and personal revelation when preparing our lessons'[17]?"

My bishop responded, "Yes. And some of that is fine, but we need to use church-published materials to draw upon."

I shared with him my process of preparing. I had both read and listened to the speech in preparation for my lesson. I had prayed about how to deliver the message to the hearts of the women so that they would feel changed by the message—not just given more to do! I had received a vision of who would be in the classroom that day, even down to where they would be sitting, and when I stood to speak in class, I was in awe—it was just as I had seen it!

---

17   This was straight out of the teacher's manual I'd been given when I was asked to teach.

"Bishop, whoever reported me to you, did they tell you how many women broke down and cried throughout the lesson?"

He looked at me curiously, "No." he said.

"Did they tell you about the lineup of women who waited long after the meeting had ended to share their experience and gratitude with me?"

"No." He said, "But they did tell me at the end of your lesson you circled back around to the article and tied it all together into the topic and message."

Fear and shame had struck me right at the beginning of the meeting, with a tightness in my chest and thoughts of, *I did it wrong! I'm in trouble!* In micro-moments throughout the conversation, I felt anger and wanted to know who the Benedict Arnold was.

I felt rage, and I could imagine myself screaming in her face, "Are you totally blind? When have you ever seen this transpire in women's class? Can you not see what these women need? How could you be so small that you go behind my back and report me to the bishop, rather than act like a grown-up and speak right to my face? You ignorant coward!" That felt like fire in my belly.

I wanted to yell at the bishop, "You weren't even in the room! How do you find the audacity to hold this conversation with me based on hearsay? Have you surveyed anyone else in the room? Is this chastisement based on *one* opinion? Why did you not have that woman who reported me sitting in on this conversation, so that truth could be established?" More fire on the tip of my tongue.

Underneath the fire of anger and rage was intense sadness. I felt so sad that I was not safe in this space, within my church. I felt captive to being judged, unheard, misunderstood, unable to be myself.

I acknowledged all of this within myself, and I breathed deeply to anchor my mind, heart, and soul in the moment and not abandon myself. Intentional breathing helps me guide the energy of love towards any part of me that calls for it; it transmutes fear into love and brings me back into connection with God so I can seek truth and release error. I asked God for help and surrendered myself to the Spirit.

The Spirit spoke to me, illuminating the fears, shame, and limiting beliefs that were at the root of my triggered reaction. These feelings were calling me to see them, love them, and transmute them. The outbursts brewing in my mind were merely the projections of my fear and shame; they were not truthful reflections of these other mortals' experiences, intent, or worth. I laughed inside at my cute, albeit raging, ego! My stories were not true. This unidentified woman and my bishop were innocent. I could see they were both doing what was *right* in their minds. They were dutifully following exactly what they had been told they *should* do in their positions within the organization.

The Spirit revealed to me the identity of the woman who had "turned me in," and I beheld her. I saw her intention behind reporting me. She desperately wanted to serve perfectly in her calling, to ensure all the rules were followed obediently and the class was spiritually nourishing to everyone. Oh, her precious heart came into view! I saw her as a little girl with so much desire to do right, to be right, and to be good.

These people were gifts, facilitators in my journey. I thanked the bishop for talking with me. A day or so went by, and I reached out to the woman and requested a visit. When I arrived at her home, her anxiety was visible. I breathed to stay calm and I envisioned circling her with light and love. I asked her about her concerns with my lesson. I could see her reasoning, and I sought to speak in love and with the desire to be one. I felt that oneness of heart I'd heard spoken of in church so many times. Several days later, I received a beautiful thank-you note from her in the mail. JOY!

"God, what do I do next with this experience? If I stay in my position as a teacher of the women, I will have to conform to the policy of using only church-published materials. That does not feel aligned, true, or authentic to me."

"Resign. Now is the time," the Spirit said.

So I met with the bishop and asked to be "released" from my teaching position. I loved how the Spirit had put it: *"Now is the time."* It was neutral. I was not angry; I felt like I had completed my service there.

This experience happened *for me*, not *to me*. As I went through things like this, I was given a choice: I could choose to attach to darkness in my energy, error in my thinking, fear in my insecurities, sadness in my stories, chaos in my mind, captivity in my soul; or I could choose to attach to light, truth, love, joy, peace, and freedom. I chose peace.

I began a new life, choosing to be less religious and more spiritual, to live in alignment with truth as it was *directly* revealed to me and for me. As I did so, I had many opportunities to observe my ego in full force, and I discovered my ability to stand firm in the truth about my immutable worth. Opportunities showed up as I counseled with male church leaders whose positions gave them authority over me. I shared small samples of my spiritual experiences to explain why I was pursuing a divorce, why I was choosing the things I was. Yes, that was my ego wanting their approval and acceptance—it took a lot of time and practice to release that. I was met with invalidation, intrusive questions, sexist and derogatory language, and other demeaning responses.

Having grown up a member of this church, I'd been taught by example to assume stories of priesthood leaders talking or behaving offensively were told only by those who had a chip on their shoulder. I rationalized that they were probably someone who was easily offended, or took things out of context, or missed the spirit of the message of their leader. I have repented of these assumptions. I now understand those who have opened up and shared the most vulnerable parts of their lives with respected leaders, and in return received responses carrying the energy of fear, guilt, shame, and judgment.

In one such personal encounter, my leader asked me if I had sought marriage counseling prior to filing for divorce. Because I had never met this man before (he was the stake president, a tier above my bishop in the chain of command in our church), I began to explain, "I have a master's degree in clinical social work . . ." and the rest of my sentence would have been, ". . . and so I value professional help and have sought it both for myself, and for us as a couple, a few times, including recently."

But I did not get a chance to finish my sentence. This leader slammed his fist on the table, laughed haughtily, and said, "Sister, I do not care what your educational background is!"

The human me felt incredibly disrespected. My body cringed, fear and shame clogged my throat and muffled my voice box, and I felt like I was going to cry. I just noticed it all, breathed, and went inward and upward. "What am I witnessing?" I asked God.

"*His humanness,*" I heard. "*He is used to dealing with people very different from you. He's perceiving you in light of his experiences with others. He is reacting from his assumptions. Be not afraid.*"

I looked at this man in his suit coat and tie, and I imagined him seated at a large table in a board room filled with men. I visualized one of the other men at the table introducing himself, "My background is in engineering and I am here bringing my skill set to this group."

I pictured this leader of mine slamming his fist on the table and laughing while saying, "Mr Smith! I do not care what your professional credentials are!" I chuckled inside. I was willing to bet that would never happen in a room full of men. I wondered why it felt okay for him to react towards a woman in such a condescending way.

I asked God what might make this meeting a more truthful and loving one. I was shown in a vision a practice I have never seen in my church: when I arrived for my appointment, this man and his wife both awaited me in the office, and as a couple, they counseled me. I saw it would be possible for them to support each other in delivering whole and perfect guidance from both the divine masculine and divine feminine perspectives. Man and wife serving together in spiritual capacities—what a brilliant concept! It held the potential for a couple in leadership together to practice and illustrate the divine design for couples.

I was caught up in this refreshing image and wondered how different things would be if women were included in every religious leadership setting, especially when a woman is entering the office of a leader for any reason.

The Spirit said to me, *"If this man's wife was here right now, this would be a totally different experience enveloped in much more light, truth, and love."*

I do not know the man's wife, but in that moment I could feel her being. I trust that inspiration was accurate. My nervous system was calmed and my body was still.

There is a Divine design to the nature of relationships between men and women, and it is in and through the collaboration of perspectives that wholeness/truth emerges. A single perspective can bring chaos, while the combined perspectives engender peace through balance, harmony, and coherence. This was a preparatory lesson in helping me to understand and appreciate the potentiality to be cultivated in partnership.

The conversation continued, and when I felt any of my leader's language was dismissive, I simply said, "That comment feels very invalidating" and left it at that. I made the statement three times during the interview. He did not seem to know what to do with that feedback. The mortal me saw the opportunity to be offended and angry at him, and I recognized that temptation as false.

The real-time dialogue between the Spirit and myself during this interview expanded my perspective on this leader, on myself, and the true spiritual purpose in our meeting. I was being taught by the Spirit how to behold another human in total understanding of his perspective while simultaneously receiving a fullness of comprehension from the Spirit. This experience resulted in feelings of compassion for him—and trust in myself and the Divine.

I was able to speak kindly, respectfully, and clearly in responding to him, and I felt the energy shift in the room. As I spoke in the spirit of love, the dynamic shifted away from the energy of patriarchal order, where I was supposed to submit. Instead, it gently settled into equality, brother and sister conversing with each other with understanding, with love, and with respect. The Spirit taught me the possibilities relevant in any relationship between the masculine and the feminine energy. Since this encounter, I have sought to counsel in cooperation with men, rather than submit or fight against their perspectives.

When my leader began glancing at his clock on the wall behind my head, I knew our scheduled appointment time was up. We wrapped things up and I left.

I felt an increase of joy. It was another awe-inspiring experience where I got to play between mortal and spiritual realms. My egoic mind could have gone—and wanted to go—to battle with this man. When I am in my ego I am very good at quick and clever articulation, sarcasm, and condescending language; I'd had a lifelong knack for triggering people and shaming them into submission. While confrontation can trigger immense fear and shut-down in many people, it puts my ego in attack mode. But this time, *I chose to not go to my egoic brain*! Instead, I relinquished the idea that I knew how to respond and turned to God for direction.

Much to my surprise, a few weeks after our discussion, this leader called me in and asked me to teach the women's class in my congregation. This was not something a stake president would typically do, but he said he felt strongly that this was an important role for me to play, and had already talked to my bishop.

Life again offered me something like an end-of-semester exam to demonstrate for myself what I had been learning about lies vs. truth and chaos vs. peace. It was the end of 2017. I had recently completed my first women's retreat to Hawaii, accompanied by fifty women. Leading the trip provided a steep learning curve for me, and it was a magnificent experience overall. I came home on a high, but that quickly crashed into a low.

Within a couple of weeks, I was filing for a child protective order and had to sit in a courtroom for the first time to discuss the drama of my family life. Additionally, I encountered several situations involving deceit and betrayal among people close to me; some were situations I was involved in, others I was simply a witness to. The theme of this period for me was deception, drama, and chaos, and it felt like I was trapped and suffocating under an avalanche of deception. *Is everyone a liar? Does everyone lie to me? Do they all think so little of me that they entertain themselves through mocking lies and betrayal?*

I was sucked into a vacuum of hopelessness as thoughts, feelings, and evidence came together in a climax. I felt totally unlovable and unworthy. Life felt purposeless. It seemed futile to continue to live in a world that was so fake and deceptive. I did not want to have any relationships. I did not want any friends. I did not want to invest my time and energy in *any* other humans, *ever* again! I felt so ashamed at having confided in individuals who turned out to be self-serving, cunning, and deceptive. The thought of ever seeing their faces again and having to relive the memories of their betrayal felt like more than I could bear. I wanted to die.

For a period of forty-eight hours, I became seriously suicidal, curled up in the fetal position in a basement room of someone else's house. It felt like I had entered hell. I was relentlessly tormented, mentally and emotionally, and my entire focus was on how to end the torment. I made a plan. My mind was racing with chaotic, destructive thoughts, running like a freight train headed for a cliff.

It was all brought to a sudden halt with a single moment of awareness: *I have five sons.*

How would my children ever process or comprehend the suicide of their mother? Which of them would feel like they were too much for me and had been a part of pushing me over the edge? I groaned in agony, releasing grief, anger, rage, and sadness. I pictured their faces. *What would this teach them?* I wondered. *How would they then cope with the inevitable adversity they face in life? Would you want this for them?*

More groans of agony escaped my mouth. "I trust no humans!" I said. "I am unable to talk myself out of this trench of darkness! Where am I to go in this moment to ask for help?" I had been wrestling with it for two days: I kept trying to tell myself I was simply experiencing depression, that these were irrational thoughts, that there were steps I could take to get out of it—but then I would be slammed with another wave of evidence that my life was worthless.

I had the impression to reach out to my mentors, The Unicorns. I sent a text to Kami and Shelby and held the phone in hopes of a quick reply. It wasn't long before I got a text. I opened it, and there were two pictures. The first was of the two of them with a hand to their mouths and their lips puckered. In the second photo, they had their hands outstretched as if they were blowing their kisses towards me. Their written text was short and simple: They told me they loved me and they believed in me.

Seeing their faces shook me out of my despair for a few seconds. I loved these two women so much, and they had walked with me and mentored me through every moment of hell over the last three years. In their classes, retreats, and one-on-one mentoring sessions, they had shown me key processes, practices, and concepts that helped clear my old patterns so I could be open-minded and open-hearted. They truly demonstrated unconditional love toward me and primed me with the necessary foundation to learn to talk directly to God, receive God's love fully, and trust in the process. They had been instrumental in all of my spiritual growth. My heart softened.

And just as quickly, it shut. I got mad. *I cannot believe I just told these two that I want to commit suicide, and they send me a text! They send me pictures? They don't even call me? They don't ask if they can come over and help me?* The tidal wave of fear washed over me again and poured out through my angry thoughts.

I noticed it, I breathed, and I asked, "What is true?"

I was shown by the Spirit the genius of my friends. They were willing to send me love; they were willing to assure and encourage me; and they were *unwilling* to rescue me.

"DAMMIT!" I yelled. "How can I stay in my victim story if my dearest friends won't corroborate it!"

The message was clear: I was responsible and capable of helping myself out of this. I reached over to a CD player and pushed play. *A Return to Love* by Marianne Williamson was in the deck. I listened to the audiobook and took in deep, slow breaths, hoping to receive any truth that might come.

It was one of the most unusual experiences of my life. As I lay there with my eyes closed, breathing and listening, every single line spoken in that book appeared in my mind as a visual scud missile: the author's words seemed to shoot into the darkness of my mind, strike, and blow up each missile of destructive thought as it came, before it could have impact. Every phrase in the book was so penetratingly true, my thoughts and heavy beliefs could not hold their form—they exploded! It was like watching a Fourth of July firework show.

I began to laugh! I laughed and I laughed and I laughed; it sounded more like a cackle at times. It was the most hilarious moment! Laughter was transmuting the intense and heavy energies that had flowed through me, releasing them into the atmosphere. I was lifted out of my pit of despair and laid back at ground level. Once again, those magical Unicorns had shown up perfectly, giving me exactly what I needed to move through that experience in light, truth, love, joy, and peace.

"Okay. I'm still here. I'm alive and on earth. God, for the past two days, I have been telling myself I am the most worthless piece of shit: that I'm unlovable, unworthy, and not good enough for anyone. Now, I am giving You the floor. What is true about who and what I am?"

Elation came like a sudden blast. I was taken places that are beyond description. I danced with God as I saw my true worth. Everything that I had been through in recent months was clarified: I had allowed myself to attach my worth to others' behaviors and absorbed their actions as evidence of my worthlessness. In truth, they were mirroring my own fears and beliefs about my worth. Like a radar, my deepest fears scanned my experience and locked onto any evidence that supported the beliefs tied to them. Without a fear of worthlessness on my radar, I would have seen the world through the eyes of my own and others' worth.

It all became funny! *Oh, look at all of us behaving this way! Acting out our deepest fears in one great melodrama!* And to think I had taken it so seriously! Our experiences were scripted by our beliefs. We were playing roles—none of it was real! At least not according to the Spirit of Truth.

I recognized that I was witnessing an unleashing of the chaotic energies built up between many interconnected lives, like an earthquake that suddenly releases the tension and pressure built up over a long period of time beneath the surface. When the tectonic plates finally slip, the impact ripples through all connected matter. I could see that the chaos erupting within my network of relationships at this time was a result of intergenerational issues finally coming to a head.

"What more is there?" I asked.

"You are a goddess."

The words came through me and I repeated them out loud. "I am a goddess."

I noticed that speaking the words of truth *out loud* brought me to a full witness of truth. The inspiration is released from the lockdown of my mind, where my ego has control and opposes it with human logic. Speaking inspiration out loud allows my body to feel the resonance of truth inside my cells.

"I am a goddess." I spoke again. I was completely cleansed from my fears and judgments about myself and others. I did not see these people through the storied lens of judgment anymore; I saw them as reflections and mirrors of my human self. I saw the beauty of human agency and experiences. All that had felt like hell was now a perfectly orchestrated heaven.

TRANSCENDENCE: CHAOS AND PEACE

Not long after these experiences, I read *The Power of Intention* by Wayne Dyer, in which he teaches that conflict is living in two-ness. He suggested that if you live in oneness—meaning you see yourself as one with others—you will always end a conflict in love. I had been taught at church that Jesus commands us to be one, as He and the Father are One. This concept had always eluded me; I had not yet had any earthly relationships that exemplified that oneness.

The lessons I learned regarding our interconnected healing on earth allowed me to truly love and be grateful for those who facilitated my growth by mirroring my fears to me. Through this experience, I was able to see myself as one with all others for the first time!

BEING: CAPTIVITY AND FREEDOM

"The most important kind of freedom is to be what you really are. You trade in your reality for a role. You give up your ability to feel, and in exchange, put on a mask."
-Jim Morrison

My daily, spiritual experiments of taking all thoughts inward and upward became like an archaeological excavation of the mind. I was looking for truth and I was continually given clues that lined up and pointed me in new directions. It felt like uncovering artifacts one at a time, laying them out to investigate, then fitting the pieces together to reveal something designed by a Power much greater than myself.

The more digging I did into the depths of my inner workings, the more truth I uncovered. I removed layers of residue from the programming and conditioning of the world. I dusted off my perceptions. I organized and pieced together my experiences. The form that emerged from this process revealed the captivity I had been living in. I had not been able to see, until now, that I had been committed to worshiping the programming and conditioning of my mortal mindset. I'd adhered to and followed voices of authority in every area of my life, instead of truly knowing how to follow the "dictates of my own conscience."[18]

All along in my prior life, I thought I was using my agency to make choices, but it was my ego that chose for me! I did not know the difference between the voice of my soul's conscience and the voice of my ego. My ego filed away the many things mortals told me to think, then assured me they were right and true and pressured me to align my life with those precepts. The ego's voice was loud and easy to follow, "This is the right way!" "You should do this!" "You have to do it that way!" And doing what the ego dictated is what earned me approval and praise from my external environment. But by following the ego's voice without reflection, I was unknowingly suffocating the voice of my soul.

I lived in soul-betrayal, obeying all my culturally programmed "shoulds," motivated by the fear of guilt and shame. My ego said things like, "I work so hard. I do everything around here. I wish other people would see how much I do and help out just a little." It planted hidden thoughts like, *I am so much smarter, more spiritual, more competent, more capable than the people around me.*

When I lived according to my ego's dictates, I projected the energy of guilt and shame onto my husband and children. I tried to guilt trip them into doing the "right things"—like me—*because,* I told myself, *doing all the right things all the time is what will make us feel happy and free.* Not! The truth was, I was miserable, tired, and resentful. Yet my ignorance kept me willing to try to guilt them into performing like marionette puppets under my control.

As I uncovered the awareness of my own behaviors, I saw that guilt is sneaky and grotesque. It tag-teams with shame. It also loves a good passive-aggressive delivery system. So the sweetest of Christian faces

---

18   LDS Article of Faith 11

can deliver the most shame-generating, worth-destroying blows, all wrapped up in the wording of "doctrines of the gospel." Throughout my life, I had been on both the giving and receiving end of these deliveries. I was schooled in it, and completely unaware!

I believe most (if not all) people start this life with clear and healthy filters for discerning truth over error and love over fear. But after running head-on into the consistent socialization of others' egos, we eventually succumb to the overbearing natural man/ego voice within ourselves. We adopt the behaviors of those around us. Over time, the majority of us fall in line, surrender our agency, and suppress our intuition in favor of the philosophies of man.[19]

My experiments led me to examine the philosophies of men, taking thoughts and phrases of indoctrination inward and upward to inquire for truth. One example that brought about a major shift within me was a phrase I often heard at church: "You came to earth to be tested." After months of conversing with God and developing my connection to my internal compass, this phrase crossed my mind, and I noticed immediately how those words created tension in my chest. I paused and asked myself, "What are you feeling?"

Afraid.

"What are you telling yourself?" I asked.

I am afraid to fail this life test and not make it to heaven.

---

[19] Those souls who refuse to do this often find ways to avoid, escape, numb, and distract themselves from the emotional turmoil they feel. The most sensitive often turn to drugs and other vices. Their choices lead them to be seen as broken and weak, and they become the societal and familial scapegoats, carrying the judgment and shame of a culture in denial. I believe these souls can be described as *empaths*: gifted people with the ability to perceive and behold the energetic frequencies of others. Empaths wrestle greatly with inner conflict because their soul's voice is so strongly opposed to captivity. I have a hunch that this may be at the root of the great exodus of members of the church I belong to. There is a global rise of consciousness occurring, and fewer people are willing to stifle the voice of their souls.

I immediately recognized the fear.

"Why am I afraid of *anything* having to do with God?" I wondered. "Who or what taught me to think this way?"

I knew where I had learned it. Mortals in my religious programming—not God.

Then I took this fearful belief to my soul for further light and knowledge. "Soul, I'm noticing I'm afraid to fail the test of life. Mortals have taught me to believe in and fear failure because of what it would mean about me: that I'm not good enough, not lovable, and not worthy. I have believed I could fail at all kinds of things in life and even fail at the 'test' of life. Is that true, or is it my story?"

"*It is your story,*" my soul responded.

"What is true about failure?" I inquired.

"*It is a human construct. It is a judgment,*" my soul said.

"What more is there?" I asked, curious and open.

"*There is no such thing as failure. You are not on trial. You are not being tested. You are the tester: you came into this life for an opportunity to test principles and develop the ability to discern from this.*"

I had a vision of myself as a science student, wearing goggles and a white smock, walking into a laboratory. I had access to all of the elements from the periodic table, and I began experimenting. When I paired certain elements together, they created a disruptive chemical reaction and I noted it on a paper. As I combined other elements, I created stable compounds. My experiments did not feel good, bad, right, or wrong—they just felt like experiences that provided me with information. I took my findings and reported back to the professor, who in this case was the Lord, Jesus Christ.

My soul taught me through this vision, "*Mortal life is like a science lab. Your whole life is like a series of experiments based on your choices. Sometimes things blow up, sometimes things are solid and stable.*

And God is right there, inviting you to be curious and ask yourself, 'What did I learn?'"

"I am not on trial?" I confirmed.

"No."

A weight I had carried since childhood fell away, and a new enthusiasm for life appeared in its place.[20] Where there had been fear and self-judgment, there was now just data. What had felt like the accumulated weight of all my failures and regrets became a collection of valuable information. Layers of fear, guilt, and shame lifted from my body as I recognized my life as an opportunity for learning instead of a test of my worthiness—HOLY SHIFT! I had been captive to my fear of failure. Now I was free to simply live, collecting all the experiences and learning this earth laboratory had to offer!

As I released my fear of failing God and the worship of my earthly reputation, I began to design my own life—on my own terms. After separating from my husband, my ego brain told me, *I should put my graduate degree to work and apply for full-time employment: a single mom has to work full-time to provide, and it is going to be hard.* I rejected that message, because every time I turned to God, I found that opportunities flowed with grace and ease. Life didn't have to be hard and painful. I didn't have to suffer.

I turned to God to ask about my employment options, and got the idea to clean houses for senior citizens—with an opportunity to start right away. Again my ego tried to shut it down: *Housecleaning? That is so beneath me. I have a graduate degree. I am smart. I can do much more sophisticated work.* I just noticed those thoughts and laughed!

---

20   Receiving correction from the Spirit of Truth is absolutely humbling, like nothing else I've ever encountered. It feels like sitting naked in front of God and not caring—having absolutely no shame about it! I have had so many "oh snap!" moments as truth shatters long-standing, fear-based beliefs. I also call them "mic drop, Jesus" moments. I love to laugh with the Spirit as it shows me the Truth.

"Who or what taught me to think this way?" I asked myself. Those thoughts were so obviously layered with judgments from the world about prestige. Once again it pointed to my conditioning to worship my reputation among humans.

I noticed that the ego's voice created tension and weight in my body every time it showed up. It brought feelings similar to an adrenaline rush, as if I were getting ready to fight. I also became aware of its snarky attitude and cocky air of knowing it is right. It is bossy, and not kind and loving at all. It provided a stark contrast to the way I felt when I was conversing with God. During those times, my body felt light and relaxed, and my mind was curious, rather than convicted. These clues within my inner compass (mind, body, heart, and spirit) made it so easy to determine which voice was guiding me. It was astoundingly simple to cast off the natural man and trust my soul!

I began calling my ego my "bitch voice," and feeling more entertained by it than annoyed. "You're so cute," I'd say to it, a response I'd learned from observing my mentor, Shelby, speak to her own ego. Although there were times I wondered if I might be—or at least look—schizophrenic as I talked to the internal parts of myself, I chose not to care, "So, what if I am schizophrenic? Can I love myself through that?" I asked. And my soul said, "Yes." I noted how, even in small moments like this one, worrying about what I looked like or how I appeared to the world was yet another form of captivity.

As backwards as it seemed to my ego, I trusted the impression to choose to clean houses over applying for other types of work. My house cleaning work began with one elderly woman who referred me to a couple of her friends, and it grew effortlessly from there. My clients were kind and flexible; I made my own schedule for my cleaning work and could change it anytime I wanted—which gave me lots of free time for my kids. The work was physical, but not hard; their houses were not messy. I loved going to their homes, where we would begin with a visit and they always asked about my life and children. While cleaning, I listened to audiobooks about consciousness and spirituality: I was cleaning out my own mindset while scrubbing sinks and toilets and tubs!

I had many spiritual moments on my hands and knees, in the most humble of postures, scrubbing these spaces. A well of love would spring up in my heart as the Spirit showed me things about these clients and their families that often brought me to tears. I gave thanks often for the privilege of cleaning for seniors and for the freedom my job gave me. I was grateful that I had listened and trusted Source rather than seeking work based on my credentials for the sake of my ego and others' opinions.

During this time, word got around that I was cleaning for work, and I was offered opportunities to clean vacation rental homes and to clean for other businesses. I tried it out and noticed it did not nourish my soul. Sure, I made money, but it did not light me up the way it did when I cleaned for my dear friends. I made this my motto: *I only clean for people I love.* My ego would tell me I needed to take those other jobs because I needed the money (notice the fear). But every time I took that thought inward and upward, I got a different answer: *"The energy you surround yourself with is far more important than the amount of money you make."*

I enjoyed my work, and I found myself tempted various times to feel guilty that I was happy cleaning houses when I saw someone at their job who looked unhappy. The increased awareness I was cultivating made it easy to perceive guilt right away. Guilt carries an energy that I can feel in my body. "What a strange thing to feel guilty for!" I thought. The ability to notice guilt allowed me to pause and ask, "What am I telling myself?"

The answers surprised me every time. My ego was promoting fallacies such as, *This won't last. You are lucky right now, because you don't have a lot of expenses, but don't expect life to always be this easy.*

Unless it will *last!* I challenged the fear. *What if it does? What if I'm always able to find ways to earn an income doing things I love doing? What would that be like?* In considering the possibilities, I was restored to my freedom.

I was freed in other ways, too—like that trailer home I was once so ashamed of! When I separated and divorced, suddenly I felt grateful for the freedom of a small place to take care of, a low cost of living, and the love and support system of my extended family. From shame to love, from captivity to freedom, all because I shifted what I was telling myself and what I believed those thoughts meant about me. I turned away from my ego's opinions and I turned, again and again, to seek the opinion of God.

During this period, I was "poor," according to the world's standards. I was receiving food assistance and never knew how I would pay for all the things we needed. And yet, I was free. I noticed I had bought into the myth in our society that freedom comes from abundant income levels. My experience taught me that money does not automatically create freedom, but a freedom mindset can generate more money. I had more freedom than ever before, and it was the result of this mindset shift and these internal practices of seeking truth over conditioning.

On the other end of the spectrum, my former captivity mindset perpetuated lies and myths about money, relationships, and happiness. I see my former, captive self often in others as we hold conversations about life circumstances. Many people use the same captive language I once used and believed:

I could never do that.

I can't afford that.

That is so hard.
That would never work for me.
Life is a struggle.
I'm too busy.
There's not enough time.
…and so forth.

I experienced life, work, and finances in a new way as I released the limitations of my fear-based, scarcity mindset around money and work while practicing trust in Divine guidance. Many of the books I listened to while cleaning helped bring about this change in perspective. A quote by Marianne Williamson from her book *A Return to Love* was one of those thought-shifting pieces.

> *Our deepest fear is not that we are inadequate.*
> *Our deepest fear is that we are powerful beyond measure.*
> *It is our light, not our darkness that most frightens us.*
> *We ask ourselves, "Who am I to be brilliant, gorgeous, talented, fabulous?"*
> *Actually, who are you not to be?*
> *You are a child of God. Your playing small does not serve the world.*
> *There's nothing enlightened about shrinking, so that other people won't feel insecure around you.*
> *We are all meant to shine, as children do.*
> *We were born to make manifest the glory of God that is within us.*
> *It's not just in some of us; it's in everyone.*
> *And as we let our own light shine, we unconsciously give other people permission to do the same.*
> *As we're liberated from our own fear, our presence automatically liberates others.*

I have heard Will Smith say, "On the other side of fear is freedom."

A close friend once told me, "I think what my soul really wants is freedom." Her statement was like a lightning bolt to my heart—it created one of the most powerful physical reactions I have ever had to spoken words. My body's response witnessed there was truth in her words. Not just truth about *her* soul, but all souls. If felt as if my soul leapt inside my body and my heart ignited with a passion for freedom.

Perhaps freedom is the truest, deepest desire we *all* have.

I have come to value the freedom of my soul above all else. I witness and honor that I am a sovereign being, free to rule myself according to the dictates of my own conscience (soul), and I seek to hold sacred the space of freedom through all parts of my life. The world sometimes teaches that an individual's quest for freedom is rebellious and dangerous. Freedom has been presented as selfish, rebellious, and dangerous to the individual, the culture, or the world at large. I see a paradox here: while the quest for personal freedom can look like all of the above as it rejects the domination and control of external forces, my personal experience has taught me that my commitment to the freedom of my soul is actually what keeps me connected to the Divine and motivated by love and truth. Ironically, when I seek to protect my ego's fear of the "dangers" of seeking freedom, my soul's connection to Source is endangered.

I found that the more I practiced operating from my soul rather than my ego, the more freedom emerged in my life. Allowing myself to be free to "choose in" to any experience I felt called to have, regardless of what I had been taught was "good" or "right," opened up an opportunity to actually discover who I was at a soul-u-lar level. While living up to others' expectations, I had suppressed my true self. I had been too afraid not to conform.

Each moment was now providing new opportunities. I began to ask my soul if it wanted to have the experience before me, rather than make decisions based on what I had been told I *should* do. Some of the most simple moments were the most liberating! For example, if I felt an inclination to sing or dance in the grocery store, I would do it and not worry about what others might think. The change came in having the ability to catch my ego's voice telling me things like, *People don't sing and dance at a grocery store.* I had to notice that thought, reject it, and then choose to trust and act on what my soul was calling to experience.[21] In little moments like these, I began to give myself permission to express what I was truly thinking and feeling and wanting to experience, and I would laugh as I caught myself exclaiming, "I feel so free!" I was not totally sure why I felt so much freer—I was a single mom with no money in the bank, cleaning houses for income, and co-parenting through some sticky situations. From the outside, my life did not appear to have more freedom, but that is the miracle—*freedom happens on the inside*!

There is freedom in *being* love, and captivity in *doing* things out of fear. As I focused more on developing my *way of being*, freedom came to me. I was choosing to *be* guided and directed by truth and love as it was directly given to me from Source moment by moment—rather than focusing on *doing* all the "right things" expected by my church and society. Recognizing the captivity in living the latter way was shocking to me. It was astonishing, after so many years of trying unsuccessfully to create more freedom through my actions and accomplishments, to realize that the path to freedom was actually just the opposite of what I had been doing.

---

21   Funny side note: I remember singing and dancing in the store and thinking, "Wow, this store is so cool, it plays the best music! When I was a kid, it seems like the stores always played oldies." Suddenly a recognition struck: "Songs from the 90's *are* oldies now!"

My Being is my soul. When I connect to my soul—my Being—I feel complete, whole, and perfect. Without all the stories of what I should, have to, or am expected to do, I am free to be me—and to know that is enough without the need to *do* my way into worth and value. When living in my ego, it was in my *doing* that I sought to prove and earn my worth and value. Separating the *being* from the *doing* happened by taking questions inward and upward regarding my worth and value. The Spirit once said to me, *"The fact that you exist is evidence you are worthy to exist."* That ended my relationship with proving my worth to myself and others.

My commitment to seeking freedom and trusting my soul expanded into all areas of my life, including my work. As I was evolving in my career path, looking at opportunities and possibilities, I found that turning to outside authorities on how to become "successful" did not light me up. I looked into many online and in-person trainings and seminars from various fields because they pitched messages right at my ego, saying, "Here are the steps to make money!" I caught myself looking for the "right" thing to do. I would begin to watch webinars or read these articles, but I couldn't finish them because my soul would not sit still, my body was tense, and my mind was fearfully thinking about how it needed money. These signs from my internal compass indicated that I was not aligned with truth.

Noticing this, I remembered to turn inward and upward for direction in this area of my life. I asked questions like, "What next? What do I have to offer or share with the world? Where do I go for income opportunities? Who do I talk to? What do I say?" And when I was told what to do, I did it.

One thing led to another, and after cleaning houses for three years, I was guided to transition into the counseling field, where I was hired by a local clinic. My master's degree in clinical social work gave me the credentials to be hired, but again, I met with a fork in the road between ego and soul: *I should take the state's licensing exam and become an LCSW,* said my ego. But my body tensed. I looked for what else might be true.

"*Do not seek licensure, be a coach,*" the Spirit said. My body relaxed, my mind began generating ideas, my heart felt inspired, and my soul danced.

"A life coach?" I asked.

"*No, a Soul Mentor,*" I was told.

"What is that?" I asked. I had never heard that term before.

My ego said, *You can't just make up a title.*

My soul rebutted, *Unless I can?!* And so I did.

It was a subtle distinction in direction, yet it paid off for me. It led me away from what I perceived (based on prior experience in the clinical field) as professional captivity in a field heavily dictated by the medical model, a view of pathologizing human behavior, legislation requirements with the department of licensure, a professional code of ethics limiting and dictating client-therapist relationships, the pharmaceutical industry's influence and lobbying power, and insurance company's games. It led me, instead, to the freedom to be me, and to interact with clients as the Divine dictated. My clients were my friends and my friends became my clients—completely unheard of in the clinical world! I had a lot of freedom to create my own schedule as The Spirit continued to guide me outside of typical nine-to-five employment.

When I asked the Spirit what to do next with my work, answers came. Each time, the answers brought up fear: *No one will come see me. I will not be able to help people. I cannot sustain myself financially doing the things that I love.* Each time these thoughts showed up, I'd sit in the face of fear and feel it. I'd let it talk to me. When I was done acknowledging my fear, I leaned in and moved forward on the directives given from Spirit. And each time, the result has been greater and more rewarding than I could have imagined! I have been led by Spirit to do things for my career that I did not anticipate I would be doing. They were not on my goals list or on a vision board—the ideas just showed up, and I trusted in them.

These promptings included:

"*Hold a women's retreat.*" (This turned into ten women's retreats over four years.)

"*Host a twelve-week class for women.*" (It became two, running concurrently, held back-to-back for four years.)

"*Host a men's group.*" (This opened my heart in so many ways.)

"*Do a Zoom class.*" (This allowed me to reach many people outside of my geographical area and even enabled me to take my work anywhere I wanted to go!)

"*Host a couples' retreat.*" (A gift to my own relationship as well as others'.)

"*Write a book.*" (You're holding it!)

A.R.T.A. (asking, receiving, trusting, and acting with courage) continued to move me out of the mental captivity of allowing my ego to drive my life and gave me the freedom to be connected to the Divine. My success with clients is directly related to my spiritual experiments and experiences. It is the because of the inner relationship I have with my soul and my ego, with my body and my emotions, that I can read and relate to my clients so well.

Every single client session is an opportunity for personal expansion for me, because I still experience fear in opposition to the energy of love, every time! One of the biggest things that comes up for me is fear around triggering people by pushing their buttons. A trigger, to me, is a thought that summons any emotion other than peace, joy, and love. Any time I bring awareness to a person in a way that makes them uncomfortable, I am triggering them. As a child, I exhibited a gift for triggering people and thrived on it! It was entertaining to be able to trigger adults. I used this ability to dominate people in order to elevate myself. I didn't realize then that I had an ego, but in this transition from living in my ego to living from my soul, I learned that my ability to recognize people's triggers is actually a therapeutic gift!

While addressing my own triggers—thoughts that led me to feel less than okay in any way—I discovered that triggers are portals to expansion. While it is a common ego reaction to build heart walls of protection to avoid feeling triggers, and devise mental blocks of self-deception to ignore them, those defenses only prolong the pain they create! "What we resist, persists," I have heard. That is very true of triggers!

I learned I could choose to lean into, rather than away from, my triggers—examining them, investigating the roots of their origins, and seeking to find the flawed and erroneous beliefs that spawned from them. Only then could I replace those false beliefs with truth handed to me from the Divine. This is what I consider to be *healing*: the replacement of fallacy with truth. I have experienced tremendous healing of body, mind, and spirit throughout this process.

I value the freedom truth brings so much that I am willing to face my own fears of offending people, or being judged by them, in order to intentionally trigger them—with love, healing, and truth as my motivation. I offer an opportunity to open that portal of expansion and walk them through it. I tend to introduce myself to new clients with this clause: *I will trigger you, on purpose. And if you'll acknowledge those triggers and ask for guidance, the process will transform you and lead you to truth.* Despite my introductory disclaimers, most people are still often shocked, some freeze, some argue, and some experience shame spirals when I trigger them. Those who admit to me what they are experiencing and open their minds, bodies, and hearts to truth have major breakthroughs. Those who stay locked down in fear and shame cannot see past, nor let go of, their own egos. These people will leave and never come back, and sometimes send angry messages to me.

My human ego can't bear being misunderstood or disliked. It wants to apologize and explain and point out the reason I intentionally triggered them. I want to unveil for them all that I could see was possible on the other side of their fears and shame—the truth is, freedom awaits them! My ego feels sadness and hurt when blamed for their painful experiences with being triggered. However, incredible spiritual experiences have come from me taking all of this and laying it on the altar before God and in total humility saying, "Here's what I'm hearing from them. Here's what I'm thinking, feeling, and believing about myself. What is true?" The answers have illuminated to me the condition of these people's lives—including their mindsets, pain, beliefs, emotions, and behaviors—as well as mine. In nanoseconds, I have beheld both parties in our entirety, with an enlarged understanding that is wrapped in compassion, love, and truth. My mind is set free. Peace is restored within me. I have nothing to prove or explain. I move on.

While freedom is a glorious state of being, the judgmental part of my ego still shows up to try to make me feel bad for the freedoms in my life. Whenever I'm experiencing a sense of freedom, the ego likes to throw thoughts at me like, *That's not everybody's opportunity. You have it so easy.* There is opposition in all things—I was taught that in church and it appears to be accurate. Feelings of freedom are opposed by feelings of guilt. Thoughts like these create restriction in my body and rob me of my sense of freedom and peace. If I do not challenge these thoughts and find the truth, I inevitably forsake my freedom and succumb to the captivity of my fear-based thinking.

On one occasion when my sense of freedom was being challenged by guilt, I took this line of thinking to God. *I feel guilty for the choices I have made that have created freedom in my life. I am thinking that it's easier for me to be free, that others have it much harder than me. Is this thought true?*

The Spirit taught me, *"Everyone chooses. Choices lead to captivity or freedom."*

My mortally programmed, egoic mind argued, *Are you telling me that people choose abuse? That they choose poverty, that they choose disease?* I recognized the energy of fear charging my thoughts; there was a defensive, ready-to-battle feeling in my body. I noticed the fear, the anger, and the attitude that accompanied the thought. "There it is!" I said. "It's my bitch voice again!" When I set it aside, I could seek for a deeper understanding.

Releasing my arguments, I opened myself up, breathed, and asked, "What more is there?"

"Circumstances are not what equate freedom or captivity. What you make it mean about you, that's where the captivity or freedom lies. It's the beliefs you develop that restrict or liberate you."

A vision illustrated the message: I saw myself standing inside of a small 10x10 foot prison, holding onto the bars in front of me.

"What is this?" I asked.

Spirit explained to me, *"The bars represent the beliefs you hold so tightly to. They are your attitudes, your perceptions, your judgments, your memories, your religious beliefs, and more. Everything you are attached to and identify with."*

I began to look at each bar individually and place a hand on it. With each bar, I asked the Spirit to identify the belief that I was still holding on to. One by one, I was shown deeply rooted beliefs I had clung to throughout my life. They were things like: *I'm not beautiful. If my kids are disobedient, I have failed as a parent. I cannot heal people physically—that is a priesthood duty. My best friends always leave me.* I was able to ask the Spirit concerning every belief, "What is the truth about this?" As the truth was revealed, the bar dissolved into sand and fell to the ground, absolving me of the captivity of that belief.

"*I am free!*" I exclaimed. Freed from my own interpretations of societal and cultural values. Freed from religious teaching mingled with philosophies of men. Freed from my addiction to doing, my own flawed perceptions, from the need to be right, or to prove and earn my worth and value. I was now free to just be!

My soul was ready to sing!

Amazing Grace, how sweet the sound,
That saved a wretch like me!
I once was lost, but now I'm found;
Was blind, but now I see.

This traditional gospel song has been a favorite of mine since childhood. I have fond memories of singing this with my three older sisters while my mom accompanied us on the piano. Now, I felt I really understood the heart of the lyrics—it felt like my life's anthem.

As I sought freedom, I recognized captivity. I had been blind to it before. If you are born into captivity, whether as an animal born at the zoo or a baby born in a country run by a dictator, you would not know you were captive because you would not know what freedom was. I did not know I was living in the captivity of fear-based beliefs until I was no longer living in captivity. Until these began to dissolve under investigation, I did not know that my beliefs—about myself, the world, others, and God—were the bars of my prison. I had thought all my beliefs were true.

I have continued to practice this exercise and it has revealed many limiting and false beliefs:

While I told myself I was not organized, I stayed disorganized.

While I told myself it was hard to find time to write, it was hard to find time to write.

While I told myself it was a struggle to lose weight, it was.

While I told myself it was hard to let go of resentment, it was.

While I told myself it was hard to love myself and believe I was enough, it was.

Anything I told myself, I made true, because I was committed to my beliefs. I unconsciously created my reality and the evidence that my beliefs were true. The "prison" I was in was entirely my own creation, and I was the only one who could set myself free.

Early in 2018, I discovered one bar in my prison that had yet to be addressed: my beliefs about men.

I had layers of limiting beliefs about men. Society had taught me, "Men are pigs and they only care about one thing," and, "In order to get a man, you have to look like a Barbie and act like a ditz."

My church had taught me, "You must be married to a man in order to get into the highest degree of heaven," and, "Men bring forth scripture, are leaders, and have the healing power of the priesthood."

My ego as a teen told me, "You are not pretty enough to be asked out. You are not good enough for a man."

My marriage taught me, "My job as a wife is to make sure the kids are neatly groomed and dressed, obedient, educated, and talented so my husband can take the credit and look good."

Following my divorce and the interactions I had with several priesthood leaders in my church, I was even more angry, bitter, and annoyed by men than I had been in my younger years. I saw men as emotionally closed off, arrogant, and less intelligent than women. This perception was created by my beliefs and cemented in my mind as truth with evidence from my lived experience.

One day, as my beliefs about men came into my awareness due to an interaction with a man that brought tension into my body and angry thoughts into my mind, I paused and took a breath. I looked at what I was telling myself and how I felt physically and emotionally in that moment. I wasn't just angry at men, I was filled with rage. There was no connection to God in that space. A thought struck me: *I am the mother of five sons! This needs to get cleared up. How can I raise my sons in true, unconditional love when I'm carrying the burden of these beliefs about men?*

The spiritual excavation project continued, digging down into deeper layers of my beliefs. I took all my attitudes, opinions, experiences, and beliefs regarding men to God and laid them on the altar of my mind.

Backing up a bit, I need to comment here that I had done some personal growth work prior to this moment that was essential to my being able to heal my relationship with men. It came in my unraveling my addiction to "doing" as a way of proving my worth.

I had been shown in that season that my "doing energy" was a masculine/yang energy, and was very high, while my "receptive energy," the feminine/yin energy, had been malnourished and depleted. I believe this imbalance of my internal energies came from multiple sources: the behaviors were modeled for me by many women in my life who were on the path of trying to do everything "right" in order to get into heaven; I also believe I carried intergenerational anger toward men passed down to me genetically from my mother's line. I had become competitive with males as early as elementary school, trying to prove I was as smart and strong as they were, and my high masculine energy was a protection from the shame I felt around believing I was not a desirable woman. I had zero formal mentoring, as far as I can remember, in the true and sacred nature of divine feminine energy. Looking back, I can identify certain individuals in my life who embodied this healthy energy, but they were rare exceptions.

Being high in my masculine energy provided me with protection in a competitive world. I was praised for being smart from the time I was small, and I became increasingly opinionated, egotistical, self-righteous, and judgmental, citing my religious testimony as justification. I felt driven by a need to be right, in order to be good, worthy, and righteous. Because my masculine energy was not balanced by feminine energies within me, I grew more and more overwhelmed, exhausted, stressed, ornery, resentful, angry, condescending, critical, and hostile—manifestations of wounded masculine and feminine energies. This mind-body awareness came from exposure to many great books by authors such as Louise Hay, Karol Truman, Wendyi Jensen, and more.

When the phrase *divine feminine energy* came into my life, I curiously examined, read about, discussed with others, and sought to observe and cultivate those traits in myself. This connection to feminine energy was crucial in getting to know my soul and coming into the presence of God.

My healing in this regard had been taking place for a couple of years by this time and had brought me to love and cherish the feminine design. When my awareness of my animosity toward men surfaced, I knew it was time to address and heal those feelings.

As I laid my beliefs about men on the altar of my mind, I said, "God, I just realized how deeply ingrained my negative beliefs about men are, and how strongly I feel about them. I am also appreciating how clever you are in sending me five males to mother. Genius! If your divine design for masculine energy is embodied anywhere in mortal form on this earth, I would like it to be shown to me."

Exactly three days later, I found myself invited to participate in a mastermind group in the home of a woman I knew. I had never met her husband, but as he shared his life story, I knew that he was an answer to my prayer. He spoke of his emergence from a culture of captivity as a child, of rising up to find worldly success in business as a young adult, of a devastating turn in a relationship, of alcoholism, and of an awakening. The way he spoke about life, relationships, and God paralleled the concepts I had been learning directly from the Spirit. It was confirmation.

Before I left his home that evening I approached him and said, "I prayed you into my life three days ago. Thank you for inviting me here today and for sharing your story." On my way out I stopped on the porch and looked up at the sky. "God, one point; Angel, zero." God had delivered my first witness.

The following year was dedicated to my quest to discover and witness the divine masculine energy embodied in mortal form. The more I sought it out and honored it, the more I found it, but a major caveat was this: I had to set aside all of my egoic beliefs. I mean every single negative thought I had about men was called to the surface. I was triggered by men in so many ways. My ego wanted to hold onto the "concrete evidence" it had gathered for decades and use it as proof to keep me convinced that men were, in fact, assholes.[22]

This was a quest, to seek to know God more by beholding the divine

---

22   The evidence I thought I had accumulated was actually a collection of examples of wounded masculine energy. I believe women who are angry toward men have mistaken wounded masculine energy with true masculine energy. Demonstrations of wounded masculine energy are not the true, divine characteristics of masculine energy. Ironically, those of us who make that mistake are the same ones who then take on wounded masculine energy in our own thoughts and behaviors as a way to protect and prove ourselves. We become our own versions of the egotistical, narcissistic beings that we hate. (The inner work just keeps going!)

masculine. With open eyes and an open heart, I began to see more and more examples of such divinity embodied in mortal form, and I was surprised and curious when I found divine masculine energy in unexpected places, such as: a man covered in tattoos, or one who had long, scraggly hair, or one who was in love with another man. These were all examples of what my religion had taught me was not upstanding, righteous, or Godly. I had to sit with that cognitive dissonance each time, and ask, "God, how do I reconcile that everything in my being is telling me this person loves like You do, and is honoring his divine design, and yet I have been told at church that You do not approve of these parts of him?" Beautiful, ego-stripping moments followed! Being able to ask God what God thinks is radically illuminating!

My heart was guided to seek and find examples of divine masculinity in relationships founded on equality, sovereignty, and friendship. Everywhere I saw an example, I openly acknowledged it, took note, and expressed gratitude to God. *Breathe and receive*, I reminded myself. I was grateful to see that loving, mutually supportive relationships existed between men and women and that—even more astonishing—male/female romantic partners could actually be best friends. This was all very new to me. It began to chip away at my biases and assumptions about men and relationships.

Prior to this investigation, I had been acquainted with primarily contractual relationships in which each partner was living the role they were programmed to live and expecting their spouse to live her/his role. Not only had I lived under the dictates of societal norms and roles about gender and marriage, I had also taken on the strict role assignments outlined by my religious beliefs. These assignments are outlined in lesson manuals, spoken by church authorities from the pulpit, and most famously declared in a document published in 1995 called "The Family: A Proclamation to the World." As with everything else taught at church, I was told this was what God wanted me to do.

The most confusing and contradictory part, for me, was that in the midst of all this guidance, we were also often given a directive to *seek personal revelation* for our own lives. Beginning with that fateful phone call in which I learned there was a warrant out for my husband's arrest, I had been powerfully guided and directed step by step in finding answers and receiving a witness of truth within my body, mind, heart, and spirit—more so than I ever had before in my life. Yet in nearly every encounter I had with a church leader, my personal revelation was confronted with opposing cultural or doctrinal beliefs. So, it seemed, unless my personal revelation aligned with what I was being told to do and believe, it was wrong.

As I sought further understanding regarding masculinity, I continued to experiment with seeking truth directly from Source. My conversations with God encouraged me to release all that programming about strict roles and gender assignments within marriage and truly trust in personal revelation. God guided me to study the topics of masculine and feminine energies, evaluate myself and acknowledge that I was out of balance, and take steps to nurture and heal both my wounded masculine and feminine energies. This completely altered my existence! The way I related to myself, to my sons, to men, and even to women, all changed! I discovered the most beautiful and sacred space inside of men is often as buried and wounded as that space is within women. I also discovered that as I operate from my divine feminine energy, I can relate to and reach the hearts of wounded men, and love them, and speak to them in a way that breathes life and love back into their whole bodies, minds, and hearts. I can call to their souls and beckon them forward. I do not think this ability is my unique gift, I feel it is the divine design of goddess energy in action. Anyone can connect to it.

My divorce was finalized in April of 2018 and I was free from the contractual egoic relationship I had co-created. Now I had a different mindset and skill set centered on practicing the sacred dance of the feminine and masculine energies inside myself. I did not anticipate what was coming. In November of that year, on a Sunday evening, God told me to create an online dating profile.

"Wait. God, I thought you had told me that for the next few years my focus was to be directed toward my career development and the nurturing and raising of my sons and our emotional healing?"

"*Yes*," God said. "*Keep that up. And if you want to expand the understanding of divine energies and increase your abilities to be in sacred alignment with a partner, it requires actual practice. Dating is your next laboratory of learning. Now is the time for your next course in conscious relationships. You will face all your fears and triggers and have the opportunity to transmute those with love and truth. You cannot fail, you can't do this wrong. It's all about experience.*"

I created a dating profile right away. In doing so, I had to face my fears: *No one wanted to date me as a teen, why would anyone date me as a forty-one-year old with five kids? Guys are going to think I'm desperate for someone to financially provide for us.* In response to the fear, guilt, shame, and judgment coming up, I paused, closed my eyes, and breathed deeply as I anchored to truth and self-compassion: *I love me. I am enough for me. I am worthy.*

In my experience with dating over the next few weeks, I discovered a new ability to behold people, and I sought to develop it. When I looked in their eyes, I saw each man's divinity, his worth and value, and I felt God's love for him. I felt what a privilege it was to be in his space. My desire was to convey those messages to them in each interaction. I did not care if I impressed them or if they asked me out again. I just hoped that being in my presence might feel different to them than other experiences. I hoped they could feel safe to be themselves in my presence.

One particular experience presented a learning opportunity. I was genuinely interested in a guy I was dating, and then our contact abruptly ended. I spiraled in shame, facing all my fears about not being enough, not being lovable, and not being worthy. It felt like a volcano erupted from within me, with fear, shame, and sadness pouring out as hot rage. I went to my storage room, grabbed a bat, and found things I could smash while I raged. I shouted and destroyed cardboard boxes until the rage melted into tears. Sobs, groans, and moans came from my lips. I had to keep coaching myself through the experience so that judgment would not shut me down.[23]

When I had exhausted my emotions through expression, I was still. It was like the ocean after a storm. Then I turned inward and upward. "Okay, God, here I am. I did what you asked. And here is what I've experienced. I've been telling myself tonight that I'm not good enough. That this ended because I'm not skinny enough, not pretty enough, not lovable, not worthy. I know these are old stories of captivity. Remind me, what is true about me?"

As I chose to suspend the old stories and seek to know the truth, glorious streams of light energy entered the room and permeated my body through the top of my head, filling me with truth. It felt like a rapid battery recharge, like I had just plugged into some accelerated charger and was fully rebooted within a couple of minutes. It was an authentic, nearly instantaneous shift from my feelings of rejection to absolute lightness and freedom!

---

23   Yes, this emotional outburst was conscious and intentional! I talk more about the importance of feeling and moving emotions in Chapter 10.

I was instructed by Spirit to get back onto the dating app and go at it again. My ego told me I was a glutton for punishment, but my soul assured me I could trust the Divine. I did, and the very next day, I matched with Eric on the dating app, Tinder. That's why I call him my "Tinder mercy!"[24]

Drawing upon all the examples and inspiration I had gathered to this point regarding the sacred nature of divine masculine and feminine energies, I began a relationship that has looked nothing like my prior marriage. In fact, it does not look like any relationship I have ever witnessed. Together, Eric and I have created a conscious relationship based on truth and love, honoring each other's sovereignty, and seeking God's wisdom each step of the way. Eric and I have often laughed with childlike delight at the way in which our lives flow with grace and ease, not only with each other but also how our relationship cascades with ripple effects into our respective professional lives. This flow is not a lucky product of circumstance, it is the result of daily, Spirit-led, ego-less choices. It is because we monitor our way of *being* and prioritize that over the checklist requirements of a contract-based relationship.

Eric and I refrain from allowing fears—which often appear in the form of "shoulds"—into our relationship. There are no binding expectations on what and how each partner should do or be to serve the partnership. No gender role assignments for our duties dictate how we run our home and family life. We cast off fear and turn inward and upward every day, receiving personal revelation to guide us in each situation that arises. We are free as individuals and as a partnership to be and do whatever we feel called to experience, and

---

[24] A light-hearted reference to the phrase "tender mercy," from the Book of Mormon, 1 Nephi 1:20. There is so much to share about meeting Eric, and our relationship, that it will be an upcoming book of its own: *Soul-u-lar Relationships*.

we champion each other's freedom to choose. These words are often exchanged: "I choose you every day." What a treasure to be chosen, cherished, and partnered with from a place of love, rather than feeling bound by fear of failure, captive, stuck, *enduring to the end* in hopes of a better relationship miraculously appearing in the next life.

I operate very differently now than I did in my previous marriage. Stemming from my former understanding of church doctrine, I had specific expectations about my husband's role, how he should show up in our relationship, how he should parent, and how he should lead our family. I estimated that he was not meeting those expectations about eight-five percent of the time. Simultaneously, I felt I was meeting my role expectations and church responsibilities about ninety-seven percent of the time.

In this mindset, I sought to quantify his worth by drawing comparisons: not only how he was doing and how I was doing, but also between how he was doing and what the ideal *righteous priesthood holder* would do. I unknowingly tried to manipulate my husband emotionally, through guilt and shame; verbally, with condescending language and criticism; and energetically, with my resentment. I thought I was reminding him of our agreements, contracts, and covenants. I thought I was being a good partner to him! This makes me feel sick to reflect on. But it was all I knew. This was the exact same way countless relationships in my culture operate. I was ignorant and therefore innocent! I choose to love myself now, and honor my innocence.

A large portion of the success of my relationship with Eric has come from our awareness that we are free to look beyond programmed expectations to what is really true and possible. For example, our programming said we had to get married and then live all together under one roof in order to be a "family." I have five sons and Eric has full custody of his three daughters. When we met, we had a combined six teenagers and two younger children. The thought of living in a home together felt like captivity to me! Instead, we chose to talk about these pressures, then challenge all the beliefs, programming, and conditioning we had around relationship and family structure.

As we acknowledged the fear, guilt, shame, and judgment around doing things differently, we cleared the way to ask God, "What is true?"

God guided each of us to a less-common path: one that allowed us to tenderly nurture our love for each other, provide space for the healing of past wounds, and honor our children's best interests. We chose to live separately for three years.

Another example of the freedom we give ourselves to be and do things differently than others was initiated on a Saturday in the spring of 2021. I was sitting on a rock to enjoy the sun while reading. I paused to look off into the distance when I heard my soul call to me, *"Go away and write by the ocean."* I wondered where I could go? My mind was drawn to one of my favorite places. "I want to go to Hawaii and write!" I declared out loud.

My ego's voice spoke up and said, *I cannot just go to a lavish destination to write.* I wondered if I was being selfish or if it was inherently wrong to have this desire.

I asked, "What is true?" and the Spirit said with love and clarity, *"It's not selfish. There is purpose in this. Go to the ocean and write."* Truth released me from the captivity of my own fears and guilt.

As I began to prepare for a trip to Hawaii, fear crept back in. I imagined potential conversations with people and being criticized for my choice. "Well that's super nice for you. How would it be? Not everyone can be so lucky to just drop everything and go to Hawaii." In my mind they were moms. Doers. Martyrs. Marthas. Nameless faces all reciting my past beliefs! They were versions of the former me, the jealous judger in me. Those were thoughts I had once had about others who seemed to do things outside of the box, outside of the norms of role assignments and expectations.

The words "judge not that ye be not judged"[25] came to mind. Suddenly I understood the scripture differently—I was now on the other end of my very own past judgments of others! I was getting to experience and comprehend another side of it! That recognition bred humility and compassion within me. I saw that I may have been wrong about my judgments of others. Those judgments may have kept me captive, locked up, not knowing how to give myself permission to just be free.

I trusted in the voice guiding me to something new and expansive. I did spend a glorious month in Hawaii that June, in my favorite area, the north shore of Oahu, an area I am drawn back to again and again. On this trip, I came with a new intention. I was returning, not just because I love the place, and not just because I needed or wanted a vacation, but because I was truly drawn there in seeking to connect with sacred space. I went to the beach daily to meditate and to write.

Toward the end of my month's time there, while meditating at Hukilau Beach, I felt a new commission, meaning, a call from the Divine: *"It's time to lose all attachments."*

When impressions come like that—thoughts that are new and different—I now notice them and repeat them in my mind, or out loud, rather than my former practice of allowing my ego to discredit and dismiss them from a place of fear: "Lose all attachments." I repeated. Then I practiced breathing and receiving, as a physical form of acknowledging the directive from the Divine. In this case, because I wasn't really sure what that phrase even meant, I asked the question,

---

25   The Holy Bible, KJV, Matthew 7:2 For with what judgment ye judge, ye shall be judged: and with what measure ye mete, it shall be measured to you again.

"What more is there?"

I received a sudden comprehension that I needed to shed my physical and emotional attachments to material objects, relationships, titles, roles, anything that kept me tied to a belief. *This is a bold move*, I thought. I attempted to clarify it in detail for myself so I could explain it to Eric. As I sat there pondering the invitation to lose all attachments, I was led to observe my attachments to food and emotion first. Then I felt guided to return home to Southern Utah at the end of June, as planned, and begin to get rid of things. The next piece of the prompting was that I would return to Hawaii soon for the next phase of this odyssey. I kept meditating on this commission, taking inquisitive questions inward and upward, and was shown that, rather than finding a place to live or rent, I would be staying right at that exact spot on Hukilau Beach where I received the commission.

"Live homeless on the beach?" I asked, incredulously.

"That's a human perspective based on fear. You will be at home MORE with yourself in Hawaii, not home-less."

I asked, "What do I need, a tent?"

"*A hammock.*"

Of course the potential threats of being a female alone on a beach at night tried to surface. But they were so blatantly fear-based, I dismissed them. "If this is what God wants me to do, there is nothing to fear, and there is a way prepared for me."

When I returned from Hawaii to Utah, *lose all attachments* was my theme. Within days, my car's transmission died and I gave the vehicle away, releasing the attachment to transportation. Next, my sister notified me that they were going to sell the home we'd been renting, and I needed to move out: lose attachment to housing. Soon afterwards, I was on my way into work to give a presentation and my favorite sandals split and fell apart, so I threw them in the trash and gave my presentation in bare feet! It felt comical how attachments began falling off left and right at that time, without any effort from me.

By the end of September, I had given away most of my belongings, and those of my kids. Our worldly possessions were whittled down to what fit in a few suitcases and one bedroom closet in Eric's house. My beloved Eric had witnessed this whole unfolding and supported me in so much love!

I returned to Oahu in October with my hammock and a tarp. My children flew to Hawaii with me and stayed at their dad's, where I could see them daily. I went to the beach with my newly purchased hammock and followed the instructions for setting it up for the first time. Prior to this, my total hammock experience added up to two minutes sitting in a friend's hammock chair, so putting up my own hammock and sleeping in it was an all-new experience.

It felt amazing in that hammock! The ocean was just yards away, and there was a constant breeze; the gentle swaying felt like being rocked by my mother. I found myself asking, "Why have I never done this before?"

The answer: *Because you did not know how to be still; you were busy proving and earning your worth and value.*

In preparing to come to Hawaii, I held the firm intention not to worry about the logistics ahead of time. I was following the *what* and *where* pattern, and I trusted God had the *how* and the *why* figured out.

As I hung my hammock, the time had come to ask the two main questions I had:

"What do I do to obey the law that says 'No overnight camping'?" and "What will I do to be safe here, as a woman alone at the beach?"

In response to both these queries, the inspiration hit me: *"Become nocturnal."*

Once again, I was struck by the hilarious genius of God. I laughed and laughed. God had the perfect, simple solution for me, and offered it only when it was actually pertinent for me to know the *how*!

I was shown that if I slept in my hammock at the beach during the day, between ten a.m. and six p.m., I was not breaking any of the beach laws. I could also sleep safely in the broad daylight, surrounded by beachgoers and nearby road traffic; I was much less likely to be the subject of a crime. At six p.m. each night, I could wake up, go see my boys, then work on my book in the university library until it closed at midnight.

Little by little, I was guided as to how to navigate my schedule. When the university closed at midnight, I went walking around town. I listened to audio books or music, or sat in stillness. Some days at two or three a.m., Hawaii time, I was able to clip a portable light onto my phone and begin Zoom sessions with my clients on the mainland whose time zones were four, five, and six hours later than Hawaii's. Just after the sun rose in Hawaii, I was finished with work and ready to return to my hammock to sleep. No law breaking, and I was safe! GOD IS A GENIUS!

This period was a very sacred time for me. I confronted so many fears as I walked through the community, alone in the dark. I had opportunities to challenge my thinking and my relationship with fear on several occasions when I was approached by men as I walked. Story after story after story about what horrific encounter or attack might happen to me rolled through my brain in a matter of seconds. I was able to halt these stories and simply ask God, "What would you have me do?"

Each response was a version of, *"Look them in the eye and send them love."*

I followed the prompting. I looked at them and thought, *You are lovable. You are worthy. You are enough. You are my brother.* I was met with kindness and curiosity, and never harmed.

I got to face something as simple as rain, and realize how pervasive the programming of our minds is. The first night it rained while I was out walking, I thought urgently, *I need to find shelter!* Then I challenged the thought. *Why is it that the human reaction is to run for shelter when it rains? It is just water. I am not afraid of the shower, and I'm not afraid of jumping into a pool. What will happen if I just stand here?* I did just that. I stood in the rain, suspended judgment, and had the experience. I felt my clothes grow heavy and saturated. I did not have to call it *bad* that my clothes were wet. And I did not have to call it *good*. I just let it be. I felt my tears flow as fear was released and freedom emerged.

I was led to the next phase of the experiment when I learned that the law prohibits loitering in any one spot for more than two hours. It was not my intention to break any laws or to disturb any locals; I wanted to be helpful. I thought, *I can be a self appointed neighborhood watchdog. I can keep an eye on things while people are sleeping.*

I wondered what people were seeing, saying, fearing, or judging. "Can I love myself through this?" I would ask—the answer was "yes" every time. I found an abandoned camp chair on the beach, and I used it to sit on a grassy space under a streetlight sometimes. I observed and learned from others I saw sleeping at the beach or the bus stop at night. I had never looked at homeless people with anything but judgment and pity. This experience changed that for me. I watched to learn and to appreciate their ability to survive. I was impressed with their ingenuity. They made multiple uses out of objects: carts that carried their possessions doubled as a frame to hold up cardboard for shelters; bags carrying clothing were used as pillows to sleep on; bungee cords secured belongings to fences; items that had been discarded as trash were pieced together to make a barrier against rain and wind. I had never looked before with curious eyes, only judgment and fear. It felt freeing to really *see* them.

I lived in the present moment. I did not know what each day would bring or if I would be prepared for it, but I chose to trust that God would tell me what to do next. I simply had experiences, evaluated the experience, and adapted. This time was not meant to be compared to others' experiences with involuntary homelessness. This was a spiritual lesson I was being taught. It was customized by God for me. I certainly didn't have real hardship. It was just new for me. I had the luxury of one close friend in the community who allowed me to keep my valuables locked in her home and I had access to her bathroom and laundry.

I often wore the same clothes for a few days at a time; I was able to sit with my judgments and attachments to cleanliness and appearance. I explored so many of my attachments: my reputation, needing to be with others, fitting in, doing what I am "supposed" to do, and more. It was such an eye-opening experience. I had fewer material possessions and felt more freedom than ever before.

It was the greatest thing I've ever done for myself. I had conversations with the ocean and sky, plants, trees, and birds, and the Being that created us all. It was so easy to feel peace and joy in a state of *being* and *receiving* rather than *doing* and *proving*. I had spent so much of my past life chasing peace and joy, doing everything I could to earn it, and now I could truly understand how unnecessary those efforts had been.

This experience came to fruition because I chose to listen to the call six months earlier to lose all attachments. My ego (and several other people) thought it sounded crazy. And it *was* crazy—crazy amazing! The results of that time were epically magical and mind-blowing, a

180-degree shift from "normal life." And where "normal life" is inundated with fear, that 180-degree shift is a walk with peace. This hammock experience lasted six weeks.

When I returned to Utah, nothing looked the same to me: not my relationship with Eric, my role as a mother, or my work as a coach. It felt like fear had no bearing on me, and all I could see were the POSSIBILITIES!

What I'd originally thought of as an existential crisis had become an *existential opportunity* in every way! That phone call in 2016 when I discovered there was a warrant out for my husband's arrest was a catalyst for me to do something different. For the first time in my life, I chose to completely trust myself, and simultaneously to trust God, over and above all others. I discovered that there was a place inside of myself that was already one with God! I learned through conversation and experience that God trusts me to experiment with life—I am free to choose anything and learn from it all!

FREEDOM POETRY

As my sense of freedom increased, I began writing poetry—something I hadn't done since high school. The spirit and energy of poetry became a natural expression; poetry is the way feelings and words dance from the mind onto paper. Writing poetry is also a way of depicting the dance occurring among my mind, body, heart, and spirit as it comes into coherence and aligns with truth.

Here are some of the poems that came through that.

You Glow Girl!
Flow with the tides
Roll with the waves
Soak up the sun
Let nothing get done,
Because it's not you
Getting things done
The Being IS you—
Doing DOES itself too!
So sail on the wind
Breathe with the breeze
Relax in the sand—
You're in God's hand.
- Written in Laie, Hawaii on 12/2/2021

And the Ocean Still Is

The sun rises and sets
And the ocean still is.
The rain pours and passes
And the ocean still is.
People enter and abandon it
And the ocean still is.
The years come and go
And the ocean still is.
I am the ocean.
-Written after a sunrise meditation at Temple Beach, Laie, Hawaii on 11/10/21

Cocoon

There are parallels to hammocks, being wrapped in cocoons
The creations of nature,
as well as of wombs.
The space holds you gently
Securely and tight
While your being evolves and expands day and night.
In a setting so still
There's a oneness with self
Removing distractions—placing all on the shelf.
Drawing inward and upward
Reaching deep in the soul
Creating a life that is epic and full
-Written 11/22/2021

Are We Separate or Are We One?

We choose our words

From what we know,

From what has been given to us.

But our hearts and our souls

All speak the same language—

Words confound

Across genders

And cultures

And generations.

We are all ignorant in our words,

Which is innocent in our words:

We do not know

What we do not know

Beyond our own upbringing

And experience,

And we fill those gaps

With assumptions.

Yet truth exists

Beyond what we think we know

Beyond what we can ever say with words,

And that truth is love.

-Written on 12/5/21

REFLECTIONS FROM "THE UNICORNS"

Following is a transcribed conversation between myself and two of my most impactful mentors, Kami Mitchell and Shelby Smith, whom I affectionately refer to as "The Unicorns." This is their response, and wise additions, to my story.

I have publicly stated this numerous times: In all my years in the clinical mental health field, in the realm of self-help, watching therapists operate, working with mentors, and learning from professors, coaches, and teachers from a range of disciplines, I have never witnessed anyone work as effectively—and with as much love and intuitive power—as these two women. They are a testament to me of trusting the power of the Divine, and trusting themselves to act in alignment with that power. They are love. Witnessing them in action in numerous mentoring settings gave me the hope and confidence to begin to trust my connection with the Divine as well.

To connect or work with The Unicorns, email them at: return2loveunicorn@gmail.com.

SHAME AND RELIGIOUS CULTURAL CONDITIONING

Kami: The pieces that stand out from our religious training are that there are definitive roles: This is the place for the woman, the wife ... So many of those pieces shaped our whole world, they defined us, they were our identity. It's so fascinating how you grew up giving time, tithing, service, everything to the church, but the one time you actually needed to receive from the church, you felt ashamed. What?? How did we mess that up? That's such a cultural faux pas. We are taught that if you're on the giving side, you're righteous, you're going to heaven. But if you're the one that needs to receive, "Oh my gosh, poor you, what on earth is happening?"

We were taught that receiving is not okay. Yet, if you do not receive, you do not know how to give. Those two are the same thing, but that was not what we grew up with. The mindset was, "Giving is righteous, receiving is selfish."

We got behind the principles, we understood that as truth, and we didn't even question it. "Okay, and this is how we do it." But then the promises of, "Then you'll be happy! And you'll have abundance!" Wait . . . where is any of that lining up? There's all this shame in our lives. For example, you (Angel) feeling like a failure because you couldn't nurse a baby. There are so many moms that are in that space, with shame riddling us, even though we were taught that "God is Love." But who is living that? That's the question. I wasn't living that. I was taught that, but I was living every mistake I made. I felt ashamed. I felt like God couldn't possibly love me. I felt like I had to earn my worth on a daily basis with all the lists like you were referring to. I had to accomplish and check this off and get this piece so I could feel worthy of His love today.

Shelby: And many of us felt like if something didn't work out in our favor, then we just needed to prove ourselves more, and try harder tomorrow, and be a better wife and do a better job of being a mom and do a better job at keeping house. No wonder so many feel like it's never enough.

Angel: I spent years confused why marriage was so difficult, while trying harder and harder to do all the right things. And I confused submission to my spouse with self-betrayal. Being willing to submit to my husband, as I was instructed in the church, was my role in order to keep my marriage covenants. And that commitment superseded listening to and trusting my spirit. I was never taught how to do that. Never. It was always to listen to leaders, listen to the Prophet, listen to others who had the authority to preside over me. Inherently, there were feelings of guilt and shame whenever I considered listening to my spirit, my intuition, when it conflicted with my husband's. My role, and he told me this repeatedly, was to obey "the priesthood"—with him being "the priesthood" in our home. I was culturally shamed into submission, which really is slavery. Submission is a choice, slavery is forced. In this environment, I didn't recognize the correlation between submission to my spouse and self-betrayal. And, I didn't know that I actually could submit to the voice of the Spirit, above my husband, in order to align with Truth. I was taught to submit to my husband, and trust him—that since he went to church and held callings, he would be submitting to the will of the Lord.

BEING VS. DOING

Angel: What does "being" mean to you two?

Shelby: I've always loved the concept, "We are human beings, not human doings."

It's that state of the human experience where there's nothing to prove. When I'm doing, I'm trying to prove my worth to God, to myself, and to other people. Trying to prove that I'm worthy to exist, that I'm worthy of blessings, that I'm worthy to have the belongings that I have. But in the state of being, it just is; your worth just exists and there is nothing to prove. And when there's nothing to prove, the being is now flow; it comes from love rather than fear. "Proving myself" energy is "I'm afraid."

Kami: The state of Being is the present moment. You can't BE if you're in the future or the past. Being is right here, right now. It's interesting that when you asked us that question, both Shelby and I automatically took a breath, because that is being. You breathe into the moment that you have right in front of you. And have that awareness that you're intentionally right here with yourself in this moment...

Shelby: ... Which is where God is, which is where reality is, it's where truth is...

Kami: ... Where love exists...

Shelby: ... It's when heaven is. I like to ask, "When is heaven?" Not, "Where is heaven?" Heaven exists right now. The past and the future is where suffering is, which is hell. So Being is choosing into bringing heaven into my existence, experiencing the heaven that already is inside of me.

Kami: And this Being isn't attached to, "Oh, then I'm going to feel great, and I'm going to be happy, and I'm going to be excited?" No. Being is: No matter what is right here, right now for me, that's the gift. That's the present the present is bringing. That awareness of, "Woah, I have tightness in my chest. I have this sensation that is coming up in my throat." And being curious, like where you went—instead of feeling ashamed and shut down, you got curious like a child. "Oh, let's hear from me right now. I'm here, so I'm okay. Even if I'm naked and alone in the wilderness, I am here." That is the BEING that I am.

It's interesting that Being, the BEing of light, the BEing of love, is me BEing all of me. It is that BEing-ness—the gift that I get to bring and deliver to this space: my vibration, my frequency, the feels that are in this body that I get to be inside of for this experience.

Shelby: And the difference is, BEing is a conscious choice. When we choose to BE, it's that choice that brings us into the space. Choose it.

Kami: That's interesting when you said that, I'm like, "Oh my gosh, if that's true, then victim cannot enter into BEing.

Shelby: No. Unless you choose the victim experience, "Oh, I want to see what it feels like to be victim in this moment.

Kami: The blaming, the roles that we play, the victim, the villain, the rescuer, are any of those being present with what is right now?

Shelby: Being, I would say, is without judgment. When we are in those spaces there is judgment . . .

Kami: . . . Filled with blindness and judgment and non-awareness. Angel, when you were driving in the car your availability to that being, right there in that moment, gave you insight into the innocence of the other car's driver. If you were anywhere else, if you were in the future, if you were in the past, if you were the victim, if you were anywhere else, that light and truth would not have been available to you. You wouldn't have been able to see it even if it was right there. You were able to see it because you were being.

Shelby: There's zero judgment . . .

Kami: . . . Neutrality

Shelby: . . . Where everything just is, and there's no label, there's no pulling from the past to define it, it's just experiencing it as it is, without judgment.

Angel: In moments like that, involving another person, I describe it as being able to "behold" them. I can understand, it is what it is. "I see what she was thinking and feeling and how it led to that conclusion." So there's no defensiveness, no judgment, just compassion.

Shelby: And you're using self-reflection, "Where do I play this same role? How is she mirroring me?"

Angel: These are the pieces that started to come forward that were so new to me. In an instant of beholding, then to do turn-arounds, that came from these pieces of trainings and books, but the spiritual piece was experiencing compassion, "Oh, I get her. She didn't know her blinker was on, she was going straight and she thought I pulled out in front of her." I drop into compassion through turnarounds and shadow work, "Where and when have I been that person?" rather than saying things to others like, "Why are you doing this? You're so stupid?"

As soon as I ask the question, the Spirit will show me examples from my past where I have been like that person and then I get to love and accept that former version of me, and when I think about the other person in my present circumstance, all there is is love and acceptance there, too.

Kami: It's interesting because you still have discernment, you still have the thoughts, you still have awareness of what's happening, but without the judgment. That curiosity, that playfulness, that self-reflection, those truths and answers, are what you're being led to in that neutral space—that the judgments would have led you to be defensive, and gotten angry, "Stupid woman, she's got her blinker on and she's honking at me?!"

Angel: . . . Proving I'm right, so I can make sure she knows I'm right and she's wrong.

Kami: Yes! And instead, that gentleness of understanding changed the whole softness of it all, where her anger was diffused immediately.

FEAR AND LOVE

Kami: When that inspiration came to you, about Mary and Martha—the only difference between the two is that Mary knew when to quit doing and she came into being—I relate that to your relationship with your husband. That is one of the hardest things to accept as humans—to know when to quit. To know when something is complete. Be it a relationship, a heart call, a job, a house where I live, all of these things. We are so attached to things and we think they are here forever. We don't even know how to ask the question, "Is this chapter complete?" Allowing ourselves to look at that is one of the hardest things for us, in our culture, to do. For example, in my marriage, I thought since I signed up for it, it was forever and ever. That's what I was taught. And therefore, quitting meant failure, it's sinful. The fear of failure overpowers our ability to recognize when something is complete. Do we know when to quit? To let go of attachments and stop doing from a place of fear, surrendering to the invitations to expand coming from unconditional love?

Shelby: We are taught that quitting means you didn't "endure to the end." We can't even say the word "quit," it has such a heavy connotation. How do we know when to complete that season, that chapter?

Angel: When I was wrestling with the impressions I was receiving to dissolve my marriage, I was replaying the cultural programming, and it was blocking inspiration. "I can't quit! This is supposed to be FOREVER! I made covenants!" Then, I got out of fear and instead of regurgitating what I had been taught to think, I asked the Spirit the question, "What are you saying to me?" I stopped looking at, "How am I interpreting this impression?" And the Spirit said, "This relationship has fulfilled the measure of its creation; it is finished." And there were the words that Christ said on the cross. Opening up the question and receiving the answer brought instant understanding, clarity, peace, and a flood of the sensation of love showed up.

Kami: That. That piece. Every piece of your growth is magical. When I notice I am holding onto something so tightly in my life that seems to be moving away from me, and I am afraid to let go of it, this is what I have learned to ask myself, "Is this part of my identity complete?" I notice the response of, "Yes. It served its purpose." In the absence of fear, there is love. And love looks different every time I ask, "What would love do right now?" That is the importance of the now, too.

Shelby: There was a piece in there where you were repenting of your fear. I discovered as I was pondering on that piece, I have heard that a root definition of "sin" is "without." When we are in fear, it is the opposite of love. And God is love. So when we are in fear, we are without God, and that is "sin." I have chosen to be conscientious to bring God in, with me, into my shameful places and teach me, rather than turn away due to fear and shame and leave God. The result is those spaces no longer feel sinful, because I am asking God to be my guide. I'm no longer hiding. I am being taught by the Spirit of Love. Another lesson linked to fear, I learned from the work of Brene Brown: the root of resentment is actually envy. A fear of what I lack. When I look back at someone I have resented, I can see that I actually was envious.

Angel: That makes so much sense. I think that I had so much resentment toward my husband all during our marriage because he never seemed to have any stress or worries, meanwhile, I was never without that! Hello, envy! I couldn't figure out how he wasn't more concerned with doing all the things the right way. I picked up the slack. I took care of everything.

Kami: How beautiful that that chapter came to a close when Angel loved herself! It had nothing to do with him! Fear is the only thing that would keep us in a chapter that was done.

FEELING JOY

Angel: What have you two noticed in working with people who cannot feel joy? How do you unlock joy in people?

Kami: It's a pendulum swing. Emotionally, people seem to shut down from feeling. When they shut off from feeling the heavy emotions, those labeled as "bad" emotions, then they shut off from feeling the light emotions too. Most of us are on an emotional swing set, sitting in the seat and not even swinging, not even feeling the range of emotions. Brene Brown says you can't cut off one side of feeling and not the other. So if you're going to cut off sadness and guilt and shame, then you're also going to cut off excitement and joy and playfulness. So we sit there, in the swing, not even moving. And how fun is it to sit there not even swinging?

Shelby: If you're not feeling joy, then what else are you not feeling? You must access all of those feelings so you can enjoy the ride. What's really cool is that when you allow yourself to feel, to meet those deep and heavy feelings in a space of love and curiosity, there is joy. You can feel so happy when you choose in to feeling the full spectrum of your emotions. Joy is a willingness to feel all of it.

Kami: Regarding that passion list that you referred to, Angel, that your therapist gave you and you just stared at it and you had no idea what brought you joy anymore—when we work with people who find themselves in that space, we invite them to think back to their childhood when they didn't have so many stories weighing them down. Judgment, attachments, and resistance to what is—that is what builds unhappiness. When they're willing to let go of those three things, they can get into this happy, playful, joyful space, to begin doing things because they are passionate about them. They begin doing things because they want to, not because they have to. It begins by going back to their childhood and thinking, "What did I like to do in my carefree days?" And they'll remember, "I liked to sing! I liked to dance!" It's crazy to rediscover those things you loved and you still love, but you stopped doing those things and the joy disappeared! When we get back to those things, and let go of the judgment of it and the fear, the shoulds, and the shame, the joy shows up again.

JUDGMENT VS. INNOCENCE, AND TRUSTING GOD

Kami: We have this ego that says, "My point of view is the right way." When I was in the Church they told me exactly what was the right way and I believed them, and so I knew that I was right! And I judged the hell out of people, out of anyone who even side-stepped off the right path. "How dare you drink caffeine! We've already been told that that is a 'no'! You have two piercings in your ear?!? I know you're going to hell! I have already been told, and I know it is right because the church told me it was right, and they said that they were speaking for God!" And I just got in line. I obeyed.

Shelby: "The Church told me." That. Not, "God told me." But, "The Church told me and said that they were speaking for God."

Kami: I was innocent in believing that I was right and in obeying what I was told to. There's nobody that is right or wrong in that position, it's just innocence. But now I get it. When I meet someone in that position, someone who is adamant that they are right, and they are judgmental of my actions because they have been told what is right, I have so much compassion because I remember being like that. For example, when someone is telling me, "God would never tell you that! God would never tell you to leave a marriage! How dare you think that?!?" Now, I am on this side knowing God has got my hand. God is walking me out of this marriage and out of this religious construct.

Shelby: When you're met with that opposition from another self-righteous person, you begin to feel this self-doubt just pouring out.
"Okay, I had this feeling…"
"But you're wrong!"

"But there's this feeling inside of me . . . "

"But you're wrong! You didn't check with me, you didn't go through the Prophet. So it can't be right. You are definitely being deceived."

No wonder we have so many people depressed and on medication in our religious culture. Because they get the answers, but everybody within this church, that they love, is saying they're wrong when those personal answers don't align with what the generalized answers and policies of the church are. They're met with, "Don't trust that! Don't trust what's inside of you! That's the devil part of you!" Confusion!

Kami: Even though the leader and founder of the whole entire church (a teenager In 1820), thank goodness he trusted that, his intuition and inspiration, went inward and asked, "Is there something more than what's here in front of me?"

"He could do that, and started the whole church, but don't you dare rely on your own truth, your own guidance system." It's so backwards!

Shelby: You've got to honor that conviction, though, of the self-righteous ones. That deep conviction; if we can harness that and have that much conviction towards ourselves and our connection with God, can you imagine the difference it would make? We are pretty capable beings.

Angel: Well, I think you're right because that is what happened to me. Once I realized what was coming by asking questions inward and upward, even though there were wrestling moments, I realized, "Of course I can trust that! I am asking questions with a sincere desire to know the truth and I am getting answers!" The same deep conviction that I had to uphold all the teachings of the Church prior, I was now able to transfer it and realize, "It's time to uphold me and what God is telling me."

COMPASSION

Kami: Early on, when you were going to other people, they were encouraging you to take on the victim card. "You're the victim here; look what your husband has chosen to do. He's the villain, you're the victim." And you refused to take on the victim role. The basis of any of those roles is judgment—and you refused, you were like, "No! That does not feel in alignment with me." I'm noticing and congratulating you; your vulnerability is astounding to me and I'm really appreciative of your willingness to be transparent with all of us in a book. Not just in a private setting, but you're letting the whole world see your innermost thoughts. Thoughts that all of us can relate to, but we don't want anyone else to know that we think that way! We judge that. And you're like, "Yeah, this is how it was." I love you so much for that. Thank you, honey!

Shelby: I love the melodrama analogy. If we just look at our lives as a comedy show, it can be pretty funny. It's why melodrama is relatable, because we know it.

Kami: From the depths of hell, you went right to the ecstasy and bliss and laughed your head off at how ridiculous it is at that blind vibrational level where truly you can't see.

Each thought is either digestible or indigestible. It's just like food; when we intake it, it's either one of those. Noticing, through replaying your story and reenactment, which of your thoughts were indigestible. You notice which thoughts cause toxic responses, illness, disease, reactions inside your body; you're learning as you go inward and upward, to catch those responses inside your body, "Oh, that's indigestible, no thanks," and kicking it off. Judgment, any judgment that we are making, lacks compassion. And yet we're taught—as believers in Christ—to be compassionate people, we are seeking after that. But judgment feels so opposite to me. If we're wanting to lean in to compassion, judgment cannot come near it. Compassion is like, "I've been there! I've done that! I've been you! You are me! I get it and I love you!" That's huge! It's so simple, but we complicate the hell out of it. When true compassion is what you're choosing, judgment has no place in it. It is that golden light. It's that third entity, taking the darkness and the light and pulling it together, it creates that gold space, our higher self. That's compassion, and judgment can't live there.

Shelby: And that's heaven! And we can all untangle and unravel the little knots of the stories within our bodies. We are unraveling each piece that ties us to the past, or ties us to the future, the worry of what happened, the regret, or the fear of what might happen. It brings us into this space of, "Oh my gosh! These experiences that I had, the use for those, isn't to put me into hell and keep me in hell, they are to offer me this compassion. I've done that. I've been that. I've tasted that. I've tried that. And I get it."

Kami: And I can still have emotion around that. I'll be emotional with it, but I'm not suffering with it, because the judgment is gone.

Shelby: I can have compassion for the bully, and I can have compassion for the bullied, because there's no judgment, because I've played both roles.

PART TWO
PRINCIPLES OF SOUL-U-LAR EVOLUTION

INTRODUCTION TO SECTION II:

"When you realize your mom had to let go of God to meet God."
-My son, Malakai Naivalu, age 9

Section two is a breakdown of the principles and processes I have extracted from my personal experiences and spiritual experiments, and from my work with clients.

I operate differently today from how I did just a few years ago, in every aspect of life. Consequently, everything in my life now looks and feels different, and I love it all! I love my life! Most of all, I love *me*—and I really like me, too. I am my own best friend! I am happy with who I am right now, and it feels good to be in an ongoing state of evolution. I am learning and expanding every day, constantly shedding former versions of myself. I feel giggly and excited when I think about meeting my future fifty-year-old, sixty-year-old, ninety-plus-year-old versions of myself!

Throughout my personal spiritual awakening—the process of coming home to myself—I have discovered certain methods that help me find a deeper and clearer connection with the Divine. By journaling regularly during this growth period, I have kept track of my processes and experiences. Certain patterns have emerged that appear to generate predictable results of light, truth, love, joy, peace, and freedom. For several years now, I have been speaking, writing, and sharing these patterns with others as a social worker and a coach. At the beginning, I wondered, *will these processes produce similar outcomes in others?* I had a sense they would, but in this, too, I claimed to know nothing.

The results I found were thrilling! It was like watching captives break their own chains and experience liberty for the first time. I witnessed individuals reuniting with their true selves and discovering that they could source truth and love from within. They learned that they could trust themselves above anything and anyone else—something many of us haven't known since early childhood! It is an honor to witness someone move out of darkness and into the light—and such joy to see them go from mental, emotional, spiritual, and physical captivity into freedom. Their whole countenance changes from dark and sad to lit up and joyful.

The process of becoming one with yourself is quite simple, with the help of a few key concepts. Two of these are *self-awareness* and *emotional intelligence.* These abilities can be learned and developed. To cultivate self-awareness and emotional intelligence, I turn to some basic tenets of cognitive-behavioral psychology: your beliefs breed your thoughts, which engender your feelings, which lead to your actions. Not everything you believe, think, and feel is true; much of it comes from the external voices of authority in your upbringing, coupled with your own limited interpretation of events.

Most people tend to assign meaning to every experience they have, interpreting their life experiences through a lens of *what does this mean about me?* Often, these interpretations of life events and experiences can lead an individual to believe they are failing, not enough, not lovable, or not worthy. In response, they can exert tremendous effort attempting to disprove these fears—seeking acceptance, approval, love, and belonging in the eyes of others. Focusing on the opinions of others obscures a person's ability to fully recognize and heal their own limiting beliefs, leaving them feeling stuck in their life because they are stuck in their mental, emotional, and behavioral patterns.

Altering the trajectory of our programming requires we take back our agency by detaching from the judgments and approval of others.

INTRODUCTION TO SECTION II

When we live seeking validation, we give up our freedom by allowing others' opinions and ideas to govern our beliefs, emotions, and behaviors. Instead of looking outward for answers, guidance, and governing, we can begin to practice going inward (to our true selves, our souls) and then upward (to God, truth, and love).

The teaching of spiritual practices, even with the best of intentions, can easily spawn spiritual confusion and idol worship. For much of my life, I was an idol worshiper and did not know it, worshiping the rituals and practices that someone else found helpful in connecting with God. I made their practices *my* practices, without question. It was like a job: I performed religious rituals (my work) in order to earn blessings through my worthiness (my paycheck). I did it to be accepted and included, and I hoped it would earn me a spot in heaven.

When a certain practice makes your life better and has a replicable result, the excitement around and belief in *that thing* grows and sometimes develops into a dogma. Because of this, I have hesitated to write about the methods I've found and wondered how to present my story without creating dogma for others to take on. God has simply urged: *"Write this book."* And so I have.

While these patterns and processes have worked for me and many people I have counseled, I'm not here to claim that they will work for you. What I have to share is *my* way, not the good, best, or right way; your way could be different.

Some people learn by being shown the steps. They want more than a theoretical framework. I feel like an art teacher: a student comes into class and says, "I want to learn how to paint." I say, "Great. Here's a blank canvas, various types of paint, and tools for application. Have fun." The student looks confused and says, "I don't know where to start. Show me how."

I understand their frustration and desire to be taught, but the request to show them how to paint feels like a trap. Of course I want them to experience the joy that art brings me. But if I show them *my way*, I reinforce the belief that they have to be taught by someone who knows more than they know, that says they need to rely on someone else to teach them the right way to make art. I believe they *are* art, and if they will look inward and explore themselves, they will find the inspiration to create art from a place of truth and joy, without judgmental comparison with any other art forms.

I have been that yearning student in so many settings: learning to dance, learning to write, learning to sing, learning to paint, learning to play the drums, learning to cook... "Show me how to do it!" I am grateful to other authors who wrote books that got me thinking and seeking new approaches and possibilities. I am grateful for mentors who were willing to challenge my thoughts by speaking their truths and living their beliefs.

These books and people all served me, and yet my processes and practices for spiritual communication evolved uniquely to suit me. I've found that once I have followed an instructor long enough to relax, I begin taking ownership of the skill and making it my own. It is my hope that my story inspires you to trust yourself and find your own connection to your Guiding Force. In experimenting with some of the steps I share, may you discover what works and what does not work, for you specifically. May my story offer you a beginning lesson that empowers you to find *your* way. May my journey be a starting point, or an extension of, your soul-u-lar evolution.

DISCERNING: DARKNESS AND LIGHT

*"Maybe you have to know the darkness
before you can appreciate the light."*
–Madeleine L'Engle

Principles and Experiments in this Chapter
- Discerning Light
  - Experiment: Seek light
- Systems Theory: Bringing External Influences to Light
  - Experiment: Who or what taught me to think this way?
- Shedding Light on Limiting Beliefs
  - Experiment: Seek an expanded perspective
- The Light Within: Tuning into Your Internal Compass
  - Experiment: Reconnect with your internal compass
- Dissolving Shame with the Light of Awareness
  - Experiment: Seeing our shame
- Breathing and Receiving Light
  - Experiment: Connecting with your breath
  - Experiment: Breathe to receive

DISCERNING LIGHT

Answers exist beyond the physical realm we live in. Therefore, to find answers, we must expand into that realm! We can transcend the box of "what I know is right and true" as we cultivate the skill of discerning light.

In this work, "light" is in reference to a frequency; it is more than the visual denotation of the word. Light is a force that can be both seen with the eyes and felt in the body. In the absence of physical tension, there is relaxation, and a feeling of lightness enters the body. Light can be felt in the heart, often described as a "heart opening," contrasting with a sense of closure, tightness, and a heaviness.

Light aids in perception, increasing mental clarity and illuminating thoughts, as when bright and new ideas flow easily into your mind. Light is what draws your awareness to the synchronicities and interrelated nature of all things around you. "Discerning light" is the ability to recognize the presence of this frequency; for example, I can be in a dark room, and if I am present, I can feel the frequency of *light* in the ideas of my mind or the emotions of my heart.

In getting curious, I have noticed there are degrees of light in everything. For example, food has degrees of light: there is a vibrance of look, texture, and taste to fresh food that is not present in fried, processed, or fast food. Music, literature, images, places, and people all hold degrees of light, or vibration. My mind, body, heart, and spirit all help me notice and discern degrees of darkness versus light in all things.

The practice of being present and mindful has heightened my awareness of the sensations of light that surround me. As I practice being still, present, and connected to my internal compass, this skill grows sharper, and I feel drawn toward experiences of greater and greater degrees of light. Each time I choose to obtain, consume, or put myself in experiences of light, I notice substantial shifts in my energy, and stimulation in all parts of my Being. It's as if light is feeding, healing, and sustaining my entire vessel—just as the sun feeds life on earth.

Experiment: Seek light

Seek to discern the degrees of light in your everyday experiences. Ask yourself:

- What do I want to eat today that contains light and life?
- Who do I want to listen to, talk with, be around, or read about that emanates light?
- Where and when can I go outside to absorb natural light into my cells?
- Can I filter my contacts and/or social media feeds to keep me connected to those people and profiles that are conduits of light?
- What words in my vocabulary carry more light than others? Can I intentionally speak using words that feel light and bright, clear, and illuminating?

SYSTEMS THEORY: BRINGING EXTERNAL INFLUENCES TO LIGHT

Many of us feel frustrated that we have worked so hard on ourselves and never seem to reach our goals for happiness, love, prosperity, and peace. We often blame ourselves when we struggle, and yet many of the struggles we experience are due, not to personal failing, but to the impact of unseen systemic forces on our perception.

Systems Theory teaches that the influence of external systems affects one's personality, choices, and perceived reality. When an individual can separate her/himself from the greater complex systems affecting them, they can begin to understand the origin of their beliefs, thoughts, feelings, and reactions to any given stimulus. In this theory, each person is impacted by three main systems:

Macro system. Includes the society the person is raised in; government policies and economics; media messaging; and widely held cultural values, beliefs, and norms.

Meso system. Includes the impact of school, employment, neighborhood, community, and religion.

Micro system. Includes family and peer relationships, biological factors, and personal perceptions, including interpretations of what every life experience means about the self.

We are each a part of a greater system, influencing and being influenced by interrelated components of our internal and external worlds.

Without a context such as systems theory, it can be difficult for an individual to identify and understand their issues, pressures, and life struggles. Humans tend to personalize everything they experience as if it is a reflection of their own strengths and weaknesses. Many of my clients express these self-judgments with statements like:

"I feel broken."

"I feel lost and confused."

"I feel like I am in survival mode."

"I am so exhausted—mentally, physically, emotionally, and spiritually."

"I am so busy doing everything I possibly can, yet I feel like I am failing! I feel like I am not enough and never will be. I feel defeated."

I thought and felt each one of these things for many years.

Even though I had a master's degree in social work, prior to 2015 I had not deeply examined the influences of the systems around me and the pressures they exerted on my internal workings. Consciously looking inward for awareness is a much different practice than just reading self-help and psychology books, attending classes, and assuming you have "knowledge." It takes a lot more humility! Though I studied systems theory in college, I was not able to apply it to my own life until I was willing to consider the possibility that some of my thinking might be erroneous.

It has been my experience that the application of truthful information—not the information itself—changes a person.

Experiment: Who or what taught me to think this way?
Consider the following:
- Where do you feel stuck?
- What might you be ignoring or pushing through, believing that it is just a normal part of life, relationships, parenting, career, or aging?
- Who or what taught you to think this way?

As you reflect, you will begin to notice the influence of systemic forces in your life. This is not to find fault or to assign blame. Instead, awareness will help you sort and separate what *you* believe, think, feel, and do, from what *any other system or person* believes, thinks, feels, and does. As you gain clarity about what is actually yours and what is not, you can release others' beliefs and take ownership for claiming truth for yourself from the Divine. This concept is eloquently reflected in these lines from the Prayer for Serenity, written by American theologian Reinhold Niebuhr and made popular by Alcoholics Anonymous:

> *God, grant me the serenity*
> *to accept the things I cannot change,*
> *the courage to change the things I can,*
> *and the wisdom to know the difference.*

SHEDDING LIGHT ON LIMITING BELIEFS

My personal belief system and convoluted thinking were not caused by church experience alone. It was *my* thinking, which was supported by the macro, meso, and micro influences in my environment. These influences included American ideals, Utah culture, LDS church culture, the school system, my friends and associates, my family, and my personal studies and experiences. Because my environment and my interpretations of my experiences reinforced my beliefs, creating a feedback loop, I did not think to question my thoughts.

For example, I believed that I was not good enough (for love, success, and salvation) unless and until I earned that status through my behavior and accomplishments. While I was a high achiever in many settings, there were always places where I thought I could have done better. Those thoughts produced emotions like guilt, shame, sadness, and disappointment. In response to those emotions, I might turn to food for comfort or put more pressure on my husband and kids to do more and be more[26] because of the stress I felt to be more and do more. My behaviors in response to my thoughts and feelings created more ways I could have done better, providing me with more evidence that I was not good enough. This evidence reinforced my belief that I was not worthy of happiness because I hadn't earned it. So the feedback loop continued. I kept trying to operate within the same paradigm, expecting to find new solutions to my problems.[27]

---

26   This is an example of unconscious psychological projection. See *projection* in the Terms section of the introduction to this book.

27   I feel like Stephen R. Covey, author of *The 7 Habits of Highly Effective People,* is turning over in his grave right now! He wrote, "If you want small changes in your life, work on your attitude. But if you want big and primary changes, work on your paradigm." I feel as I write this that he is sending me a message: "Angel, I wrote about this more than forty years ago and you read it as a teen." All I can say is, "Well, it has taken me a minute. Thanks for planting the seeds, Mr. Covey."

DISCERNING: DARKNESS AND LIGHT

I was caught in a repetitive pattern. I would feel frustrated, always wanting something to change so I could be happy. I would pray for help and ask for blessings, and repent of my sins so I could be worthy of what I'd asked for. And very little ever changed. So I repeated the pattern and tried harder to do more of the same type of things, even though they were not working. When life felt especially hard, or I felt I was falling apart, I resigned myself to the delusion that it was because I had done something wrong and I was supposed to feel that way. I had a distorted paradigm that included the idea that punishment and suffering were a sanctifying part of life.

Experiences like these are often marked by frustration and confusion: you are doing everything you've been taught to do, but all that obedience is not bringing you the happiness you thought it would. This leads to a lack of joy, feelings of resentment towards others, controlling behaviors, and even clinical depression. The confusion stems from seeking the solution from the sources of the problem! "We cannot solve our problems with the same thinking we used to create them."28

The answers we seek lie outside the patterns of our old thinking, in what I like to refer to as the space of what we do not know we do not know. We can find answers if we are willing to look outside the boundaries of our usual thinking and question every assumption. Be aware that true answers to our problems will often not make sense upon the initial delivery. They will look and feel foreign because they are! We may first be tempted to reject the information because it does not match anything we already think; it may even be offensive to us.

Experiment: Seek an expanded perspective

In place of perpetuating the cycle of frustration that came from the

---

28   This quote is attributed to Albert Einstein.

behavior patterns of my existing beliefs, I began to ask questions, to seek an expanded perspective, and to look for what I could not see. These questions expanded the focus of my thinking. I invite you to begin your journey by asking some of your own questions.

Breathe, soften, and consider:
- What if what feels "right" to you is not necessarily right, but rather, seems right/true because it is familiar or comfortable?
- What if the source of your suffering (all that is painful, stressful, overwhelming, exhausting, and unbearable) is the result of your implicit trust in the belief systems woven by your micro, meso, and macro cultural messaging?
- What if what feels like darkness is simply a lack of light?
- What if your perception of your experience involves error and lacks truth?
- What if the presence of fear is pushing away the spirit of love?
- What if sadness and grief are the thieves of your joy?
- What if the chaos in your life is blinding you to the prospect of peace?
- What if the captivity you feel is limiting your innate capacity for freedom?

THE LIGHT WITHIN: TUNING INTO YOUR INTERNAL COMPASS

Throughout my life, my mind, body, heart, and spirit were sending me messages of truth, each in their own language, but I missed and even rejected their signals for a long time because I had come to trust external influences more than the truth inside myself. For the first several decades of my life, I devalued these parts of my Being;,misunderstanding their functions and underestimating their power. I separated them because I didn't know they were meant to communicate with one another and work as a whole.

I saw my **physical body** as my enemy—its appearance, desires, and appetites something to be ashamed of and struggle against—so I detached from it completely.

Emotions were something I misinterpreted too: I judged them as "good" or "bad," seeking only pleasant feelings and repressing the others. I feared, at times, that I might drown in the depths of my emotions.

I did not recognize how much impact my **thoughts** had on me. I didn't connect the dots between the unconscious beliefs I carried, the heavy emotions I felt, and the physical health problems I struggled to overcome. I was shocked to learn that my own limiting beliefs were at the core of my moods and physical health challenges, and had even blocked my connection with my soul.

Oddly, I did not recognize my soul as a relevant entity at all. Although I had been taught at church that I had a "**spirit**" inside my body, I did not know how to relate to it—or even that I *could* relate to it.

As I'd been culturally conditioned to do, I compartmentalized these dimensions of my Being into separate categories by symptoms: mental health, emotional health, physical health, spiritual health. I believed that the heavy emotions I experienced, particularly stress and overwhelm, were normal for the stage of life I was in. I had lots of young kids, I was socially isolated as a stay-at-home mom, and we were barely making ends meet—of course I was stressed!

The process of evolving from a state of ignorance to awareness was one of *re-membering,* a restoration of the *members* of my Being: mind, body, heart, and spirit. Together, these comprise what I now call my *internal compass.* Through stillness, self-honesty, and deep listening, I learned to tune into and trust each of these four dimensions of my Self, and developed a relationship with each part of me. I now check in regularly with these aspects to discover what I need and desire; they act as a compass, offering direction in my life.

At times, I will receive mixed messages from the various parts of my internal compass. I have learned this means there is some part of my Being that believes an untruth—whether that is in my mind as a belief, in my body as a past experience, or in my heart as fear. When I recognize the sensation of dissonance, it's easy to identify the lie by investigating which facet of my internal compass is misaligned and seeking to get to the heart of the misunderstanding. There, truth can correct error, and resonance is restored.

This process is explained throughout the subsequent chapters. When the witness from within creates a resonant reaction from all four facets of my internal compass, discernment is easy. This process breeds new levels of self-trust and a sacred relationship with myself.

Experiment: Reconnect with your internal compass

To gain an awareness of the ways in which you may be disconnected from your internal compass, I invite you to try these practices and observe the thoughts and feelings they evoke.

Mind. Practicing meditation and mindfulness helped me to increase my awareness and detach from personalizing my experiences as a reflection of my worth. It helped me cultivate the ability to observe the ongoing *dance of life* both within myself and in the outside world without judgment or fear. Mindfulness allowed me to begin to challenge my thoughts instead of attaching to them.

Try this: Set a timer for five minutes and sit with your eyes closed. Pay attention to your breath, as you inhale and exhale. Notice how busy your mind is, and how often you are distracted by thoughts. When you notice that you are thinking, pause, take a deep breath, and label what's happening in your mind: "Oh look, a thought!" Instead of holding onto it, allow it to pass across your consciousness.

Body. Learning to be still, practicing methodical breathing exercises, and noticing my body's responses to fear and love connected me to my body.

Try this: Become aware of how your body responds to fear vs. love. When you are feeling fearful (or any emotion related to fear, such as anger, stress, or shame), notice how your body feels. On the other hand, when you are feeling loving (or any other emotion related to love, such as joy, hope, or peace), notice how your body feels. Typically the body will contract, tighten, and harden when experiencing fear—and will open, loosen up, and expand in the presence of love.

Heart. Giving myself permission to feel, express, and witness all my feelings connected me with my heart.

Try this: Check in with yourself periodically throughout the day and ask, "What am I feeling?" Name the emotion and just observe it for a moment without judging it as good or bad, or trying to change it. "I am feeling fear," or, "I am experiencing sadness." This acknowledges and validates the emotion while separating it from you. You may even talk to it: "I see you, Fear. I understand why you're here." It is a simple step to form a connection to the heart.

We feel a range of emotions each day, and yet it is common for us to ignore, deny, and bury them. As a result, we are often unconscious about what we are actually feeling. When the pressure of unaddressed emotions builds up, we can erupt in irrational ways and project our emotions onto others through anger and blame.

These brief check-ins with emotion bring awareness and aliveness to the emotionally disconnected individual.

Spirit. Taking questions inward and upward to converse with my spirit body and the Divine Source of Truth connected me spiritually. ***Try this:*** Close your eyes and take in a few deep, calming breaths. Notice how this assists you in directing your awareness within.

Closing your eyes seems to turn the volume down on your ego's voice and the voices of external programming and conditioning. With your eyes closed, you get to experience a personal and sacred space that no one else can enter. This gives you an opportunity to tune in to your internal compass. You can then think the words, "Show me my soul." Just notice what comes into your mind (or what doesn't). Try to allow what comes to just be, without judgment or any attempt to steer or control it. Your experience is perfect, regardless of what shows up for you.

Ask the question, "What am I?" This goes beyond "Who am I?" where we normally list our roles or relationships. Again, breathe deeply as you contemplate the question, "What am I?" and notice what thoughts come to mind.

DISSOLVING SHAME WITH THE LIGHT OF AWARENESS

Fear loves to call on shame, which is often tied to a deep fear of being unworthy. Shame's core message is that there is something inherently wrong with us. It tells us that we are burdensome or unlovable, and that we should hide. "Hiding" can manifest as withdrawing socially, avoiding taking risks, and never asking for help.

Fortunately, the truth about shame is that it can only survive in darkness.

When we recognize that we are experiencing shame, instead of immediately following its order to withdraw, we can approach it with a gentle curiosity, asking questions that help us see the stories we are telling ourselves and illuminate the truth. The light of awareness will dissolve shame and its damning fears.

Experiment: Seeing our shame

Our unconscious beliefs are often embedded with shame. I discovered I had this belief: *You need to earn or be worthy of service and love.*

Although this sounds absurd and unbelievable when put into words, we may still unconsciously believe that it is true.

To bring awareness to shame, ask yourself:

"Where or when have I felt shame (or embarrassment) recently?"

"Whose love have I felt I needed to earn or did not feel deserving of?"

"What have I thought or done that I do not want anyone else to know about?"

When you find answers to the above questions, ask, "What was I afraid of in that situation or relationship?" Then ask, "Who or what taught me to think this way?" Identifying the mortal source of your beliefs can free your mind to look for truth.

Even the first simple step of intentionally looking at the areas in your life where there is shame can begin to free you from its grip. Awareness enables you to make a conscious choice to pivot from the shadow of shame toward the light of love in your beliefs, thoughts, feelings, and behaviors.

Next, speaking to or about the shame, expressing it verbally to yourself or to a trusted friend, seems to escort the shame out of the body. Bringing shameful thoughts, beliefs, and behaviors into the light of acknowledgment—into a space where they can be met with unconditional love, non-judgment, and acceptance—dissipates shame's power.

BREATHING AND RECEIVING LIGHT

"The depth to which you breathe is the depth to which you can receive."
-Unknown

Breathwork was foundational in my experience of learning to identify and connect with light, but because I wasn't familiar with it, I was originally skeptical. In seeking how meditation and breathwork practices tied in with my church's doctrine, if at all, I searched the words "breathe," "breath of life," "I am the breath," and "meditation" in the LDS canon of scripture. They led me down a rabbit hole, where I uncovered key insights.

John 20:22 teaches, "And when he [Jesus] had said this, he breathed on them, and saith unto them, Receive ye the Holy Ghost."[29] This scripture account depicts Christ conferring the Holy Ghost on his apostles after his resurrection. He used the *breath* to accomplish this, not the laying on of hands as is done in my church today.

Curious about the term *Holy Ghost*, used by the LDS church, rather than the common Christian term *Holy Spirit*, and where the term came from, I found this information in Wikipedia[30]:

The English terms "Holy Ghost" and "Holy Spirit" are complete synonyms: one derives from the old English, *gast*, and the other from the Latin loanword, *spiritus*. Like *pneuma*, they both refer to the breath, to its animating power, and to the soul.[31]

---

29   The Holy Bible, KJV, John 20:22, KJV

30   I have discovered so many illuminating concepts by looking outside of the church-published materials (something I was discouraged from doing). These concepts have brought me back to the scriptures with a deeper understanding of doctrines.

31   Wikipedia reference: https://en.wikipedia.org/wiki/Holy_Spirit_in_Christianity.

DISCERNING: DARKNESS AND LIGHT

The last line: BREATH—ANIMATING POWER—AND TO THE SOUL! Everything I was experiencing and connecting in my own breathwork and meditation practices was right there in the root origin of the term *Holy Ghost*. When I was invited, at eight years old, to "receive the Holy Ghost," I was invited to *receive the breath* as the power to animate and connect to the soul.

In the Church, it is often taught, "At baptism, you are given the gift of the Holy Ghost," but this statement is actually incorrect. During the confirmation blessing in the LDS church, individuals are told, "Receive the Holy Ghost." We were not *given* this gift, but *commanded to receive* the Holy Ghost—and then never instructed on how to do that! Even though I was baptized and confirmed a member of the church at age eight, I actually *received* the Holy Ghost at age *thirty-eight*, when I began to practice breathwork and meditation, finally opening my body, mind, and heart to receiving the messages from my spirit and from God!

Breathing is tied to receiving, and *breath holding* is physical evidence of resistance to an idea or experience, in reaction to fear. Simply noticing when I was holding my breath allowed me to become aware that I was feeling fearful and resistant to something. I could ask myself, "What am I afraid of?"

Through this practice, I noticed how often I held my breath: when I was cut off in traffic, receiving a phone call that brought bad news, feeling reprimanded or corrected at work, or experiencing frustration with the disobedience of my children. I was surprised to find that I even held my breath when offered pleasant things, like money, service, and gifts. When I applied the *breathing and receiving* technique, it helped me become more receptive in all areas of my life.

In conversation with God one day, I was invited to look at how I reacted when someone gave me a compliment. Despite saying "thank you" out loud, I noticed I habitually discounted or downplayed compliments in my mind with thoughts such as, *I could have done better if . . .* or, *If they really knew what kind of a mom I am, they wouldn't say that.* I would hold my breath for a split second, blocking myself from truly receiving the compliment.

The Spirit of Truth simply said to me, *"Angel, if you can't accept the compliment of a mere mortal, how well do you think you're doing at receiving the love I have to offer you?"* I was shown there was a direct correlation between my shallow breathing, my resistance to life, and my distance from God.

Experiment: Connecting with your breath
Take a deep breath by inhaling through your nose and exhaling through your mouth. Repeat. What do you notice?

Intentional breaths throughout the day are a starting point for expanding your ability to be open to new information from the realms beyond what you think you already know. Simply inhale through your nose as deeply as you can, then exhale slowly through your mouth. Notice how deeply you're able to breathe and how it feels in your body.

Experiment: Breathe to receive
Practice taking intentionally deep breaths when someone gives you a compliment, invites you to something, or offers you feedback, or anytime you feel you are resisting or rejecting what is taking place. Intentionally choose to receive by saying, "I receive that, thank you."
Take it one step further by repeating the compliment in your mind in first person. For example, if someone said, "Angel, you gave a great presentation today," I would say in my mind as I inhaled and exhaled, "I gave a great presentation today."

DISCERNING: DARKNESS AND LIGHT

Try to gauge, by the depth of your breath, your level of resistance to a statement. This helps bring to light the places in which you may be harboring self-doubt, judgment, and limiting beliefs.

Consider how you typically react when given a compliment. Do you usually totally agree with the person, or do you have some resistance in your mind, discounting the credibility of their positive words? Start watching yourself. Do you hold your breath, even for a split second?

You can also use the breath to receive spiritual guidance. When you connect with your soul or God and ask for guidance, breathe deeply to receive the messages and exhale to release any resistance you may have.

SEPARATING: ERROR FROM TRUTH

"Truth will sooner come out from error than from confusion."
- Francis Bacon

Principles and Experiments in this Chapter:
- Finding Truth: Going Inward and Upward
    - Experiment: Recognizing truth
    - Experiment: Tuning in to your inner lie detector
- Identifying Your Inner Voices
    - Experiment: Who's talking?
- Using the Internal Compass as a guide
    - Experiment: Practice using your internal compass
- The Truth About Your Worth and Value
    - Experiment: Am I still good?
- Trusting Your Truth
    - Experiment: Ask - Receive - Trust - Act
- The Courage to Move
    - Experiment: Calling on courage

FINDING TRUTH: GOING INWARD AND UPWARD

Many of us automatically identify with our perceptions and assume our thoughts are true without ever looking at them. One of the more common therapeutic modalities used today, and one I studied extensively in graduate school, is Cognitive Behavioral Therapy (CBT), an approach that seeks to bring awareness to a person's thinking patterns, helping them recognize irrational beliefs and cognitive distortions. The intentional self-awareness required to recognize and separate truth from error in one's thinking provokes profoundly liberating results, such as:

- Freedom from addiction
- Relief from emotional and physical pain and suffering
- Release of traumatic memories
- Freedom from repetitive and debilitating mood cycles
- Removal of limiting beliefs
- Enhanced self-esteem and self-worth
- Increased feelings of joy and peace

The practice of going inward and upward takes the therapeutic approach of challenging irrational beliefs a step further, into spirituality, by seeking answers from a source of truth. In addition to simply recognizing thinking errors of the mind, by relating with your body, heart, and spirit as an internal compass, you can turn to your Source of Truth and begin to seek and receive answers and new beliefs to replace erroneous ones. When truth replaces error, our entire perception changes; we feel and react differently to our experiences.

Experiment: Recognizing truth

Make a goal to notice at least one judgment thought—meaning a thought that expresses anything that lies outside absolute, indisputable fact—each day.

An easy way to find these thoughts is to notice your emotions. When you are feeling stress, guilt, shame, resentment, or anger, it is likely that there are some judgments creating those emotional states. Ask, "What am I telling myself right now?"

You might be thinking something like:
- He is being so selfish.
- I should sign up to volunteer for the school activity.
- I shouldn't be eating this.
- They are making a terrible mistake.
- What those people are doing is wrong.
- There is not enough time to get everything done.

When you've identified a thought, breathe deeply. Invite your body, mind, and spirit into the conversation. Say, "Here's what I am telling myself." Restate the thought you have noticed. Then ask, "Is it true, or is it my story?"

Listen, breathe, and receive.

Then ask, "What is true?"

Listen, breathe, and receive.

Then ask, "What more is there?"

Listen, breathe, and receive.

Trust the answers that come to mind.

Experiment: Tuning into your inner lie detector

A lie detector test monitors physiological changes to help identify when a person is speaking truth or telling lies. If the body can lead us to truth in a forensic setting, why not use it for the same purpose in everyday life?

Try performing what I refer to as a "personal polygraph test" on yourself. Focus for one day on noticing your body's physical reaction to your thoughts and feelings, words you hear or speak, the emotions of others, and even the impact of energetic frequencies given off by people, places, and things. Notice:

- When during your day do you feel physical restriction, tension, or tightness in the body?
- Where do these sensations show up for you in your body?
- What emotions are present when you feel physical tension?
- What causes your body to relax and expand?

IDENTIFYING YOUR INNER VOICES

As I began to take all of my thoughts and beliefs inward and upward to discover truth, I asked the Source of my spiritual impressions to help me discern between ideas coming from my mortally-programmed ego's voice and those coming from my Divine Creator's voice. With practice, I gained an awareness of what my ego (or "natural man"[32]) voice sounded and felt like. Once identified, I could begin to easily separate and distinguish the origin of the thoughts within me!

When I watch a movie, I listen to understand each character's personality, attitude, and the roles that she or he will play out in the course of the film. I notice their tone of voice, speaking cadence, and the energy and intensity of their words. All of this occurs rapidly and intuitively. The longer I watch, the more familiar I become with each character. Before long, I can close my eyes and distinguish which character is speaking and discern their motives in the moment.

Noticing which "character" is running the show in my mind is very similar to watching a movie and getting to know its characters. When I am observing my thoughts, I seek to feel the *tone*—the energy and attitude—of my thoughts. This helps me identify whether these thoughts are coming from fear/ego or love/soul. I often refer to my ego's thoughts as my *bitch voice* because its tone, energy, and attitude

---

32   The Book of Mormon, Mosiah 3:19.

are judgment, blame, criticism, fear, defensiveness, sarcasm, and the like. My soul's thoughts, in contrast, are pure, loving, compassionate, peaceful, and liberating. Just as I would not likely confuse the voices of Leonardo DiCaprio and Kate Winslett, I do not have any issue discerning between the voice of my ego and that of my soul.

Experiment: Who's talking?
Notice times when you feel pulled—in your mind—between two opposing perspectives in a situation. Take time to look at the messages that are coming from each one. It can be helpful to write out the contrasting thoughts. Feel into the tones and approaches of each perspective. How do you feel physically (constricted or open) when you listen to and align with each separate voice?

USING THE INTERNAL COMPASS AS A GUIDE

I rely on my internal compass to assist me in discerning truth vs. error. Each voice of influence I encounter represents a distinct direction, and I like to visualize them in place of the cardinal directions on a traditional compass. By determining the source of a belief, I am able to orient myself to the direction I truly want to go.

I label my Internal Compass as follows:

North: Soul (Spirit)
North represents truth, love, light, God, and my soul. My soul points me in the direction of my truest desires and highest potential. It never lies, has no fear, and is unattached to the world's ideas. It operates on unconditional love. I believe all truthful thoughts—whether inspired by God, my ancestors, nature, or other sources—come to me through my soul.

South: Ego (Mind)

My ego voice and the fear-based thinking of the mind point south—180 degrees from north. You can find your way to truth (north), by looking for the direct opposite of the fearful statements and beliefs that come from the ego. Notice and pivot—it is that easy. This analogy has helped me let go of the belief that I need to get rid of my ego/natural man thinking in order to be a "good" or "better" person. I now view my ego as a reliable reference point for navigation and guidance, just as south on a compass is a reference point when I want to go north.

East: Emotions (Heart)

Emotions are bred by our thinking. They serve to identify the source of the belief, as a kind of "second witness" regarding the truthfulness of our thoughts. If the source is fear-based, the emotions will be heavy and unpleasant, such as resentment, frustration, anger, rage, shame, guilt, etc. If the source is love-based and truthful, the emotions that follow will complement the truth with feelings of peace, gratitude, excitement, energy, delight, awe, etc.

West: Body

I have a hypothesis that the body is a vessel of truth—it cannot lie. Polygraph tests are based on this psychophysiological connection. The body responds to truth as a resonance, just as the body responds to harmonious music. Have you ever noticed how music feels in your body? When music is resonant, there is a physical expansion: the body relaxes, expands, and even breathes more deeply. There may be tingling or goose bumps (one friend calls them "truth bumps"). Conversely, when tones are dissonant, or unpleasant, like clashing notes, the body

SEPARATING: ERROR FROM TRUTH

reacts in tension—a cringe.[33] The physical response to truth and falsehood feels the same. In this way, the body's responses can also help determine the source of an idea. I see my body's responses to these disparate frequencies as evidence that I am equipped to discern light and darkness, love and fear, truth and error.

Chronic health problems, like the ones I experienced while living out of integrity with myself, can be a sign of habitually believing in and making decisions based on false, or ego-based, thinking.

Learning to use my internal compass to guide my navigation through life has been my greatest discovery. I live in awe of how we are each equipped with this flawless guidance system! Every day is a grand adventure of exploration and navigation as I hone the skills of seeking truth, listening to my internal compass, and then directing my course.

My worth is reaffirmed as I rely on my divinely designed Being and instructions from God to chart my life's course. God and I hang out together and miracles happen. Acting in truth, light, and love illuminates that I am Divine. There's nothing more glorious than existing as the ME that I am!

I went from thinking I was separate from truth, and therefore from God, to discovering that my true essence—my soul, or spirit—is always in the presence of God. Any belief that I am separate from God is an illusion created by my ego/natural man. When I discovered how to align with my soul, I came home to TRUTH. There is not as much a sense of having to "choose truth over error" anymore, because to be anything other than truth would be to deny myself. When truth

---

[33] The Spirit told me that truth is like a diatonic chord in music, such as a C major chord. I had never heard the word "diatonic" before, so I looked up the definition. I learned that something that is diatonic uses only the notes assigned to that key. I was taught that if truth is diatonic, then error would be chromatic.

arrives in my awareness, it is a simple, "Oh, there it is." It is like finding your way home at night. You recognize the streets, you know your neighborhood, and when you see those, you naturally turn in the right direction.

Advaita Zen Master Mooji puts it this way:
When there is a YOU and TRUTH,
Effort has to be made to bring two things together.
When there is you as Truth, effort falls away.
What brings this about?
The understanding
That transforms
You and That
To you as That.

Experiment: Practice using your internal compass

Choose a concept you would like to look at: a decision you're trying to make, a new idea you're considering, or a long-held belief you're reevaluating.

Check the concept with each of your internal compass directions. I like to begin with east and west because the emotions and the sensations in the body are easier to discern. The ego can often try to convince me that my fear-based desires are coming from love (i.e. my ego-driven and fear-based desire to control my child is coming from my love for him).

East (heart & emotions): Notice the emotions you feel surrounding the idea. If it's a decision, notice the emotion you feel when you think of one choice versus the way you feel when you think about another. Do your emotions feel peaceful and light or heavy and fearful?

West (body): Pay attention to the physical sensations in your body. What do you feel in your chest, shoulders, and gut area when you think that thought?

South (ego mind): Look for the warning signs of your tricky ego regarding the concept. Do you notice the word "should" anywhere? Do you have "what if" questions coming up? Do you feel drawn to something for fear of what will happen if you don't choose it?

North (soul & God): As a final check, does the concept hold a feeling of love, light, and truth? Is it devoid of fear? Go inward and upward, asking your soul, "What is true?"

Note: To calibrate your attunement to these internal compass directions, you can perform these same check-ins using a concept you already know to be true, such as your love for your child or your desire to seek truth.

THE TRUTH ABOUT YOUR WORTH AND VALUE

In the process of going inward and upward when seeking truth, I was always met with love. This taught me that my choices do not define me. It is so easy to love myself in *all* my experiences now, rather than judge myself as I did before.

Choices give us experience and teach us things that can then inform subsequent choices. Contrary to what many of us learned in religious contexts, they do not make us more, or less, worthy.

Experiment: Am I still good?
Look back on a choice you've made recently that didn't turn out as you would have hoped. Something you might be inclined to call a *mistake*.

As you think of this choice, breathe deeply and release your preconditioned judgments or the answer you expect to receive. Allow yourself to relax and center in a feeling of neutrality or peace. (Note: if you carry a lot of shame around this particular choice, you may not be able to come to a peaceful, neutral frame of mind. In that case, try a choice that is less triggering for you.)

Go inward and upward asking through your soul, "Am I still good?" or "Has this changed Your love for me?"

Observe your thoughts. You might receive opposing answers.

Try on any thoughts you have one at a time and notice the sensations in your body.

TRUSTING YOUR TRUTH

From the time we are small, we receive messages from every direction that imprint us with beliefs about who and what we should be—things like: *Stop crying, you are not hurt. Sit like a lady. Act like a man. That's a dumb idea, why would you think that? Don't be selfish, share your things. You are too much. You have to suffer to be beautiful. Children should be seen and not heard. It is better to give than receive. Don't be angry. The smart ones sit in the front of the classroom. Play dumb so boys will like you. Good girls like bad boys.* We are led to believe that others know what is best for us and we quit trusting ourselves.

We will inevitably have mortal experiences that teach us not everyone is trustworthy. This can lead us to develop "trust issues"—neither trusting ourselves nor others fully. The conundrum is this: we are conditioned to distrust ourselves, and when we discover that the sources we were taught to look to are unreliable, we don't know where to turn.

As you begin to go inward and upward, you may receive some surprising answers to your questions, as I did when God told me simply to put chicken in the crockpot when I expected a much bigger answer for my life. The practice of trusting and acting on the first answer you receive when you turn inward and upward will strengthen your confidence in the answers that come.

Experiment: Ask - Receive - Trust - Act

Pick a day to really hone in on experimenting with this. When you wake up in the morning, review your commitments and schedule. Then close your eyes, breathe, and ask, "What do I do next?" Receive the next thought that comes to you. Trust that it was inspired. Then act with courage. When you complete the activity you've been guided to, ask again. "What do I do next?"

Remember A.R.T.A.:
1. Ask a question
2. Receive the answer
3. Trust myself and the Divine
4. Act with courage & commitment

Avoid asking *why* something is being asked of you, or *how* you are going to accomplish it. These are fear-based questions that can put you into a state that does not support a connection with the Divine. Instead, choose to trust your guidance and ask *what* and *where* questions to clarify your next steps.

If you find yourself triggered emotionally, stop, identify clearly what you're telling yourself, and ask, "Is this true?" and "What more is there?"

Follow this process over and over throughout the entire day. Cultivate a spirit of playful lightheartedness as you practice—this is a dance with the Divine! You don't have to do it "perfectly." Relax and enjoy the experience!

THE COURAGE TO MOVE

It requires courage to trust and act on the messages of truth we receive. It can feel scary to do things differently than the way you were taught or have done them in the past. Fear can paralyze us, literally taking away our power to move. Courage, in contrast, is a sort of fuel, propelling us forward and into action.

One day, as my internal compass pointed me to a new way of being, my ego-mind began kicking and screaming like a terrified child, and I felt paralyzed. I said out loud, "Courage, I need you right now!" and—BAM—it showed up! I do not know, and I do not need to know, how that happened. But in that moment I learned that courage *is*. It is an energy or perhaps an entity. When I call for it, it comes and empowers me.

Experiment: Calling on courage

To experiment with this, think about something in your life you feel is true for you, that you need or want to do, but you've been hesitating to take action on.

Hold this action in your mind, and then call on courage by speaking the words out loud: "Courage, I need you now!" Or, "Courage, accompany me through this." Or "Courage, show me how to move through this situation."

Note the sensations in your body, particularly at your heart center, in response to this request.

Breathe and consciously trust in the action to which you feel called.

PERCEIVING: FEAR AND LOVE

"Your ego is rewriting your biography; Your soul has the original manuscript."
-Spirit, to Angel Lyn

Principles and Experiments in this Chapter:
- Identifying the Source of Your Thoughts and Feelings
  - Experiment: Be love
- Noticing the Red Flags of Fear
  - Experiment: Shift from fear to love
- Making Peace with the Body
  - Experiment: Love your body
- Becoming Acquainted with the Fearful Ego
  - Experiment: Can I love myself through this?
- Fear-Based Core Beliefs
  - Experiment: What does this say about me?
- Accepting the Law of Innocence
  - Experiment: You are innocent
  - Experiment: Ho'oponopono

- If I Cast Off Fear, I Am Prepared
  - Experiment: Find the opposite.
- Lovingly Encountering Your Shadow
  - Experiment: Use judgments to uncover truth.

IDENTIFYING THE SOURCE OF YOUR THOUGHTS AND FEELINGS

My mentors The Unicorns were the first to introduce me to the idea that fear is the antithesis of love. There are many scriptures that suggest that fear is not from God. One of my favorites says, "For God hath not given us the spirit of fear; but of power, and of love, and of a sound mind."[34] Curious, I began to experiment by observing my thoughts and noticing the fear in them. At any moment of contraction, I could simply ask, "What am I afraid of right now?"

Our relationship with fear is so funny: we know it is there, but we do not normally challenge it; we simply regard it as a part of life. Some people live consumed by it. Imagine a child who is afraid there is a monster under her bed. Every night, she worries about and imagines what this horrible creature could do to her. She deals with this darkness every single night until someone else says, "Let's look under there." They both look, and there is nothing under the bed! The "monster" is revealed to be something created in the child's mind. Once it is looked at and labeled for what it is, it no longer has power; the fear story is finished.

As adults, we have many "monsters" under our beds. We have perpetually occurring stories and emotions that accompany them. The fearful emotions we think of as monsters are actually here to serve us. They *want* us to look under the bed so that we can see the beliefs that are not serving us and let them go.

---

34 The Holy Bible, KJV, 2 Timothy 1:7

PERCEIVING: FEAR AND LOVE

Cognitive Behavioral Therapy suggests that our thoughts birth our emotions, which drive our behaviors. Fearful thoughts breed emotions like anxiety, anger, depression, guilt, shame, judgment, resentment, loneliness, and rage. These are just a few examples. Such emotions spawn behaviors like control and manipulation, hostility, rescuing, martyrdom, mis-giving, hustling to prove or earn our worth through busyness, overachieving, perfectionism, etc.

The Spirit of Truth does not operate by the spirit of fear. To override our conditioned response to attach to fear, we can pause and choose the path of love, utilizing our agency to promote our own growth and freedom.

Experiment: Be love

Making a conscious choice to show up differently in your life is often called "setting an intention." You could also call it "choosing your target." What do you want to commit to being? How about setting an intention to "be love"?

The more acquainted you become with the sensations in your mind, body, and heart, while feeling the frequency of love, the easier it becomes to monitor and self-regulate when you are in a loving state or outside of it.

Love is a frequency that has been identified at 528 Hz. You can search online for samples of music at that frequency, and observe the impact on your mind, body, and heart as you listen to it.

Picture a person you have felt absolutely adored by. Imagine yourself walking into their presence and being greeted by their enthusiasm, love, and embrace. Notice what happens in your mind, body, and heart. This is what love feels like.

It becomes increasingly easy to discern the energy you are operating from just by setting an intention to do so. Watch for and perceive shifts within yourself that mark the presence of fear creeping in. Then choose love.

NOTICING THE RED FLAGS OF FEAR

Each part of your internal compass waves red flags to let you know that fear is present.

Mind - ruminating thoughts, seeking for control, resistance to what is

If you are a worrier, then it is obvious you run on fear. You ruminate on thinking about how you "shoulda-coulda-woulda" done things differently in the past and/or you plan and overthink things that have yet to happen.

A more subtle sign of fear in the mind is seeking to control situations and outcomes. Many of us are controlling but deny it, preferring to think of ourselves as "capable, take-charge, get-things-done" people. We do it all, or tell others how to do everything, because we secretly think others are stupid, less competent, or less dependable than we are. Some of us pride ourselves on how kind we are, and therefore we cannot see our controlling sides. We covertly control through passive-aggressive means such as performing acts of service for others, then casually applying pressure to return the favor or align with behavioral expectations.

When we resist anything, it is because we are afraid, but our egos will not admit it. Instead, they look for and latch onto evidence that validates our reaction to situations and people. The justification mounts as we gather "evidence" to validate ourselves. Then we go to battle: we confront, accuse, blame, and attack another person or group. Sometimes humans take this to the death on a quest to defend their "rightness." Yet, even in conquering the enemy, what is won? The prize is merely self-deception.

PERCEIVING: FEAR AND LOVE

Heart - heavy and intense emotions

Anger is a mask for fear. Resentment, guilt, shame, rage, loneliness, jealousy, sadness, hurt, offense, and many more emotions are also rooted in fear. Your emotions arise from what you are telling yourself.

Body - tension, tightness, knots, restriction, fatigue, fight/flight/freeze

As you watch your own thoughts, you will begin to notice when you are triggered—meaning taken out of an emotional space of peace and love—by something someone says or does, and you will notice your body's reactions. You will become more aware that your emotions carry a weight and take up space in your body. Some people describe knots in their stomachs or heaviness in their chests that restricts their breathing. You may notice a feeling of combativeness, or feeling like you want to run and hide, or even feeling stuck—like you are frozen and do not know what to do or say next. These are all manifestations of the fight, flight, or freeze mechanism in your nervous system. Emotional reactions range, but feelings rooted in fear *do not* make you feel free and like you are flying. Quite the opposite, they can seem paralyzing.

Soul - internal struggle

Every person I coach (including me) has some area in their life where they are at war with themselves or others. I often hear individuals express frustrations in their lives, saying they "feel stuck," or are "struggling" with things in their lives. When examined closely, there is often evidence that the perceived struggle is actually a wrestle between the loving desires of the soul and the fearful resistance from the ego. The struggle is a trust and courage issue: we are unfamiliar with the feeling of trusting ourselves, and are uncertain about how to summon the courage to act in accordance with truth.

Through the process of inquiry, we find the fear driving that war. Then we find the lie(s) tied to it and the story that goes with it. We investigate it and are led to the truth. In the light of truth, the lie surrenders itself. When we choose to receive love, we are set free.

Experiment: Shift from fear to love

Any time you notice any of the red flags of fear, you can pause and ask yourself, "What am I afraid of?" This question will illuminate why you are really struggling, feeling stuck, or carrying heavy emotions. The question will bring an enlightening answer. The next step is simple. Ask, "If I were to operate from love right now, what would I think (pause and listen), what would I feel (pause and listen), and what would I do right now (pause and listen)?"

When you are seeking and asking, ideas show up. You can start listening to your heart and soul, and trusting them. New thoughts, great ideas, and loving possibilities will surface from right inside of you!

MAKING PEACE WITH THE BODY

A significant area of false programming in our world has been directed at the body. We have been taught to focus on the size, shape, and appearance of our bodies while ignoring the sacred and miraculous nature of its divine design. Few of us have any education or awareness around the magnificent elemental structure of the body. As a result, we overlook the potential power our body offers us as one of our greatest guides for identifying truth.

Many people perceive their body as an enemy. They hate it, they complain about it, and they feel inhibited or restrained by the body when it is sick or injured. They criticize it when they look in the mirror. All of these approaches are linked to fearful beliefs that say, *If my body is not "perfect," I'm not enough, I'm not lovable, I'm not worthy.*

When you are at war with your body, you cannot access the truth it holds. Loving your body is imperative to connecting to it and then receiving the messages it holds for you. These messages are delivered through light, truth, and love.

Experiment: Love your Body

Create an opportunity to spend time with your unclothed self—near a mirror or in a tub or shower, for example—and look at your body.

Ask yourself what you think about different parts of your body. Notice which parts you love and which ones you judge, condemn, and criticize.

Ask yourself, "Who or what taught me to think this way?" Recall past experiences and cultural influences and notice the impact they have had on your relationship with your body.

Place your hands on the unloved parts of yourself and simply observe the thoughts and feelings that emerge. If you are open to the idea, say, "I am willing to learn to connect with (or love) this part of me." Notice if there is resistance to that phrase. Keep your hands in place and take a few deep breaths, intentionally connecting with this area and sending love to it.

BECOMING ACQUAINTED WITH THE FEARFUL EGO

I became aware of my ego when, at the advent of my existential reawakening, I began to observe my thoughts like a curious outsider. I began to catch the frequency with which I used words like *should, shouldn't, have to, must, need to, right, wrong, good, bad, worthy, unworthy, righteous, unrighteous, not enough, too much,* and myriad other comparative and judgmental words.

I was surprised to discover I had this know-it-all, fear-driven voice in my mind, and that it was my ego talking. I mean, I was familiar with the voice because I had called it my "personality" for a long time. But I had not noticed the prevalence of fear and judgment in it, and all that time I thought it was *me*: that confident, outgoing, achievement-oriented, goal-driven gal. Well, it was not the authentic me, it was a character I had created in response to all the environmental influences I grew up with.

After I recognized the true source of this voice I'd identified with, I sought to learn more about my ego through conscious books and mentors. I was taught that my ego's primary goals were: 1) to keep me safe and protected, and 2) to protect its own reputation by being "right," regardless of the cost.

The ego seeks to keep me safe by guiding me to avoid anything unknown or unacceptable. It disproportionately emphasizes and magnifies the significance of all perceived dangers. It acts as a kind of behavioral immune system, seeking to eradicate anything foreign or unknown, just as the body's immune system is programmed to destroy foreign objects.

It also has a primal need to seek safety through belonging, which means the ego is most protective of its own reputation. It works to shield me from the dangers of embarrassment, feeling awkward, and feeling excluded or lonely. It propels me to want to fit in, conform, and/or be liked by others. The ego drives me to obsessively seek after approval, acceptance, and love from other people.

The ultimate covert narcissist, ego seeks to sustain itself by proving it is right with justifications, validation, and carefully selected evidence. It is tireless in this effort and will go to any length to survive. It will dismiss information that threatens what it believes is true. It will criticize any person who threatens its position with their own beliefs, words, or actions. It will hide its own existence to keep me from investigating or questioning it, disguising its judgments as part of my innate personality or core values.

When I'm in my ego, I quietly think, and sometimes overtly speak, words of disapproval, condemnation, and shame towards myself and others; I use guilt and shame to manipulate people into changing their thoughts, feelings, and actions to serve my ego-based beliefs. Ultimately, the ego will persuade me to ignore the truth, sabotage relationships, and even relinquish my own freedom in order to prove itself right.

Experiment: Can I love myself through this?
In her famous Ted Talk "The Power of Vulnerability," Brene Brown taught that the difference between guilt and shame is simple: Guilt says, "I made a mistake," while shame says, "I *am* a mistake."

When you encounter information or situations that bring up shame, pause, breathe, and ask, "Can I love myself through this?"

Allow your soul to remind you that you are always worthy of love, and capable of giving it to yourself. This will empower you to choose *humility* over *humiliation*, and grow as a result of your new understanding, rather than hide in shame.

FEAR-BASED CORE BELIEFS

My ego doesn't just prefer to be right; it is terrified of being wrong! Many of my clients have found the same deep fear. Facing the potential of being wrong puts the ego in an identity crisis. Being wrong leads the ego to feel like it is facing its death. If the ego is wrong, then it has failed. The ego also fears failure. Perceived evidence of failure is a clear message to the ego that it is not good enough.

These ego fears are the source of the most common, unconscious, limiting core beliefs humans carry. The five most common fear-based limiting beliefs I encounter in people are:

1. I am a failure
2. I am not good enough
3. I do not belong
4. I am unlovable
5. I am unworthy

Every person I interview is affected by these five statements. Most often, we have to use cognitive behavioral tools to get into the unconscious mind for the awareness to surface. People generally react to these five beliefs in one of two ways:

1. They either already believe they are true and unchangeable, and they suffer great emotional turmoil as a result.
2. They are afraid of them becoming true. They would never want to see themselves that way. They perceive people who feel these things as weak or insecure, so they achieve and perform their way feverishly in the opposite direction.

These two ways of being are two sides of the same coin.

When operating from an attachment to these limiting core beliefs, we either, one, exist in a state of fear, drowning in perpetual worry, sorrow, insecurity, and scarcity; or two, create fear-driven personality complexes to overcompensate for the existence of these fears.

An overcompensating personality complex can develop through a sense of superiority. This presents as the "highly functional," the "overachiever," the "perfectionist," the "performance junkie." This complex is driven by the ideas of proving one's worth by achieving success and productivity in all its forms: high achievement; constant personal growth and progress; prestigious titles, awards, and advancements; beauty, wealth and material possessions; or—if you have begun to tune out because this is *not you* we are talking about, you may want to look at this last example—righteousness. Whether seeking worldly pursuits or religious worthiness, it is the same.

Experiment: What does this say about me?
Notice when an ego response comes up. (For example, you're feeling frustrated with your spouse, who failed, yet again, to call and let you know that they would be late coming home from work.)

Ask yourself, "What does this say or mean about me?"

Initially, accusations toward the other person may show up. (You may think *your spouse* is thoughtless, forgetful, self-centered, or just plain unkind.) These thoughts come from your ego's unwillingness to look at an uncomfortable belief about yourself.

Pause and ask again, "What does this say or mean about *me*?"

Your ego will likely resist turning this inquiry inward rather than outward—remember, the ego is terrified of being wrong. Be patient with yourself and keep asking. It may be helpful to put your hand on your heart and remind yourself that you are safe and can love yourself through this process.

Once you move past your ego's resistance, it's likely that something will come to the surface, such as, *It says that he doesn't care about me.*

Then ask yourself: "If this statement were true, what would it say or mean about me?"

Continue to inquire into each subsequent thought until you come to a fear about your own essential worth, value, or worthiness. You may move through layers such as:

- He only loves me for the service I perform for the family.
- He doesn't value me as an individual.
- No one values me as an individual.

Ask again, "If this statement were true, what would it say or mean about me?"

When you follow your ego's judgments down this line of questioning to focus more specifically on the fears you have about yourself, you will likely eventually uncover a core negative belief like the five mentioned above. (You may think, *If this were true it would mean that I am not important, that I am not lovable,* or *that I don't belong.*)

Reflect on the way you tend to respond to your core negative belief. Do you tend to overtly believe it is true and react with shame, or do you work to avoid the possibility it could be true by working to prove it's not true?

If you absolutely knew that this core belief were *not* true, what would you think, say, or do in this situation? (What would you think of your spouse? What could you say or do to address your needs when he is late and doesn't call?) This is living in love, rather than fear.

ACCEPTING THE LAW OF INNOCENCE

Tremendous amounts of suffering come from attaching to and perpetually reliving our past experiences. This happens when we look back on our lives through the lens of fear and judgment and assign blame, guilt, and punishment to ourselves and others. By applying shoulda-coulda-woulda perspectives, these judgments become part of your story. Each time you revisit a judged memory, you re-experience guilt and shame.

We see others as we are, so when we live in retroactive self-judgment, collecting and holding onto our mistakes, regrets, shortcomings, and failures, we project that same perspective onto others. Even when we have tried to "learn from our mistakes" and "better ourselves," there is a common lack of forgiveness of the self. We may have moved on, but have not let go. Those who believe they have progressed beyond their past limitations, but have yet to acknowledge their own innocence in the past, judge others the most harshly for demonstrating the same behaviors. This breeds a lack of forgiveness, which then becomes pride.

What I term *The Law of Innocence* is the reality that in every moment, each person is doing the best they can with what they have. People do exactly what they know how to do, based on their current beliefs, thoughts, and feelings. Stephen R. Covey said, "To know and not to do, is really not to know."[35] If someone truly doesn't understand a concept, they cannot live that principle. Everyone, including ourselves, is doing and being what they know to do and be right now.

Embracing this truth expands our ability to love and accept ourselves. As our hearts open to the truth of our own innocence, the suffering created by guilt and shame vanishes; self-compassion replaces self-judgment. As we have compassion for ourselves, we begin to see the innocence in everyone else. By removing judgment, first for ourselves, and then for others by extension, The Law of Innocence grants freedom and engenders love.

This simplifies the idea of being Christlike, making forgiveness doable for any of us. The ego-driven stories we tell ourselves about how we were wronged begin to unravel, and the common inner wrestle to forgive another naturally dissipates. We no longer need to prove we are right because there is no threat of guilt—no need to point fingers—when we see everyone involved as innocent. Love, compassion, and true charity are inherent in the absence of judgment.

Receiving The Law of Innocence opens the channels of light, truth, and love from the Divine. It enlarges our comprehension of unconditional love through felt experience.

---

35   Covey, Stephen R. *The 7 Habits of Highly Effective People: Powerful Lessons in Personal Change.*

As we see ourselves as innocent, we begin to see ourselves as lovable; we are able to love ourselves and receive Divine love as never before.

There is a common fallacy in humans. We tend to believe once we have learned a concept, we should now "know better," and never forget or fail to act on that knowledge. For example, as we gain greater awareness, we might think that now we've discovered our ego, it should go away or no longer control us. Once we discern truth over error, we should never be fooled again. We might expect to "arrive" somewhere—at the pinnacle of knowledge, I suppose.

However, the truth is that life is a constant experiment. Seemingly oppositional forces are at play all the time. The glorious nature of this is that if it were not so, we would be stuck in a Garden of Eden state, as described in the Bible with Adam and Eve, living in innocence, with no true choices. In the laboratory of life, we are able to enact the gift of agency and create our experience. We will vacillate between light and darkness, truth and error, love and fear, sadness and joy, chaos and peace, and captivity and freedom, again and again. And regardless of where we are in those cycles, at any given time we can meet ourselves in compassion with this question, "Can I love myself through this?"

Experiment: You are innocent

Imagine I'm sitting across from you, and I say to you, "I'm about to ask you a question. Do you know what it is?"

You'll answer, "No," right?

So do you know how you'll answer my question when I ask it?

"No" again?

So now, ask yourself, "In this moment, in our conversation, am I guilty or innocent?"

You're innocent, right? You've done nothing wrong in this moment, in this conversation, because you didn't know what you didn't know.

What if your entire past is a compilation of one innocent moment after another, where you did not know what was coming and what to expect, but you did the best you could with what you had right then in the moment?

It's only after the fact, when you look back and judge yourself with *I should have...* or *I could have...* stories, that the guilt and shame show up. But remember: they're just stories. In the moment, you were as innocent then as you are right now.

Think about something from your past that you feel guilty about or ashamed of.

Take a deep breath and sit with the following questions:
- What if you were as innocent in each moment of your past as you are in this present moment?
- What if your entire life is a compilation of present, innocent moments?

After a few moments, check in: How does this new perspective feel in your body?

I invite you to experiment with replacing judgmental words in your thoughts with the word "innocent." When you find yourself thinking, "I am so thoughtless," think, "I am so innocent." Or instead of, "He is really selfish," try, "He is really innocent." Notice as you do this that love and compassion for yourself and others begin to surface with ease.

Experiment: Ho'oponopono

Rather than looking back on yourself after the fact and applying what you know *now* to what happened *then* with shoulda-coulda-woulda judgments, remind yourself what it felt like in the moment. Under all the pressures present, can you see and acknowledge that you did the best you could with what you knew and felt right then? To argue against this idea is to resist reality. Can you have compassion for who you were then, offering yourself grace and compassion and acknowledging your innocence, while understanding that, in your awareness today, you are capable of choosing and operating differently?

Ask yourself: *Where am I holding on to feelings of guilt and shame?*

Begin to notice how often you feel guilty. (Do you ever feel guilty for *not* feeling guilty for something you think you *should* feel guilty for?)

Think about something you have not forgiven yourself for. Can you see where the belief that you are *guilty* is part of what prohibits forgiveness?

Notice where judgment comes into play to determine guilt, and become aware of the belief that being guilty warrants punishment and repayment.

In these moments of recognition, I apply within myself the Hawaiian relationship resolution practice known as *Ho'oponopono*. I close my eyes and picture a former version of myself in a time that holds guilt and a lack of forgiveness. I talk to that younger version of me, using these prompts:

1. "Angel, I'm sorry that . . ."
2. "Angel, I forgive you for . . ."
3. "Angel, thank you for . . ."
4. "Angel, I love you!"

I then picture my current self embracing my former self and assimilating her into me, as a healed, loved, perfectly innocent entity. As I do so, I feel light replace darkness, love replace fear, and truth replace error. I feel free!

I invite you to experiment with this sacred process.

You may notice once you have gifted this forgiveness to yourself, it becomes a process that you naturally access when interpersonal conflict arises. You are now equipped to replace judgment and criticism of others with the same perspective of innocence and compassion you have gifted yourself.

You cannot give what you don't have! When we cannot forgive ourselves, we tend to struggle to forgive others. When self-compassion replaces self-judgment, grace, forgiveness, and compassion for others flows effortlessly.

IF I CAST OFF FEAR, I AM PREPARED

A scripture quoted often during my upbringing was, "If ye are prepared ye shall not fear."[36] Whenever this doctrine was brought into lessons, the focus that followed was on the steps of preparation. We were taught to physically prepare for disasters by fortifying our homes with food storage and supplies, to mentally prepare with a good education, and to spiritually prepare by keeping commandments.

These things are not inherently bad or wrong; but I found that when they were my focus, I was missing the mark.[37] It seems to me that the security this type of preparedness offers is limited: I can do all the things on a preparedness checklist and still have fear. Life can still throw me a curveball I am not prepared for.

By observing the frequency of the presence of fear in my mind, body, and heart, I began to recognize fear is the direct opposite of love; therefore, I can use it as a reference point for turning toward love. I have found that learning to cast off fear *is* my preparation. By tuning into the Spirit with the courage to do whatever I feel inspired

---

36   Doctrine & Covenants 38:30

37   This is a common phrase used to describe sin. The Hebrew word "hata," "sin," is used in the Old Testament. Literally translated it means "to miss the mark." It is also a reference to Jacob 4:14, in the Book of Mormon: "Wherefore, because of their blindness, which blindness came by looking beyond the mark, they must needs fall."

to do, I have been prepared 100% of the time because God filled my needs as they surfaced. I believe true safety comes through believing in miracles and God's goodness.

If I cast off fear, then I am prepared. That is my motto. When I release myself from fear, I have "put off the natural man,"[38] reconnected with my spirit, and put myself in alignment with the voice and direction of God. In that state, I am prepared to ask, receive, trust, and act on anything and everything God directs me to do right now.

In Proverbs 3:5-6 it says: "Trust in the Lord with all thine heart; and lean not unto thine own understanding. In all thy ways acknowledge him, and he shall direct thy paths."[39]

The truth of this concept has been proven to me over and over again in all aspects of my life: in finances, in my career as a coach, as a public speaker, as a parent, and in all my other relationships.

Experiment: Find the opposite

When you notice fear manifesting in your life (remember to watch for the red flags!), stop and ask, "What am I telling myself right now?"

Identify an opposite thought. Love is 180 degrees from fear. Reorienting to love empowers you to make a clear choice between fear and love.

The energy of love is peaceful. It calms the mind, enabling you to find solutions and receive inspiration—to be prepared in any situation.

LOVINGLY ENCOUNTERING YOUR SHADOW

Many of us want to be loving towards others, yet we are not aware that when our relationship with ourselves is rooted in fear, it sets the precedent for how well we treat others. The Bible teaches, "Thou

---

38   Mosiah 3:19
39   The Holy Bible, KJV

shalt love thy neighbor as thyself."[40] Clearly there is a directive to love yourself unconditionally in order to be able to love anyone else. Following this commandment becomes simple as we remove fearful resistance and judgment, challenge our beliefs with truth, and choose love over fear.

I have yet to encounter anything that cannot be healed by truth and love.

When you find yourself in judgment, get curious. Curiosity and judgment cannot co-exist. Ask, "What is going on in my unconscious mind?" My mentors taught me this question as part of a practice called *shadow work*.

The *shadow self* is a term coined by Swiss psychologist Carl Jung, referring to the unconscious, dark side of one's personality. These are the parts that have been tucked away and hidden from conscious awareness due to the feelings of shame and fear surrounding them. They are the parts of you that you are unwilling to claim.

Even though they are hidden from your conscious awareness, your shadow parts are still shaping your life. When you bring them to light and learn to own and integrate them into your conscious being, you will no longer be subject to the negative thoughts and behaviors they create.

Shadow work is the process of looking inward to find one's own hidden shame, inferiority, and irrational beliefs, which are the origin of any projected blame, criticism, and judgment.

Experiment: Using judgments to uncover truth

A powerful tool in shadow work is noticing when you are standing in judgment of someone else. When you are feeling emotionally triggered

---

40   The Holy Bible, KJV, Mark 12:31

by someone else's way of being, it is often because they are manifesting an aspect of your shadow self that you do not want to see.

Note the things you are judging about that person and the statements you are making about how they "should" be doing things. Note the thoughts that assert your own superiority in this area. (*I would never . . .*)

Now take a minute to connect with your soul. Say, "This is what I'm telling myself. Is it true?"

Breathe, and receive the answer.

Then ask, "What is true?" And then perhaps, "What more is there?"

Continue to breathe and love yourself through the answers, reminding yourself of your own innocence.

EXPERIENCING: SADNESS AND JOY

"Joy is the infallible sign of the presence of God."
-Pierre Teilhard de Chardin

Principles and Experiments in this Chapter:
- Ending Self-Betrayal
    - Experiment: Is this a soul's yes or a soul's no?
    - Experiment: Following "should" to your source of resistance
- Learning to be Present
    - Experiment: Make a Sensory Kit
    - Experiment: Meditate
- Dropping the Addiction to Doing
    - Experiment: Why am I doing this?
    - Experiment: Ignite your passions
- Getting Comfortable with the Pendulum Swing
    - Experiment: Feel it!
- DON'T Stop Crying
    - Experiment: Holding Space
- Emotional Triggers: The Alarm Clocks of Our Awareness
    - Experiment: Triggers can lead to joy

ENDING SELF-BETRAYAL

Self-betrayal is the act of ignoring your soul, the Spirit, and therefore, the Truth. It is at the root of our stories about others, the lies we tell ourselves, and the pressured emotions we carry. It is present in every scenario I have investigated in which there is a lack of satisfaction. We betray ourselves without even noticing, and where there is self-betrayal, there is deep grief at being separated from the true source of our worth, our own integrity. This leads to behaviors that seek to bring a sense of validation from external sources, such as:

- Mis-giving - Saying "yes" when you truthfully want to say "no." Doing things, not because you want to, but because you are capable of doing them and think you should. Doing things for others from a place of fear, guilt, shame, obligation, or judgment.
- Comparison - Looking at others and thinking you are better or worse than they are, contribute more or less than they do, etc.
- Copying - Modeling your rules for life on outside sources and doing what you see others do.
- Judgment - Settling on your perceptions of self and others as the truth.
- Resentment - Feeling tired and unsupported in your efforts, feeling bitter, alone, and unloved.
- Blame - Projecting the shame of your mis-giving and self-betrayal onto others. Blame is the ego's way of deflecting shame.
- Guilt - Feeling bad for being mean, critical, judgmental, and/or vengeful, even if it is just inside your head.
- Justification - Seeking evidence to validate your poor choices.

These behaviors only reinforce your patterns of self-betrayal, and the cycle repeats. You are caught in a spiraling trap that starts and ends in self-betrayal. It is a prison of living under the fear and pressures of the external compass: the macro, meso, and micro system influences in your life. Living this way chips away at your relationships with yourself and with God—you cannot trust yourself when you are in self-betrayal; you cannot trust God if you do not trust yourself.

In contrast, turning inward and upward and utilizing your internal compass as your guide is where you will find joy.

Experiment: Is this a soul's yes or a soul's no?
The next time you are asked to do something, check in with yourself and ask, "Is this a soul's yes or a soul's no?" Listen and feel in your body, mind, heart, and spirit whether it's a "yes" or "no." Trust the answer that feels like resonance, or harmonious alignment, and act on it. This is a way to honor yourself (the opposite of self-betrayal), and to honor what is true for you.

When you listen to your soul's desires and align with your inner compass, you are not trying to prove or earn your worth and value. You escape the drama triangle dynamic and the resentment it creates. You step away from being motivated by shoulds, guilt, fear, shame, and judgment. These motivations are created by the ego seeking someone else's approval, acceptance, love, or belonging—essentially denying God and worshiping these sources as idols!

Remember, you are not responsible for how anyone else reacts to you trusting yourself and your Source of Truth. That's not your business. Things are so simple when you let this go! You can just find truth and align, and move on.

Experiment: Following "should" to your resistance
As you observe your motivations, thoughts, and words more diligently, you will increase your self-awareness. Notice whenever a "should" or "shouldn't" is present in your mind or language. The word "should" is

an indicator that you are judging and resisting what is real and true in your soul. "Should" is telling you what external voices of authority and your own conditioning want or expect you to do. This pressure to conform creates a sense of resistance to the soul's longing for freedom and its inherent ability to experience joy over sadness.

Ask yourself, "Where am I *shoulding* on myself? What am I resisting in this moment?"

Through investigation, you can become aware of the programming and conditioning of your thinking: someone or something taught you to "should" on this moment.

Ask yourself, "If I removed the 'should'—if that rule didn't apply in this moment—how might that change the way I feel?"

LEARNING TO BE PRESENT

Mindfulness enables us to be in the present, the only space from which we can access the voice of God. In the present, we can see clearly to dis-identify from our thoughts, and recognize that they may not always be aligned with truth.

We practice mindfulness by focusing on our present, embodied experience. Engaging the senses, focusing on the breath, stillness, and meditation are all great ways to do this.

When I first attempted meditation, I got tripped up and had difficulty relaxing and focusing because I was unsure of how to do it the "right" way. I tried listening to soft sounds or instrumental music, but my mind would ruminate on my worries and the tasks waiting for me. Then someone told me about guided meditations, and it opened up a whole new world! Meditations by Sarah Blondin are my favorite, hands down! I practiced following her voice and noticing her words and tones, tuning in deeply to my sense of sound. Through this, I learned (or perhaps *remembered*) to be present!

Experiment: Make a sensory kit

Make a Sensory Kit to help you easily access the present through your body. Find a box, bag, or container to hold items that stimulate your five hard senses. These are just examples:

- Choose a scent that you love. An essential oil, perfume, or scented candle work great for this.
- Select an object that fits in your hand that has a pleasing texture, like a smooth rock, a soft or furry fabric, or a squeezable ball.
- Choose an item that is visually pleasing, like a photo of your favorite place, a small piece of art, or something in your favorite color.
- Create a playlist of soothing sounds or songs on your phone, or add a bell, a chime, or a sound bowl to your kit.
- Add something edible like a mint or candy, something you can suck on for a while and savor its flavor.

When you feel emotionally triggered, choose one or two items from your sensory kit and focus on stimulating your senses for 1-2 minutes. Notice what shifts for you. You can decide if you need more time with your senses to help you stay in the present moment. (This has also been very helpful for my adolescent and younger clients who deal with anxiety.)

Experiment: Meditate

Meditating every day, even if it's just for a few minutes, can make a profound difference in your mental and emotional well-being.

Look up guided meditations on YouTube, where there is an almost unlimited array of options. Or download the free app Insight Timer. There are thousands of guided meditations available, searchable by topic or by the meditation leader. (This is where you can access most of Sarah Blondin's work.)

DROPPING THE ADDICTION TO DOING

Are you being fooled by the DO-HAVE-BE myth? It goes something like this:

If I DO...
(...complete some goal: finish my to-do list, lose weight, make more money, find a partner, have children, finish college, launch a business, etc...)

Then I will HAVE...
(...something you feel will make your life better: a better self esteem, more friends, more freedom, a loving relationship, meaning and purpose, a marketable degree, entrepreneurship status)...

And so I will BE...
(...more valuable: good enough, lovable, worthy, successful, accomplished, happy, fulfilled, content, at peace, etc).

Do you believe achieving your goals will bring you happiness, worthiness, joy, peace, or approval?

Seeking to earn these feelings through action is a sign that you are driven by fear-based beliefs. You may believe that you are currently lacking, not enough, not lovable or worthy *right now*. If your goals are aimed at obtaining external approval, acceptance, love, and belonging, it's probably because you believe in this myth: that DOING is the way to HAVE what you need to BE who you want to be.

But what if you recognized that you are already enough? What if you knew that, at your core, you *are* love? What if you understood that you don't have to prove or earn your worth or value? What if you lived from the satisfaction of who you know yourself to BE, without waiting for an accomplishment to give you permission to feel the joy you're looking for?

What if that were your starting point?

When your starting point is *your own* approval, acceptance, love, and belonging, then you know you already *are* all you want to BE—*right now.*

This recognition can help you to see that you already HAVE everything you've been looking outside of yourself for—inside of you!

With the BE & HAVE in order, can you see how you are now able to DO life from a motivation of love?

Some people worry that being content, peaceful, and happy with life will strip them of their ambition and leave them idle, unable to progress. That is a myth! An expansive way of being fills you with the energy of love, rather than fear. Your DO-ing aligns with your innermost desires. This empowers you to do things because they're right for you, not because of external pressure or expectations. Peace is no longer something you chase—it is something you *are*. Your operating paradigm becomes: BE-HAVE-DO.

Experiment: Why am I doing this?

To break your addiction to doing and to stop living in self-betrayal, periodically ask yourself: "Why am I doing this?" Bring this question into every moment and situation. Notice how many of your choices are determined by a desire to HAVE or BE something.

If you find that you are doing something because you are seeking to obtain something outside yourself, stop. Breathe. Say, "I'm telling myself that if I am not (*trait you wish to possess*), or that I don't have (*thing you're trying to earn*). What is true?"

Receive the answer. Now, grounded in this information, ask yourself: "Do I still want to do this?" If you don't, stop doing it! If you do, keep going. Either way, notice how it feels to choose to do something (or not do something) from a place of worthiness, rather than lack.

Experiment: Ignite your passions

Make a list of activities that light you up, give you energy, and bring you joy. These can be simple or complicated, mundane or exciting.

If you struggle to remember things you enjoy doing, like I did, try asking what you might like to try or what activities used to bring you joy. Consider talking to your siblings, parents, or partner for ideas.

Make it a non-negotiable priority to do something from your passions list regularly. You will be amazed at how this changes your life, infuses you with energy, and enables you to show up fully for others!

GETTING COMFORTABLE WITH THE PENDULUM SWING

In my experience, the practices of seeking awareness of light and darkness, discerning truth and error, and choosing to operate from love over fear builds a kind of momentum. This momentum provides an energetic thrust that speeds the individual through subsequent phases of soul-u-lar evolution: sadness and joy, chaos and peace, and captivity and freedom.

When I began my journey, it felt like hard work to challenge my beliefs, change habits, and to pivot behaviors—but eventually, these things began to flow with grace and ease. The undercurrents of joy, peace, and freedom in my present life have come as dividends from a wise investment of energy and focus.

I think it is only fair, however, to tell you that, while transitioning from the realm of absolutes, there have been moments when I wondered if I was losing my mind. The shift away from black-and-white thinking can lead a person to feel like they have bipolar disorder. As you consciously and intentionally interact with life, rather than defaulting to programmed mental and emotional habits, you may swing dramatically between light and darkness, truth and error, love and fear, sadness and joy, chaos and peace, captivity and freedom. That swinging pendulum can resemble mental illness as emotional highs and lows became exaggerated.

The bliss I experience in connecting with my soul and the Divine is beyond any happiness I have ever felt before—and this bliss is often followed by a backlash of depression, like an emotional gravity seeking to pull me back into the homeostasis of my past stories. *Am I going crazy?* is a programmed reaction of fear and judgment to all these changes.

Instead of falling into that judgment, I invite you to consider what happens when a rocket takes off into space. At first, there is so much resistance from the gravitational pull of the earth that rocket boosters are needed to counteract its effects. But as the rocket moves out of earth's gravity, it takes almost no energy to maintain its course.

Similarly, fear and past programming will try to pull you down, particularly at the beginning, and it will take a lot of energy to continue your climb. But your new way of being and seeing things will feel like rising higher and moving faster than ever before. These moments of freedom and bliss will blast you right out of the atmosphere. For me, these intensely opposite emotions seem to have evened out over time, but the initial contrast was significant.[41]

If this shows up for you, I invite you to celebrate your aliveness! Welcome yourself back home to your heart! What a gift it is to feel! It is much more fun than life in survival mode, avoiding, escaping, numbing, and distracting! A gift I have found in this deep and intensely emotional space is that I have become more gentle with myself and others, and gained an awareness of the sacred nature of all

---

41   Individual experience may vary. :)

things. Rather than running *from* life or running *through* life, I can choose to simply live *in* life—being present here, now, feeling all the feels; therein lies peace and joy.

Grace and self-compassion are essential here. Developing the ability to be with your emotions will help you move through these phases with greater ease and less resistance. This ability depends on first releasing judgment for the emotions you feel. Expressing your emotions through sound and movement then allows these feelings to move through you with greater flow.

Experiment: Feel it!
When I allow myself to truly process my emotions, I walk away with a sense of healing that feels more effective than months of clinical talk therapy sessions.

Give yourself permission to feel all your emotions. Try the following:
- **Begin to notice and name your emotions.** If you can, talk out loud about anything that is bothering, annoying, frustrating, hurting you, etc. Then ask yourself, "What am I feeling?" Going back to noticing and naming the emotion. Say, "I feel _____!"
  - **Note:** It's not uncommon for people new to this practice to feel stuck in identifying the emotion they're experiencing. If you're having a hard time identifying your emotion, an Emotion Wheel might help you figure it out. There are many free printable options available online.
- **Witness yourself.** This means, rather than run away from what you're feeling, be your own source of validation. See how it feels to say this: "I give myself permission to feel." Notice how your body feels the emotion; where do you feel it in your body?

- **Ask yourself what judgments you have on each emotion.** For example, we often label anger as "bad" and happiness as "good." Remove the judgment words and sit in the awareness that emotions are morally neutral and natural.
- **Make a sound to express the intensity of the emotion you feel.** You can begin practicing this in private. For example, scream into a pillow, curl up in the fetal position and groan and cry, yell in the privacy of your car. Shout the things in private that you feel like shouting at another person.
- **Move your body to move through emotions.** Ask your body, "How do you want to move this energy?"
- **Play a song (or songs) that feel aligned with any emotion you are currently feeling.** Give your body permission to move to the music. Explore and experiment with movement.

The energy of emotion wants to be moved. With awareness, you will begin to read the frequencies of your emotions and, rather than obstruct them, let them move you—your body, your voice—in the way they want to move. There is no wrong way to do this. The act of moving emotional energy is so joyful!

DON'T STOP CRYING!

I believe the western world is emotionally constipated. Most of us have heard the words, "Stop crying! You're not hurt!" or at least a well-meaning, "Don't cry, it will be okay." We are taught that there are good emotions and bad emotions, positive and negative emotions, acceptable and inappropriate emotions. We are taught to fear emotions that feel anything but pleasant.

I invite everyone to try something new: *Don't* stop crying! And don't suggest that others stop! Emotions are part of the human design!

Can you come into alignment with the truth of that statement? How can we know we are meant to feel? Because we *do* feel.

Author Neal Donald Walsh has referred to emotion as "energy in motion." The Latin root of the word emotion is *emotere*, which means *to move*. Many people experience emotional release during exercise. This is not a coincidence. As I move my body and breathe with the intention of giving myself permission to release emotions, my emotions respond and rise to the surface.

My increase in self-compassion has given me an increase in compassion for others, along with the ability to make room for other people's emotional experiences. Remember, you cannot give what you do not have. When we live in emotional restriction, we unconsciously shut down others' emotions. We allow our discomfort with emotions to cause us to feel uncomfortable in the presence of others' emotions, and we attempt to quickly distract them from feeling.

Instead, we can shift to *holding space* for someone else, creating a safe emotional environment that allows them to express their emotions. When you are well-acquainted with your emotions, the thoughts and beliefs that govern them, and the art of moving the energy of them, you gain insight into observing and understanding all of the above in other people. Compassion grows. You are developing emotional intelligence.

Experiment: Holding Space

When you see emotion surfacing in others, you can say, "It's okay to let it out," or "You are safe to feel here."

Then sit with that person, allowing them the space to express in whatever way they need to without offering advice or trying to fix their problems.

Allow yourself to move and breathe deeply in order to release the energy of emotion you may feel while sitting in this space. Intentionally focus on inner peace, gratitude, and love. This allows you to transmute the emotion for yourself and emanate an energy of peace for those you are supporting.

EMOTIONAL TRIGGERS: THE ALARM CLOCKS OF OUR AWARENESS

Many people have limited emotional intelligence because we are culturally conditioned to avoid, escape, numb, and distract from uncomfortable emotions. With repetition, these behaviors can become habits and, eventually, addictions. When coping behaviors reach the level of addiction, it is easy to become distracted from the root issue by a concern for the behaviors, symptoms, and consequences of the addictions. Yet we struggle to break the addiction cycle without understanding its cause. It is essential to understand that at the root of the behavior is an underlying, unconscious, fear-based belief.

Our unpleasant emotions are the alarm clocks of our awareness: they have the potential to wake us up. When we set an alarm clock, and then hit snooze and go back to sleep, we are ignoring something. Likewise, ignoring our heavy emotions is like hitting the snooze button on our alarm clocks: we often miss something important!

For example, until I began to investigate my negative reactions, I didn't recognize my belief that my husband and sons were the source of my suffering as a projection of my ego. I was a prolific author without knowing it, writing countless stories in my mind every day! I framed my relationships within the drama triangle, creating vibrant egoic characters for myself and everyone around me. I was the protagonist in my story, and I grandiloquently depicted heroes, villains, and victims in my perception of every experience. I judged those I considered my antagonists and wrapped them up in incriminating evidence. While my ninth grade English teacher would be proud of my creativity, the lack of personal awareness of this process was at the core of my self-deception and unhappiness.

Erroneous thinking like this—thoughts that resist and reject reality—are at the root of pain and suffering. The easiest way to discover our erroneous thinking is to pay attention to our emotional triggers. A *trigger*, in my definition, is any emotion that moves us out of a space of peace and love. I have learned to love triggers. I get and give triggers every day! When people tell me I trigger them, I respond with, "You're welcome!" because triggers offer important messages about ourselves and our beliefs. They alert us that something is out of alignment with truth. When we are living in a place of non-resistance and non-judgment, triggers create portals of self-discovery and gateways to truth and love.

Heavy emotions, which are always rooted in fear, can alert us to the presence of self-deception in our thinking. Anger, whether it shows up as frustration, annoyance, or just plain pissed off, is always a mask for fear. The belief that an emotion appears because someone or something else is *making* you feel that way is your *story*.[42] We can seek out the lies we are telling ourselves by asking, "What am I afraid of?" when these emotions appear.

If you find yourself arguing internally at this point, I invite you to breathe. When we begin to choose radical accountability, the ego will often become obstinate and defensive. It begins to argue by piling up evidence of one's grievances towards another person. The ego protects and justifies itself by blaming others. The ego's need to avoid blame is the source of emotional imprisonment and relational drama. As long as you are trying to defend your ego, you cannot transcend your ego.

---

[42] A story is the set of assumptions, perceptions, and judgmental conclusions a person has compiled for their interpretation of any situation.

Our ego operates in drama, believing there must be a good guy and a bad guy—that we must place the blame on someone else to avoid being bad ourselves. This is called *black-and-white thinking*. Looking at ourselves to acknowledge the fear behind our anger does not excuse the harmful actions of another person, nor does it invalidate our feelings. We can have compassion for the pain we feel while also taking responsibility for ourselves. This allows us to escape the ego's lies that keep us stuck.

When we are in projection, believing something outside ourselves is making us feel anything, we are helpless victims of our circumstances, needing something or someone else to change so we can feel better. Challenging this delusional and disempowered state is the first step to uncovering the truth and setting ourselves free. Unmasking the fear underneath the anger shows you the real problem hiding under your projection or story. It takes you to the true source of your anger, making resolution much easier and more effective.

Experiment: Triggers can lead to joy

Think of an experience where you were emotionally triggered. When was the last time you were angry, for example? Use that experience and follow the eight-step process below. If possible, write out your answers to these questions, or at least speak them out loud. This helps prevent your mind from spinning in circles and sneaking back into storytelling.

1. Ask, **"What was I feeling?"** If you can, identify not only the name of the emotion but where you experienced it in your body.

2. Ask, **"What was I telling myself about this situation?"** This takes you to your thoughts. Many of us have a tendency to believe and agree with the things we think. We affiliate with our thoughts as if they are us, and we are them. We think our thoughts are true and right simply because we think them and can find justification for them. This is a breeding

ground for darkness, self-deception, and error. Thoughts are to our being as weather patterns are to the sky: the clouds are not the sky; rain is not the sky; wind is not the sky. These elements of the natural climate shift and pass by, constantly, just like our thoughts. In the same way that we observe weather patterns, we can begin to observe our thoughts and separate who we really are and what is really true from what we are thinking at the moment.

3. Ask, **"Are these thoughts coming from fear or love?"** Quite often it is fear. You will be surprised at how many of your thoughts originate from fear.

4. Ask, **"If these thoughts were true and permanent, what would that say (or mean) about me?"** This is a challenge for some because our egos want to stop us from going into the unconscious mind. The ego will say things like, *It says nothing about me! It says this other person was a total jerk!* If that comes up, breathe deeply and ask the question again. As new thoughts surface, continue to repeat this question to uncover more unconscious beliefs and fears that were present and pertinent during this encounter.

5. When you find a fear-based belief that really stings, meaning you almost choke saying it, or tears suddenly show up, or you feel embarrassed to even admit it, ask yourself, **"Who or what taught me to think this way?"** Reflect on your entire past. We can always find influences, whether it was a person, a cultural message, or a situation, that imprinted the beliefs that are affecting the thinking. It could be many moments or people that taught and reinforced these fear-based beliefs. When we notice the imprints came from a human experience, I invite the client to consider, *"Perhaps there is a potential margin of error. Maybe this thinking is not 100% true."*

6. Next, close your eyes and seek with intention to see and feel an image of your soul—the unstoried version of you. The part that is

ageless, fearless, and egoless. Picture yourself approaching your soul with a sincere desire to know the truth. Present your beliefs to your soul, **"This is what I have been telling myself. Is this true, or is it my story?"** Watch what perceptions occur. It could be in your mind as thoughts, in your body as a physiological response, as a message from your soul, or all of the above.

7. Ask your soul, **"What is true?"** Breathe and receive the answer. Remember, "The depth to which you breathe is the depth to which you can receive."

8. Finally, ask for further enlightenment, **"What more is there?"**

These steps can help you separate what you have *believed* was true about yourself and others from what is *really* true and possible. Embracing the truth that shows up during this process is a way to instantly access the peace, joy, and freedom that many of us are chasing externally or trying to get others to fill for us. Receiving truth escorts in a flood of love and allows us to release the fear, fallacy, lies, shame, guilt . . . all the sadness born from our thinking.

OBSERVING: CHAOS AND PEACE

"We can never obtain peace in the outer world until we make peace with ourselves."
-Dalai Lama

Principles and Experiments in this Chapter:
- Suspending Judgment
  - Experiment: Drop the judgment
- When Others Judge You
  - Experiment: Addressing anger in others
- Resolving Trust Issues
  - Experiment: Honoring yourself
- Releasing Resistance to Darkness and Confusion
  - Experiment: Tune into your tension
- Speaking Truth
  - Experiment: Say it out loud

SUSPENDING JUDGMENT

To me, life is like a tornado: physical, mental, and emotional forces creating massive pressure as they spin rapidly around me. I used to think this pressure was inescapable, just "normal life" for everyone. Now, I see the tornado of life differently. The image offers valuable insight about what is really true and possible.

The center of a tornado is often referred to as *the eye of the storm.* The conditions within the eye of the storm are said to be calm enough for a bird to fly around in without being harmed, even while the outer winds are wreaking havoc and destruction on anything that stands in their path.

I have found that suspending judgment is one of the most powerful tools available for getting my Self away from the chaos of life's storms and back into its calm, peaceful center. Awareness moves me out of the winds of chaos and into my peaceful center. Now, when I feel oppositional forces pulling at me, potentially robbing me of peace, I choose to pause and notice, to carefully examine my thoughts, and to realign with truth. There is no need to force my Self in any direction. When I recognize the truth, it draws me effortlessly into the eye of the storm.

In the Bible, Moses asks God what name he should use to tell the children of Israel who sent him, and God responds, "I AM THAT I AM . . . Thus shalt thou say unto the children of Israel, I AM hath sent me unto you."[43] This simple response contains no additional qualifiers, no judgmental words. I have observed each time I remove judgment words from my thoughts, I am left with an awareness of things as they actually are, and I stop resisting reality. In the absence of judgment, there is truth. This allows us to "separate the wheat from the tares"[44] and untangle the "philosophies of men, mingled with scripture."

In the book *Loving What Is,* by Byron Katie, I was introduced to the concept that my thoughts are judgments shaped by programmed

---

43   The Holy Bible, KJV, Exodus 3:14

44   The Holy Bible, KJV, Matthew 13:24-30

perceptions—they might not actually represent the truth. I began to observe my bias for or against things based on what I had been taught. In the absence of these programmed judgments, I can accurately identify truth and discern light from darkness for myself. When judgment is present, however, my perception is tainted; it is easy to believe I see light and truth or darkness and error in something based more on what I've been taught to expect than on actual experience.

The Spirit helped me make this shift of suspending judgment through an impression to look at things with the curiosity of a scientist, to be an observer rather than a judge. I adopted the practice of experimenting and observing. I look at all things in my life, including my own thoughts, feelings, and behaviors, with my third eye—my spiritual sense—with the intent to discern their frequencies and draw conclusions. As I do this, I seek to keep my conclusions tentative and stay open to further understanding.

Experiment: Drop the Judgment

Pause when you notice a thought or spoken sentence that feels heavy or creates tension in your body.

Look for the judgment word(s) in that thought or sentence, including statements of value (i.e. good/bad/right/wrong) or the word "should."

Notice the way you feel and respond when you are judging yourself, others, or a situation.

Visualize crossing out the judgment word(s) then repeat the new thought/sentence.

Notice how different the sentence feels without judgment.

Example: I am such a bad mom.

The judgment word is "bad."

Remove the judgment word and say the sentence again:

I am such a mom.

Ask yourself: is that new sentence true?

Keep the truth and discard the story.

Example: He is so stupid

The judgment word is "stupid."

Remove the judgment word and say the sentence again:

He is so. And it then could be shortened further to:

He is.

Ask yourself: is that new sentence true?

Keep the truth and discard the story.

Example: Everything is just so hard.

The judgment word is "hard."

Remove the judgment word(s) and say the sentence again:

Everything is just so.

This one could be further reduced: *Everything is.*

Ask yourself: is that new sentence true?

Keep the truth and discard the story.

Self-Judgment

Where are you critical of yourself? Write down your judgments and criticisms. For example, *I'm too heavy/skinny, I am too tall/short, I should be more kind, I am lazy, I am a perfectionist, I am a procrastinator, I don't belong* ...

Think back to childhood, and write down any judgments that others put upon you that you still carry and get reminded of: *I am too much, I am so smart, I am too loud, I am too busy, I am very obedient, I am not quick enough, I am a good kid, I laugh too much, I am too bossy, I am very responsible.*

Review what you have written and cross out every word that is a judgment.

For example: I am too tall. "Too" and "tall" are subjective judgments. They are human comparisons and evaluations. Therefore, they might not be the absolute truth.

Read the new sentence with those words removed: *I am.*

"I Am." The same words God spoke to Moses.

Speak these words again and ask yourself if that new sentence is true. Does it feel true in your body as you speak the words out loud?

This activity will help you pay more attention to the things you think and the way you talk to yourself. As you begin catching your thoughts and recognizing judgments, you can practice backing up and challenging those judgments. Notice how frequently you make up stories about who and what you are and believe those stories are true. Judgments carry degrees of light and darkness, and the vibrational frequency of your words affects you physically, mentally, emotionally, and spiritually.

Judging Others

Watch your thoughts and seek to catch a "rude" (judgmental) thought about someone else—one you would likely never say out loud.

Tune into your internal compass and notice how you feel when you think that thought. You may want to describe the feeling to yourself in a few words.

Ask yourself why it is a hidden thought, not one you would say to the person directly.

In this process you begin to observe the difference between your inner and outer persona: how you inwardly think and judge vs. the outward way that you treat people. Watching your thoughts brings awareness to the internal dissonance and chaos of your judgments.

Next, classify your thoughts by category:

Is this coming from fear or love?

Is this absolute truth or is it my story?

Ask yourself, "What am I afraid of?" Where there is judgment, there is often fear. You may discover a fear of the guilt and shame you would feel if you were to do the thing you're judging. Often the fear underlying our judgment of others is rooted in the threat their differences pose to our own "rightness." Or you may even be secretly jealous of the one you're judging for this behavior—something I call *jealous judgment.*

Now say, "This is what I'm telling myself. What is true?"

By paying attention to your thoughts and the presence of judgment in them, you can bring clarity to the fears that weigh you down and keep you in chaos.

Experiment: When others judge you

When your spouse, child, family member, coworker, or fellow churchgoer is behaving in a way that feels judgmental, shaming, manipulative, or controlling, it can be difficult to feel love and compassion for them. Especially when a situation is tense and you're reacting physically, mentally, and emotionally to both their judgments of you *and* your own fears and judgments of yourself.

Here's why: YOU CANNOT GIVE WHAT YOU DON'T HAVE. It's that simple.

The power is in starting with yourself. The key question is, "Can I love myself through this?"

That question takes you inward and upward—back to a remembrance of what God has told you about your worth. From that perspective, the answer is always, *"YES! You CAN love yourself because you are enough, lovable, and worthy!"*

If you don't fully feel it, begin to consider by asking yourself, *"What if this is true? What if I was created whole, worthy, enough?"*

The peace that comes with knowing who you truly are brings you the clear opportunity to choose: "Am I going to operate from a place of fear or love?" This is so simple, yet it has the power to change every interaction we have with other people. When someone is yelling at you, when you find yourself in conflict, when you feel judged and misunderstood, you can return to peace by asking, "Can I love myself through this? Am I going to operate from a place of love or fear?"

As you anchor to truthful beliefs about yourself and your worth, you can respond with an energy of love and override the energy of fear.

"For the natural man (EGO) is an enemy (OPPOSITE) to God, and has been from the fall of Adam, and will be, forever and ever (there's no escaping it—the ego will lead you away from God in the OPPOSITE direction every time, no matter what religious practices you're performing) unless he yields to the enticings of the Holy Spirit, (*"come follow me," "love thy neighbor as you* love yourself") and putteth off the natural man (EGO) and becometh a saint (embodying the characteristics of unconditional love, compassion, peace) through the atonement of Christ the Lord, and becometh as a child (unattached to fear, guilt, shame, and judgment—egoless), submissive, meek, humble, patient, full of love, willing to submit to all things which the Lord seeth fit to inflict upon him (not resisting *what is*), even as a child doth submit to his father."[45]

Experiment: Addressing anger in others

The next time you're in the presence of someone who is angry with you, try this:

First, calm your body's natural reaction to confrontation by breathing deeply.

Now, remembering that anger is always a mask for fear, ask yourself:

---

[45] The Book of Mormon, Mosiah 3:19, with lots of commentary from me.

"I wonder what he's afraid of?"

Seek to perceive the answer in your whole body, your being, your heart space, the whispering of your soul. We're not just trying to figure it out in our heads—the mind will keep you wrapped in judgment for yourself and others—we're really intentionally seeking to know what the fear is.

You'll get an impression. Present that impression to yourself or the other person.

Bring awareness to what is true. "I'm noticing you're really angry right now. I'm wondering, what is it you're afraid of?"

Wait for their response. If he denies it or tries to justify it, simply deliver an invitation with an intention of curiosity and love: "You might want to look at that." Whatever the person chooses is their business; there is no need to probe more.

If they are open to sharing the reasons for their anger, listen and then thank them for sharing. You will be tempted to step into proving, explaining, or defending yourself. Don't. Keep your ego out of it. "Thank you for sharing," is sufficient. You can focus on processing your own stuff internally; no need to talk yet.

Stay in your own lane. Do not engage in a fight and don't try to prove that you're right.

If anyone is using guilt and manipulation to try to get you to do something for them, either by bringing up past things they've done for you, or things you've done "to" them, for example, just bring awareness to it: "I'm noticing that you're using guilt to try to motivate me to do what you want. I no longer choose to be motivated by guilt and shame. If you would like me to help you with something, you can invite me to do it, and I will choose to honor what's true for me."

If you're feeling open, you may ask, "Do you have a request for me?" as an invitation for them to say what they would like you to do or say differently. If they share, you can tell them, "I'll take a look at that and get back to you." You get to check in with yourself and decide if their request is a *soul's yes* or a *soul's no* for you.

This is how we "yield to the enticings of the Holy Spirit"! We take time to slow down and look both ways, to see the fear on one hand and the truth on the other, then intentionally choose.

RESOLVING "TRUST ISSUES"

As I have reflected on my past, I have reframed the situations where I used to tell myself the story that someone else *broke my trust*. The Spirit of Truth has shown me that the only trust issue I ever had was that I did not know how to trust myself. Upon investigating such instances, I have found evidence of times when I ignored my gut instincts in favor of seeking approval, acceptance, love, and belonging from others. I obeyed the "precepts of man" because I did not know how to challenge them to find truth. By ignoring my soul's cues, I broke my own trust!

I betrayed myself through my choices, and then at times felt let down by the way people treated me or lied to me. By interpreting others' actions as a reflection of my worth and value, I broke my trust again because I could not trust myself to stay in alignment with the truth of my own worth.

In contrast, I have been shown that when I live in self-trust I have nothing to fear in others' behaviors. When others have lied to my face, intentionally sought to use me, and threatened my safety, I have maintained my own peace and well-being. I am able to check in with myself any time and ask, "What do I do now?" My soul always responds with truth and gives me the courage to act on it.

I have learned that when I stay connected with myself, I am always safe. Yes, someone could slander my name, rob me, or attack me, but I will not attach my worth to it; they can take whatever they take from me and I will love myself through it. Ultimately, no one can take my existence: even if they take my physical life, they cannot touch, harm, or alter my essence, my soul, the *real* me! I have nothing to fear!

Christ taught, "I am in my Father, and ye in me, and I in you."[46] This was a confusing concept for me until I was led through these processes to become one within myself and one with the Spirit of Truth. Now it's simple and clear! Though my goal had always been to become Christlike and to have a relationship of unity with Him, I felt I was always falling short due to mortal weaknesses, and I felt separate from Christ. Now I feel that it is amazingly simple to be like Christ, with Christ, and in Christ. I discover more every day about what is really true and possible through aligning my being with the light, love, and truth of Christ—healing, miracles, and peace beyond words.

I now choose not to give any energy to the idea that someone else might *break my trust* or not be trustworthy. It is an extinct worry. I've got me and I am safe with me; I will not abandon or betray myself again. I love me, and I listen to me. As I have learned to trust myself and God, these have become my core commitments. Peace emerges as the result of a reunification, the *re-membering* of mind, body, heart, and spirit, into a state of wholeness. My experience has shown me that oneness with self is necessary to and preparatory for oneness with others, nature, our Creator, and anything and everything in the universe.

Experiment: Honoring Yourself

Investigate your "trust issues" by looking at people and situations with which you don't feel safe. Consider the past experiences you have had with this person or situation. What happened in those past experiences that left you feeling hurt or unsafe?

---

46   The Holy Bible, KJV, John 14:20

OBSERVING: CHAOS AND PEACE

Ask yourself: "What did I do to betray myself in that situation?" Did you say "yes" when you wanted to say "no"? Did you betray your own safety or values by *not* doing or saying something? Did you believe the hurtful thing that was said to or about you?

Take some time to sit with that past version of yourself in love and forgiveness. Acknowledge that she was doing the best she knew how at the time.

Hold that hurt part of you and let her know she's safe now, that the stronger, wiser version of yourself that you have become is someone you can trust.

Commit to making self-honor your highest priority. This means remembering that nothing is worth the cost of self-betrayal. This also means showing compassion to yourself when you fall into self-betrayal again. You don't have to do it perfectly; as with any relationship, trust will grow as you keep coming back to loving kindness for yourself.

RELEASING RESISTANCE TO DARKNESS AND CONFUSION

I have noticed that I often had, and sometimes still have, resistance to feelings of darkness and confusion. It is easy to judge darkness because we have been taught to fear it. Darkness has been identified with evil, sin, deception, wrongdoing, danger, etc. These are all judgments of darkness.

Darkness is not the presence of evil, but simply a lack of connection to light, truth, and clarity. It is a reference point—being the opposite to sources of peace: light, truth, love, and freedom. Rather than fearing darkness, noticing it can help guide you toward the eye of the storm. Darkness in thoughts looks like chaos and confusion in the mind, when it's hard to make a decision or I feel like I'm "struggling" or "stuck." Emotionally and energetically, darkness seem like a collision of turbulent emotions that feel difficult to sort through or calm. Darkness in behavior shows up as a response to fear in fight, flight, or freeze reactions, sometimes called trauma responses. These all simply indicate a need to reconnect to our sources of peace, to still ourselves and allow clarity.

Judgments breed fear, and fear spawns the protective reaction of resistance. When we resist anything, including what we see as darkness, our engagement with it keeps us stuck, giving it power over us. As I notice the many things I have been afraid of—particularly things I considered "evil" or "sinful" due to my religious upbringing—I can see how much power I was giving away when I judged darkness as bad. This realization is liberating—and sometimes hilarious.

Darkness is a part of everyday life; it is an inevitable occurrence—it is the chaos that precedes clarity. And yet, because I feared and judged darkness, I also feared and judged myself: if darkness is bad and I think or feel something dark, then I must be bad too. I was at war with darkness, and therefore at war with myself.

Judging and resisting the inevitable darkness we all encounter daily creates fear, guilt, and shame. These feelings actually give the darkness power: we allow our perception of darkness to create a downward spiral of self-destruction. Fearing and judging darkness fuels the repetition of behaviors as we push these thoughts into the shadows, leading to the formation of habits which can evolve into addictions.

In place of fearful judgments, we can open ourselves to the guidance these thoughts and feelings are offering and follow them to the Divine truth and peace on the other side of the chaos. This is a path to captivity. Removing judgment is a path to freedom. Rather than fear and resist darkness, consider: what might happen when you lean in, and sit in the darkness to discover the truth it is offering?

"How long must one remain in the dark?" Someone once asked.

"Until one can see in the dark."[47]

It is my experience that when I become still and choose to sit in my dark moments, I am able to notice. I allow myself to feel without shame, and I am able to choose wisely for myself. I discover that I am safe in darkness. Darkness can be around me and can even feel like it is in me, but it is not me. Darkness is separate from me and has no power over me when I am able to identify it. The longer I sit and observe darkness in the absence of fear and judgment, the greater my perception of it becomes.

Now I have a new relationship with darkness. To me, darkness is a way to describe a lack of light, love, and truth: it just is. Like mashed potatoes without salt, it is not good, bad, right, or wrong, it just is. I can be in, near, and around influences of darkness and not worry, because I give them no power over me. I allow myself to experience degrees of darkness and light in different forms, and simply experiment with the ways they affect my mind, body, heart, and spirit. I call these *experiences*, and I learn from them.

I have found that when one can "see in the dark," one is able to sit in darkness, without suffering, until light shows up. Dark spaces are illuminated by awareness and insight. While sitting in those moments, I discover I have power over fear and can see through many fallacies and illusions in my thinking.

Suspending judgment of the darkness we encounter goes hand in hand with releasing the suffering that comes from our resistance to life. When there is nothing to judge, there is nothing to resist. By removing judgment, we suspend the false, mortally influenced stories we have attached to reality. The false story is what engenders suffering; once it is set aside, peace is naturally present.

---

[47] Florence Scovel Shinn, *The Game of Life and How to Play It*.

Experiment: Tune into your tension

As you go about your day, practice checking in with your body by periodically scanning it with your mind's eye, looking for tension. Breathe in, and as you exhale, command those tense places to "relax." Imagine them melting like butter.

As you practice this awareness, you will become more able to notice sudden physiological reactions to your thoughts and experiences—when your body suddenly tenses, it is telling you that fear is present. You can then ask yourself, "What am I resisting in this moment?"

Remind yourself: fear is a liar. Take a few deep, cleansing breaths and release the fear as you exhale.

Look for what is true, and speak it aloud to yourself. Some of the grounding phrases that help me eradicate fear and tension in my body are:

"I am safe with me."

"I love and approve of myself."

"I will not abandon me."

"I love me and I'm listening."

Once you are centered in truth, you can lean into (meaning engage with) whatever is present, rather than resist it.

SPEAKING TRUTH

Growing up, I was taught in church there is a value in bearing my testimony publicly; I had opportunities to stand up at appropriate times and share my beliefs with others. I was taught that not only would bearing my testimony edify others, it would allow me to feel the confirming witness of truth of the Holy Spirit as I spoke. Now I practice this alone, speaking ideas out loud solely for myself.

Speaking words aloud greatly assists me in discerning the truth and error in my own thinking. It helps me recognize when a thought truly is inspiration from the Divine and when it has come from my deceptive ego's programming. The sensation I feel in my body when I speak truthful thoughts out loud is very similar to the sensation I feel in my body when I hear music that is on key. There is a resonance within me. I can "try a concept on" by speaking it aloud and tuning into the resonance or dissonance in my body to gauge the level of truth the words contain.

Experiment: Say it out loud

When you encounter a new thought or idea, try speaking it out loud. Notice how it feels in your mind, body, heart, and soul.

Practice this process with the answers that come when you are seeking guidance from your soul, or while investigating the thoughts and beliefs you have carried.

Your whole being can respond to truthfulness or error of the words you speak with either expansion or contraction:

- The **mind** contains thoughts that are clear in response to truth and confused in response to error
- The **body** feels resonance in the presence of truth and dissonance to error
- The **heart** feels peace and joy in the light of truth, heavy and fearful in error
- The **soul** gives off a sense of assurance to truth and a repulsion to error

PLAYING: CAPTIVITY AND FREEDOM

"You can't separate peace from freedom because no one can be at peace unless he has his freedom."
-Malcolm X

Principles and Experiments in this Chapter:
- Exercising Agency
  - Experiment: Is it a problem or a choice?
- Creating Space for New Freedom
  - Experiment: Is it hard or is it new?
- Breaking Out of Captivity
  - Experiment: It's okay to be wrong
- Eliminating the Captivity of Judgment
  - Experiment: Release the captivity of guilt.
- Finding Freedom in Opposites
  - Experiment: What is really true and possible?
- Uncovering the Female Ego
  - Identify your wounded feminine and masculine traits
- Playing Your Way to Freedom
  - Experiment: Go play!

EXERCISING AGENCY

Everything I experience, perceive, believe, feel, and choose to do is MY CHOICE.

Agency, the ability to choose, is considered a foundational principle in the LDS religion. I was always taught that we are free, agents unto ourselves. And yet the religious culture around me was filled with immense pressure to stay on a very narrowly defined path.

I heard the motto "choose the right" often, followed by being told what the "right thing" was on every scale and in every aspect of my life: the "right way" to dress, to eat, and to speak; the "right" music to listen to and entertainment to watch; the "right" way to dance. I was told the "right" decisions to make about my life, including education and career, dating, marriage, and having children, and the "right way" to prioritize each aspect of my life. I was taught the "right" way to pray, worship, serve, and repent; the "right" way to be grateful, and the "right" way to love and connect with others.

These prescribed ways of being were consistently spoken or written with "should" statements, as in, "Members of the Church *should*..."[48] The word "should" carries an inherent sense of shame for noncompliance. When we "should on" ourselves and each other (yes, it sounds like "shit" for a reason!), choices are often motivated by fear of guilt, shame, and judgment. Does that environment honor choice? When we are operating from fear and shame, are we truly exercising our agency?

I believe that following the counsels and guidance of the Church *could* lead people to love, joy, peace, and freedom. But I also see that people can learn how to discern truth, sometimes more clearly and

---

[48] Just open any chapter of the old LDS Gospel Principles manual and start circling the number of times you read "should." Try the chapter on the Law of Chastity, for example.

effectively, through the unforgettable lessons that can come when they *choose* the exact opposite of those counsels. As poet James Russell Lowell wrote, "One thorn of experience is worth a whole wilderness of warning."

Throughout my life, I put my faith in the things I thought were logical, safe, and familiar. Sometimes, honestly, I believed that the things I learned were from God simply because they were taught by someone of authority in the Church or in my life. My father, whom I respect and adore, had a philosophy that he occasionally repeated to our family: "Just do what you're told." I got really good at living that way.

Then, at thirty-eight years old, I was practicing something totally new—I was studying, experimenting with, and recording *my own experiences*! I began to see myself as a science student in this "laboratory of life." I had never felt like a scientist before; now every day I sought to continue the fascinating experiment to uncover truth. I asked questions that challenged my ideologies, and I learned through the sensations and guidance of my internal compass. I held no assumptions and chose to stay open to any and all possibilities, without expectation—honestly seeking the truth, knowing nothing.

I often experimented with word substitutions in my thoughts, looking for a truer word than those that seemed to automatically come to my mind. I discovered how one word exchanged for another could significantly shift the entire thought from fear to love and from error to truth.

The simplicity and power of this exercise felt so significant, I asked the Spirit, "What is happening here?"

"You are reinstating your agency."

After living by predetermined "shoulds" for decades, I was now free—through intentional awareness—to really exercise my agency, in both word and action. I was choosing to trust impressions that came to me and act on them. I was allowing myself to choose experiences that had formerly been forbidden; I could then intentionally evaluate within myself how each choice affected me and felt within my internal compass. I was free to experience anything and everything!

The gift of agency—in the absence of fear, guilt, shame, and judgment—began to feel like a *gift* for the first time, given with real, unconditional love. I treasure it as my greatest tool for freedom and learning. I use it deliberately, monitoring my thoughts, words, and actions to align them with the energy of truth and love.

Experiment: Is it a problem ... or a choice?
The word "problem" has a connotation attached to fear, and its energy can make you feel like a victim. The word "choice," however, consciously and intentionally enacts your agency, bringing forth the energies of freedom, empowerment, and truth. It reminds you that you are free to create your experience.

Substituting the word "choice" for "problem" can offer an empowering energetic turnaround of awareness. Try it!

> Former thought: *I have a PROBLEM with this person at work.*
> New thought: *I have a CHOICE with this person at work.*
>
> Former thought: *I have a PROBLEM with my weight.*
> New thought: *I have a CHOICE with my weight.*
>
> Former thought: *I have a PROBLEM with my finances.*
> New thought: *I have a CHOICE with my finances.*
>
> Former thought: *I have a PROBLEM with my self worth.*
> New thought: *I have a CHOICE with my self worth.*
>
> Former thought: *I have a PROBLEM with feelings of grief and loss.*
> New thought: *I have a CHOICE with feelings of grief and loss.*

PLAYING: CAPTIVITY AND FREEDOM

Former thought: *I have a PROBLEM with the fear of failure perfectionism.*
New thought: *I have a CHOICE with the fear of failure/perfectionism.*

Former thought: *I have a PROBLEM with anger.*
New thought: *I have a CHOICE with anger.*

Former thought: *I have a PROBLEM with forgiving someone.*
New thought: *I have a CHOICE with forgiving someone.*

Former thought: *I have a PROBLEM with an illness/pain.*
New thought: *I have a CHOICE with an illness/pain.*

Speak the new thought aloud, and notice how your mind shifts with the change of just one word.

When I emphasize that a situation presents a choice, rather than a problem, I feel a flood of loving, truthful, peaceful possibilities begin to pour into my mind. The pathway to light, truth, love, joy, peace, and freedom clears. The acknowledgment of my agency is the master key that opens a portal of revelation where ideas about that situation and my choices in it come through. Seeing my options frees me from the captivity of believing I am stuck with a problem.

CREATING SPACE FOR NEW FREEDOM

Many of us have spent years, even decades, repeating strenuous cycles of self-deception, but feeling trapped in these patterns. We are often aware of the emotional and behavioral loop we are caught in, but don't know what to do to break it. The repetition of unsuccessful attempts to break our patterns typically leads to the development of a belief that change is "hard."

Changing our patterns of thought, beliefs, and habits can feel like a struggle. But I believe that when someone says they are "struggling" with something, what they mean is that there is an internal wrestling match taking place between their soul and their ego. A client will tell me that a part of them dreams of something, but another part shuts that dream down, using loads of evidence to illustrate why the desire is illogical or impractical.

As I have inquired further in many situations, it appears to me that the soul is speaking truth by presenting a desire or dream or hope, and the ego is resisting the soul's call with fear and judgment, producing the sensation of a struggle. Trusting and acting in alignment with the soul's desires can, indeed, appear to be hard. When a person has lived in chronic deferral to the ego, talking themselves out of trusting their soul as I did for so many years, making a switch from operating from fear to operating from love and truth can feel difficult.

Change takes time and practice. It requires patience with ourselves as we gradually learn to think, speak, and behave in new ways. When I hear my clients say, "But that is SO HARD," I invite them to try a word substitution, saying "That is SO *NEW*," instead. Like this, "It's SO *NEW* for me to hear and trust my spirit, but I'm willing." Or, "It's SO *NEW* for me to practice new beliefs." Words are powerful, and so much freedom is uncovered when we choose words that emphasize our agency. Simply choosing a different word changes the energy from stuck to flowing; the hard is now possible. We are given the ability to recognize that we are progressing even when an old pattern repeats in the process of practicing something new.

Experiment: Is it hard or is it new?

The next time you find yourself thinking, *This is SO HARD,* stop yourself and try saying out loud, "This is SO *NEW*."

Notice the physical shift in your body from tension and tightness to expansion and relaxation.

PLAYING: CAPTIVITY AND FREEDOM

This practice can take you yet another step out of captivity into freedom. You can transmute your perspective to a new awareness and free yourself from the emotional constriction of your old beliefs.

The substitution of the word "new" for the word "hard" came to me through the exercise of seeking words with greater truth. Continue to pay attention to the words you choose and play with word substitutions. When you notice constriction in your body in response to a thought, take the thought inward and upward by asking, "Here is what I'm telling myself. What word or words are truer than the ones I'm thinking?"

Notice the words that come and repeat the phrase with the substitution you receive. Witness the reactions in your body and heart. True words evoke resonance in your entire internal compass: clarity of mind, relaxation in the body, increased love in your heart, and a sense of freedom in your spirit.

When an individual chooses to consider the truth of their thoughts and open to what contains more truth, it is astounding how quickly long-held beliefs and attitudes about certain people or situations can be overturned. This is a HOLY SHIFT!

BREAKING OUT OF CAPTIVITY

The greatest prison, and the origin of our suffering, is that of our own thoughts and beliefs.

In his book *Man's Search for Meaning*, Viktor Frankl observed that he, a prisoner in a Nazi concentration camp, had more freedom than his prison guards. While they had more liberty to come and go at the gates of the prison, their minds were controlled by their superiors to the point that they were willing to harm and even execute other people. These guards were prisoners to their fears and beliefs. Intentionally choosing thoughts and actions that were aligned with light, truth, and love, Dr. Frankl maintained his peace, found moments of inner joy, and granted himself ultimate freedom—the freedom of his mind.

Circumstances, in the absence of judgment, are neutral. It is what we tell ourselves these circumstances mean—about ourselves, other people, and God—that imprison us in suffering. We erect our prisons, one bar of belief at a time, cementing them in fallacy, fear, and error. The programming and conditioning of our ego minds keeps us captive by guarding the perimeter in an effort to keep us safely within the bounds we have learned to be "right" and "good."

Finding my beliefs and challenging them is like removing the bars of a prison one at a time. It is where I find freedom and peace of mind. The process of challenging my beliefs becomes easy with these commitments in place:

1. I am not afraid to find out I have been wrong.

2. I am open to anything my soul, and Divine Source, has to say.

3. I am willing to test out any new ideas, no matter how radical they seem to my brain.

Experiment: It's okay to be wrong

It is common to be so incredibly attached to our programming of what is "good" or "bad" and "right" or "wrong" that we are afraid to allow ourselves to believe something new and different. We fear accepting new ideas would mean we have been wrong—perhaps wrong about major ideologies, and wrong for a long time! We connect being wrong with being bad, stupid, not enough, unworthy, or failing. I have seen people so afraid of being wrong about anything that they would sacrifice their own happiness to defend their belief that they are right. Therein lies the captivity.

Instead of fearing and shaming ourselves for being wrong, we can choose to love ourselves in our innocence and see these moments as opportunities to grow. As we do, we become more open to receiving the truth. I use gentle, compassionate statements to accept my mistaken beliefs, like:

"I was wrong, and I love me."

"Well, look at that! I thought I was right, but I'm not. I love me, and I'm learning."

"I have simply believed what I was taught. I am innocent and I love me."

"That was right for me back then, but it no longer serves me to think that way, and I can let it go. I choose freedom over captivity."

"I'm open to being shown by Spirit that I'm wrong about anything because I can then pivot and find the truth! There's nothing to fear!"

ELIMINATING THE CAPTIVITY OF JUDGMENT

Now that I am no longer afraid of doing things "wrong," I try things that call to my soul, rather than shutting myself down with fear. I have the courage to do things differently, to challenge the status quo, because I don't believe I can get it wrong or fail. There's nothing to fear, only new experiences to learn from.

Sometimes when others see me doing things in uncommon ways, they feel inclined to comment. I have had people say things to me, such as:

- "It's nice that you can write in Hawaii. Not everybody has that opportunity."
- "It's nice that you can have a flexible schedule cleaning houses. Not everybody has that option."
- "It's nice that you have such an easy relationship with Eric. But relationships are not so easy when you live under the same roof as your spouse."

For a season, such commentary about my choices would summon feelings of guilt—a heaviness in the body and thoughts of self-doubt. I went inward and upward to ask the Spirit why I was feeling guilt for the freedoms in my life—that seemed so off!

The Spirit taught me that when others aren't free, they compare, judge, and make excuses to unconsciously rationalize the captivity created by their own choices. Spirit then showed me times I unconsciously judged others for the freedoms they enjoyed because I did not realize it was my own choices that led to the limitations in my life. I was judging the other person in jealousy of their freedom—a situation I have termed *jealous judgment*. As I looked at that, I could feel the victim energy underlying such judgments. The unconscious thinking behind it goes something like this: "This person has chosen what I haven't chosen, and I haven't chosen that because I can't."

When I accessed true personal freedom, human conditioning first led me to respond to others' captivity by feeling guilty for what I had gained. Essentially, I was feeling guilty because my life was so good and theirs wasn't. What a spiritual trap! Feelings of guilt for my peace, joy, and freedom tempted me to think I didn't deserve it, or to feel it was wrong to have it. Can you see the obvious opposition to truth? I laughed at the irony!

The Unicorns introduced me to the concept of *victim consciousness*. This is the insecure energy that comes when judgment is present. According to psychologist Stephen Karpman's Drama Triangle model, victim energy takes on one of three character roles:

- Victim - judging the self and others from a sense of helplessness
- Prosecutor - the angry victim who blames others
- Rescuer - the "I have to do everything" victim trying to prove their worth by saving others

Comparison is a way to determine who is right and who is wrong, who is good and who is bad. It's a function of the ego, a self-deception it uses to protect itself. These judgments prevent us from seeing what is really true and possible, defending why we can't do the thing we are jealously judging instead of considering that perhaps we can!

Since this pattern was revealed to me, I have observed it frequently. I have come to recognize that when we put guilt or shame onto others for their choices and experiences, we are not only disempowering their use of agency, we are disempowering ourselves. In contrast, when we eliminate comparison, judgment, and the assignment of worthiness, we take a step toward more freedom—not only for ourselves, but for everyone.

Seeing possibilities from a lens of freedom and love releases myself AND the other person from the captivity of my thinking. I don't always verbalize possibilities. I check in before speaking, and sometimes the spirit tells me, "Angel, this awareness is simply for you."[49]

Other times, the Spirit directs me to speak of possibilities out loud. I sometimes ask the person, "Are you open to me sharing what I see?" Many times when the other person says they are open and I share what the Spirit is telling me, we have a refining, unifying experience, enveloped in unconditional love. Other times, the awareness is rejected, and the person feels offended by what has been said. Whether they will receive or reject my message is a gamble, yet either way, it's always an opportunity for me to ask myself, "Can I love myself through this?"

Even if I don't say anything in situations like these, the presence of love and freedom offer a silent invitation to the other person to be released from the captivity of their own thinking. When I relinquish

---

[49] Sometimes my ego wants to share the awareness with another to *teach* them, and because it loves to be right. Yet I have come to love the wisdom the Spirit offers, gently guiding my practice in releasing my attachment to the rightness of my ego.

fear and step into a perspective of truth, I bring an energy of presence, non-judgment, and unconditional love. This energy is so different from the way people typically interact that its contrast to what is expected invites awareness of new possibilities.

Limiting beliefs, whether coming from ourselves or others, are like prison bars—barriers to truth, expansion, and evolution. Yet we can use limiting beliefs as a catalyst for seeking the opposite possibilities. The ultimate purpose in becoming aware of and changing these beliefs is freedom.

Experiment: Release the captivity of guilt
As you choose to uncover and align with truth and welcome more and more freedom into your life, you may encounter similar feelings of guilt as a result of others' comments and judgments around your expanded circumstances. Guilt and shame will show up every chance they get. When others offer judgment toward the choices we make in our freedom, it can be tempting to step back into our old prisons of guilt, shame, and fear.

One of my mentors, Diana Dokos, taught me a simple and clever way to maintain my mental freedom in the face of others' judgments as well as my own limiting beliefs. I can explore what else is possible with one word: *unless*. This invites me to look at the exact opposite of the judgment or belief that is holding me back. For example, I will repeat what I heard in my mind, and then add, *unless it's not that way*. This creates a mental about-face.

- **Judgment:** "It's nice that you can write in Hawaii. Not everybody has that opportunity."
  Inquiry: ... *unless they do! What if everybody DOES have that opportunity, but few act on it?"*

- **Judgment:** "It's nice that you can have a flexible schedule cleaning houses. Not everybody has that option."
  Inquiry: *. . . unless they do! What could people do to create flexibility if they tried?*
- **Judgment:** "It's nice that you have such an easy relationship with Eric. But relationships are not so easy when you live under the same roof as your spouse."
  Inquiry: *. . . unless they are! What would it take for others to give themselves the space needed to create an easy relationship?*

FINDING FREEDOM IN OPPOSITES

Beyond using the ". . . unless it's not," tactic, Diana also taught me to next ask the universe and God, "Show me what is really true and possible in this moment." This simple seeking question empowers me to further separate limiting beliefs from truths as curiosity expands my perception of what could be.

When I stopped creating my own captivity out of fear, I ceased living in self-deception and self-betrayal, and I stopped projecting my shame onto others through blame. Then I was able to escape the egoic programming and conditioning that limited my freedom. My false beliefs about myself and others had brought me sadness, depression, fatigue, and despair. In the absence of that emotional weight, joy surfaced, and I began to see my freedom to create my life the way I wanted it.

Experiment: What is really true and possible?
We don't have to remain captive to unsubstantiated, limiting beliefs! Watch for the red flag words in your thoughts and speech that often precede limiting beliefs: "should," "shouldn't," "have to," and "can't" are

big ones. When you catch one, try the opposite statement on for size: "Unless it IS!" "Unless it's NOT!" "Unless I CAN!" "Unless I DON'T!"

Then breathe deeply, connect with your soul, and ask, "What is really true and possible in this moment?"

- "I can't take a vacation from work" . . . *unless I can! What is really true and possible in this moment?*
- "Son, you shouldn't stay out so late" . . . *unless you should! What is really true and possible in this situation?*
- "I can't come this weekend, I have to be home" . . . *unless I don't! What is really true and possible for me?*
- "I should host my relatives for this holiday" . . . *unless I shouldn't! What is really true and possible this time?*
- "I have to keep working this job I hate because it pays the bills" . . . *unless I don't have to! What is really true and possible for my life?*
- "I shouldn't go on a trip with my girlfriends and not my husband" . . . *unless I should! What is really true and possible in my relationships?*
- "I can't break this habit, I've been in it too long" . . . *unless I can! What is really true and possible for me now?*

This practice allows you to stop and evaluate whether what you're telling yourself is actually true. It then guides you to seek for more truth from the Divine. This is so simple and so expansive!

UNCOVERING THE FEMALE EGO

I was really shocked to discover that I had an "ego" because I had linked that word in my mind to men! This was one of the most humorous discoveries of my life. I thought of cocky, arrogant, male chauvinists as the only ones with "egos." I had never heard the term "female ego."

I love bringing this up with women because 100% of the time, to date, the women I've spoken with have said that they, too, think of men when they hear the word "ego"! This is a major cultural blindspot. Ironically, the lack of awareness around the existence of the female ego perpetuates the tendency for women to blindly operate from their egos.

My hypothesis is that wherever females are blindly operating in their egos, cataclysmic encounters with males in their egos will be created. Through the clashing interactions of female and male egos, both women and men encounter cultural stereotypes about each other, and therefore miss opportunities to discover the divine design within. This leads women to continue to label men as "narcissists," and men to continue to label women as "crazy bitches," without either being able to understand how to find the truth.

When both women and men acknowledge and heal the *wounded* masculine and feminine energies within themselves, aligning instead with their *divine* masculine and feminine energies, all are freed to interact with both males and females with confidence and compassion.

Experiment: Identifying wounded energies

When we are young, we learn by the examples of those around us how to think, feel, and act towards ourselves, in relationship with others, and in relationship to the world. When the examples in our lives demonstrate "wounded" energies, we take those examples on and perpetuate the wounded versions of masculine and feminine energies.

Read through each of the characteristics listed below and ask yourself, "Which of these traits do I see in my mother and my father (or other parental figures or role models)?" Remember, women and men both have feminine and masculine energies. Therefore, descriptions from either column could apply to either parent.

Review the lists again and ask, "Which of these traits do I see in myself?" (Refer to both columns).

WOUNDED FEMININE
- Low self-worth
- Afraid to speak his/her truth
- Compromises his/her integrity and values
- Easily attached
- Manipulative
- Stuck in victimhood (waiting to be saved)
- Drowning in (or stuffs) her emotions
- Passive-aggressive
- Uses guilt and shame to motivate

WOUNDED MASCULINE
- Extremely critical
- Emotionally unavailable
- Controlling
- Constant inner and outer conflict (reactive)
- Selfish
- Needs to be right
- Stuck in mind
- Aggressive
- Afraid of failure

Now consider the way these traits manifest when they are transmuted into their fully healed, divine manifestations. As you read these words, notice how they feel to your mind, body and heart.

DIVINE FEMININE
- Creative
- Intuitive
- Accepting
- Unconditionally loving
- Empathetic
- Receptive
- Vulnerable
- Nurturing
- Fluid
- Speaks truth

DIVINE MASCULINE
- Confident
- Protective
- Supportive
- Disciplined
- Clear
- Responsible
- Directed
- Logical
- Assertive
- Courageous

Wounded energies are rooted in darkness, error, fear, sadness, chaos, and captivity. They are traits perpetuated in society by judgment, stereotypes, and misrepresentation of truth. All of the prior principles and practices mentioned in this book equate to moving out of a state of wounded energy and into a state of wholeness. This transmutation is the natural byproduct of soul-u-lar evolution. When you align your beliefs, thoughts, feelings, and actions with truth, the divine feminine and masculine traits become the way truth and love are expressed.

I have observed that a person who shows up operating in alignment with truth and love, according to their divine design, seems to unlock that same capacity for those around them. They become a model, a blueprint, a roadmap. And once their partners (or children, friends, or coworkers) are able to see divinity in action, they often match it. Without pressure or force, coercion or convincing. It's really similar to singing with someone or tuning one instrument to another. When truth and love are the frequencies held in place with intention, others nearby will shift into that same frequency (or remove themselves). It's like their souls can "hear" (feel, perceive, etc.) when they are out of tune.

PLAYING YOUR WAY TO FREEDOM

Another very profound lesson my mentors The Unicorns shared with me is the power and potential of play.

When they first introduced this idea to me, I was very resistant. I saw their playful nature as immature—and ridiculous. I did not think that I, as an adult, needed to play. The reality was, shame around play was unconsciously programmed into my mind. I harbored a hidden belief that adults *should not* play. When the Unicorns invited me to play, my triggers of discomfort and resistance became obvious signs of this hidden and unconscious belief.

Although my egoic mind wanted to refuse to play, my soul was prodding from within to participate, to let go, to have fun, and I finally conceded. I jumped on a trampoline with grown women, I participated in theatrical improv exercises, I put on costumes and wigs and danced. These are just a few examples; I started to play often and in many ways.

I discovered that principles of truth entered into my mind, body, and heart with greater ease and less interruption when I played! Instead of being lodged in my brain, the concepts being taught permeated my body and opened my heart. Learning through play brought a depth of understanding that was changing the nature of my whole being.

Curious, I took this question to God: "What is going on here? Why is this 'ridiculousness' bringing such depth of understanding and expansion of my being?"

The Spirit responded, *"You have heard it said to 'be as a child.' Play is the gateway to that. When you play, you suspend the natural man, release the judgment of mortal perceptions, open your heart, and receive love."*

I gained more understanding and self-awareness in that moment than I know how to describe with words. All of my years of "adulting," where work replaced play as the priority, had disconnected me from my *inner child*—which I realized through this experience was my *soul*. I had left my soul behind and attached to my ego! I laughed at myself for having judged the Unicorns. Turns out, it was *me* who was immature and ridiculous—on a spiritual level!

I took pride in my ability to "work hard" and "be productive," but that approach actually held me back. As I tried to make changes in my life, surrender my stories, and turn the volume down on my ego's fearful voice, I often thought to myself, "This is so hard!" I called it "personal development," or "inner work." But "work" is no fun! The word denotes difficulty. Author Bob Proctor has said, "What you think about, you bring about." When I viewed seeking intentional awareness as "work," the illusion of "hard" was bound to accompany my experience.

But play is different. Playing is done just for the sake of having fun, rather than to create an outcome, eliminating the possibility of failure. Instead of doing "inner work," I've started doing "inner fun." When I'm playing, I cannot mess up or get it wrong—it is all about the experience. Living life, drifting between captivity and freedom and all the layers in between, is a playful experiment of mortality. When play is a valued priority, everything becomes an experiment. I know nothing, I have nothing to prove and no need to earn my worth and value. Life is fun!

Learning to play like a child again took practice, and it is something I still need to consciously choose, or I forget. When I do choose to play, I feel creative, I feel present, I feel loving, I feel curious, I feel open. My whole experience feels *free*!

Experiment: Go play!
I must warn you, this concept seems to be the one most often dismissed. I initially disregarded it when my mentors encouraged it, and many of my clients have as well. The dismissal tends to lead to fixation to the ego and a stagnation in personal growth.

I challenge you to give it a try right now, rather than waiting until you're feeling stuck, desperate, and frustrated. Time and time again, I have seen the initially rejected idea of play affect a breakthrough where other approaches have failed.

Reconnect with the innocence and energy of your inner child. Try something you liked to do as a child, like:

- Jumping on a trampoline
- Climbing in a tree
- Splashing in water
- Finger painting
- Waterslides
- Running through a sprinkler
- Creating something without worrying about making it perfect
- Walking barefoot on the earth
- Dancing freestyle

Notice how play loosens up your mind and heart. Notice how it energizes your body. Notice how it connects you to your spirit. Notice how it frees you to see things in a different way.

EPILOGUE

"Be ye therefore perfect."
-Jesus Christ

I'm currently working on my book in the library of BYU-Hawaii. Loving it. Loving my life. Loving being in Hawaii, alive, with resources that support me in doing this. Loving the energy and ideas coming through me.

I am reflecting on my past life. I spent years trying to "do the right thing." Just trying, again and again, to do what I "should" and what I "had to." I look back at that version of Angel and I see frequent anger, annoyance, impatience with others, resentment, exhaustion, depression, and excess weight. I see limited (and guilt-ridden) time for myself. I see my never-ending to-do lists—shit-lists. I see a chicken running around with her head cut off, a woman who is busy, burdened, and exhausted. A woman who feels like she is drowning, but holding on tightly to a firm resolve to JUST. KEEP. GOING.

And now—WOW—here I sit in so much freedom: time freedom, money freedom, with abundant creative space and energy to do what I LOVE! I just caught myself questioning, "How is this possible? How is this my reality? It's my DREAM and it is REAL RIGHT NOW! And how is it SO DIFFERENT from my former life? I wanted the same things for myself back then—I wanted to wake up with the sunrise, I wanted to have the energy to go for a run in the morning, I wanted income that I could generate from home and on my own schedule,

I wanted to visit Hawaii, I wanted to read great books. Most of all, I WANTED TO WRITE! To write and write and write my thoughts for hours at a time. I wanted to feel creation energy pour from my heart into my mind and turn into words that could be written on paper and SHARED—with myself and then the world!

The difference is this: the former me attached to, lived by, and was controlled and limited by fear, guilt, shame, and self-judgment. I told myself I couldn't do these things. I told myself it wasn't possible yet. It wasn't realistic. I had to somehow *earn* the right to be able to have this. I had to be a wife and do XYY. I had to be a mom and do XYZ. I had to do my daily list of things that did not fuel my fire! Marking off those checkboxes did not light me up. It did not bring me the peace, joy, love and fulfillment as advertised. To the contrary, by living this way, I was writing and administering my own life sentence—a slow death by suffering, sacrifice, and sorrow. Captivity. That's what I created for myself. Bondage (and not the fun kind!) Imprisonment.

NOT ANYMORE, BABY!

Perfection, adj: Whole. Complete. Including all opposites.

What if this is a true definition of perfection?

It is not the definition I was taught growing up. From my youth, I understood "perfect" meant "to be like Christ; without sin, no mistakes, obeying all commandments," and I often heard adults say things such as, "No one is perfect. Jesus Christ is the only one who ever lived on earth that was perfect." "I'll never be perfect, but I'll keep trying." "I'm far from perfect, but I do my best."

I experience the contrast of opposites constantly in my life:

Light and darkness

Truth and error

Love and fear

Joy and sadness

EPILOGUE

Peace and chaos

Freedom and captivity

And what if I suspend all judgment in, and of, these moments? Suspending judgment of the situations, all people involved, including myself, while assigning no meaning to any of it? What if it all . . . just . . . is? True. Opposite. Whole. Complete. Perfect.

If my experiences in all their opposition are perfect, then my life is perfect.

If my life is perfect, then I am perfect.

If I am perfect, then there's nothing for me to prove or earn.

If that's true, then I'm free to be love.

Follow the clues: light - truth - love - joy - peace - freedom. They are available in every moment. I have watched this pattern surface in my life, and this has been my experience. One leads me into the next. Yet it is a cyclical process rather than linear; it is an expansion and evolution of the consciousness of the soul. It is Divine!

Thank you for choosing to sit with my words and receive these thoughts and experiences. May you play with the principles and experiments in this book and become even more curious about life. And whatever patterns you are led to uncover, it is my prayer that they will set you free, too!

I do not wish to leave out the truth that opposition in all things is a natural part of life for *everyone*. Fear, ego, and constriction are a daily occurrence for me. In an instant, I can shift from a sense of freedom, feeling expansive and open, to suddenly feeling shut down and captive once again. The egoic mind can react to these moments with judgment, and tends to spiral in humiliation, telling itself things like, "I can't believe I did that again. I have worked so hard on myself, and now I'm back at square one. I should know better." The temptation to take on self-judgment, guilt, fear, and shame—it's a red flag and an invitation to recognize that life is not a ladder, it is not a race, it is not linear. When we stop comparing ourselves, it helps us to stop judging ourselves, which then frees us from causing damage to our own self-worth.

Nature has weather patterns and seasons, but they are neither good nor bad, right nor wrong—they just *are*. They are elements; they are cyclical. Imagine greeting a season with the same attitude that we apply in our own lives, "Winter? It's YOU, again? I thought we did that already. This is wrong. This is a setback. This means nature has failed!" Our lives and growth are also cyclical. Though every moment is new, we may experience similar things and learn similar lessons repeatedly, but in each moment, there is something new to observe. There is an opportunity.

The end.

And . . .

The beginning.

FOR FURTHER READING

The following are some of my favorite consciousness-oriented books. This is the list I provide to clients who ask for book recommendations.

- *A Return to Love,* by Marianne Williamson
- *Conversations with God,* by Neale Donald Walsh
- *Conscious Living,* by Gay Hendricks
- *Conscious Loving,* by Gay Hendricks
- *Dangerous Love,* by Chad Ford
- *Leadership and Self-Deception,* by the Arbinger Institute
- *Love is Letting Go of Fear,* by Gerald Jampolsky
- *Love Without Conditions,* by Paul Ferrini
- *Loving What Is,* by Byron Katie (I *highly* recommend this one!)
- *Man's Search for Meaning,* by Viktor Frankl
- *The Anatomy of Peace,* by the Arbinger Institute
- *The Dark Side of the Light Chasers,* by Debbie Ford
- *The Game of Life and How to Play it,* by Florence Scovel Shinn
- *The Mastery of Love,* by Don Miguel Ruiz
- *The Power of Intention,* by Wayne Dyer
- *The Untethered Soul,* by Michael Singer
- Search "Brene Brown books" and her TED talks on YouTube dealing with shame, vulnerability, and empathy. They're *all* great!

Specifically about the mind/body connection:

- *Feelings Buried Alive Never Die*, Karol K. Truman
- *Heal Your Life* and *Heal Your Body*, by Louise Hay
- *The Body Keeps the Score: Brain, Mind, and Body in the Healing of Trauma*, by Bessel van der Kolk, MD
- *The Healing Questions Guide*, by Wendi Jensen
- "The Body, Mind, Spirit Connection," by Matt Townsend (LDS perspective, an audio talk, only available on Deseret Book's "digital bookshelf.")

Made in the USA
Monee, IL
28 April 2024

57526126R00174